Renaissance Literature

Edinburgh Critical Guides to Literature
Series Editors: Martin Halliwell, University of Leicester and
Andy Mousley, De Montfort University

Renaissance Literature

Siobhan Keenan

Edinburgh University Press

© Siobhan Keenan, 2008

Edinburgh University Press Ltd
22 George Square, Edinburgh

Typeset in 11.5/13 Monotype Ehrhardt
by Servis Filmsetting Ltd, Stockport, Cheshire and
printed and bound in Great Britain by
CPI Antony Rowe, Chippenham, Wilts

A CIP record for this book is available from the British Library

ISBN 978 0 7486 2583 3 (hardback)
ISBN 978 0 7486 2584 0 (paperback)

The right of Siobhan Keenan
to be identified as author of this work
has been asserted in accordance with
the Copyright, Designs and Patents Act 1988.

Contents

Series Preface

The study of English literature in the early twenty-first century is host to an exhilarating range of critical approaches, theories and historical perspectives. 'English' ranges from traditional modes of study such as Shakespeare and Romanticism to popular interest in national and area literatures such as the United States, Ireland and the Caribbean. The subject also spans a diverse array of genres from tragedy to cyberpunk, incorporates such hybrid fields of study as Asian American literature, Black British literature, creative writing and literary adaptations, and remains eclectic in its methodology.

Such diversity is cause for both celebration and consternation. English is varied enough to promise enrichment and enjoyment for all kinds of readers and to challenge preconceptions about what the study of literature might involve. But how are readers to navigate their way through such literary and cultural diversity? And how are students to make sense of the various literary categories and peri-odisations, such as modernism and the Renaissance, or the prolif-erating theories of literature, from feminism and marxism to queer theory and eco-criticism? The Edinburgh Critical Guides to Literature series reflects the challenges and pluralities of English today, but at the same time it offers readers clear and accessible routes through the texts, contexts, genres, historical periods and debates within the subject.

Martin Halliwell and Andy Mousley

Acknowledgements

I am especially grateful to the Series Editors for their invitation to write this book and to Andy Mousley for his advice and encouragement throughout the process. I am, likewise, thankful for the support of staff at Edinburgh University Press (Máiréad McElligott, especially) and for the helpful suggestions made by the Press's anonymous readers.

My passion for Renaissance literature and my thinking about it have been shaped by those who have taught me and by my colleagues and students. I am indebted to them all but would especially like to thank the following: Catherine Bates, Charles Butler, Bernard Capp, Deborah Cartmell, Kate Chedgzoy, Peter Davidson, Rebecca D'Monté, A. S. G. Edwards, Scott Fraser, Takako Kato, Peter Mack, Clare McManus, Andy Mousley, J. R. Mulryne, Melanie Ord, Amanda Penlington, Claire Preston, John Reid, Carol Chillington Rutter, Jane Stevenson, Christiania Whitehead, and the late Julia Briggs.

The completion of this book has been assisted by a period of research leave, granted by the School of English, Performance and Historical Studies at De Montfort University (Leicester), for which I express my thanks. My last, and greatest, debt of gratitude is to my husband David Morley, for his encouragement and support during the writing of the book, and to my son Gabriel, for his patience.

Abbreviations

ELH	*English Literary History*
ELR	*English Literary Renaissance*
MLQ	*Modern Language Quarterly*
MLR	*Modern Language Review*
MRDE	*Medieval and Renaissance Drama in England*
PMLA	*Publications of the Modern Language Association of America*
REED	Records of Early English Drama
RES	*Review of English Studies*
RQ	*Renaissance Quarterly*
ShS	*Shakespeare Survey*
ShSt	*Shakespeare Studies*
SQ	*Shakespeare Quarterly*
SEL	*Studies in English Literature*
TLS	*Times Literary Supplement*

About this Book

This volume provides a concise introduction to the literature of Elizabethan and Stuart England (1558–1649). It is aimed chiefly at undergraduate students taking courses on sixteenth and seventeenth-century English literature, but will hopefully be useful, too, for taught postgraduates looking to refresh or consolidate their knowledge of the period's literature, and lecturers preparing or teaching Renaissance courses.

The beginnings of what we now describe as 'Renaissance' or 'Early Modern' English literature precede the accession of Elizabeth I (1558), but Renaissance literary culture only became firmly established in England in the second half of the sixteenth century. Similarly, while the literature produced between 1649 and the Restoration of the Monarchy (1660) could be said to belong to the Renaissance, the unusual historical context in which it was produced marks the Interregnum as a distinctive literary era. This is why this book concentrates on the literature of the late sixteenth and early seventeenth centuries. For pragmatic reasons the focus is, likewise, on printed literature and literature in English. Although many Elizabethan and Stuart authors wrote in manuscript and some wrote in Latin, such texts are not generally readily accessible in student editions and anthologies.

The book opens with an overview of the original context in which English Renaissance literature was produced, and a discussion of its contemporary and modern critical reception. Following chapters focus on the major literary genres: drama, poetry and prose. Each chapter offers a survey of the genre, and illustrative case studies of key sub-genres and texts, including traditionally canonical and non-canonical works. At the end of each chapter readers will find a summary of its main points. Further support for those studying Renaissance literature can be found in the Student Resources section at the end of the book. This section includes essay writing advice, sample essay questions and plans, a glossary of terms and a guide to further reading and electronic resources. The conclusion summarises some of the most significant developments in Renaissance literary culture, and considers the future direction of Renaissance scholarship. This includes a discussion of research opportunities that may be especially useful to students devising undergraduate or postgraduate dissertation topics.

Throughout the book quotations from Shakespeare are taken from *The Norton Shakespeare*, edited by Stephen Greenblatt, Walter Cohen, Jean E. Howard, and Katharine Eisaman Maus (London: Norton, 1997). Quotations from other Renaissance authors are generally taken from student editions or *The Norton Anthology of English Literature*, edited by Stephen Greenblatt, 8th edn (London: Norton, 2006), volume 1. Biblical quotations are taken from *The Bible (Authorized King James Version with Apocrypha)*, edited by Robert Carroll and Stephen Prickett (Oxford: Oxford University Press, 1998). Direct references to, or quotations from, textual editions printed prior to 1700 have been cited from the facsimiles of those editions accessible via the subscription service *Early English Books Online* (http://eebo.chadwyck.com). Unless otherwise specified, the dates given for the literary works cited in the text are their dates of publication (rather than composition or performance).

Chronology

Note

Authors' names are given in full the first time that they are cited; thereafter they are listed by surname only.

Date	Historical and Cultural Events	Literary Publications and Events
1558	Accession of Queen Elizabeth I	John Knox, *The First Blast of the Trumpet Against the Monstrous Regiment of Women*
1559	Acts of Uniformity and Supremacy passed, re-establishing Protestantism after the Catholic reign of Mary I (1553–58)	
1560		Anne Locke's *A Meditation of a Penitent Sinner*
1561		Performance of Thomas Norton's and Thomas Sackville's *Gorboduc*

Date	Historical and Cultural Events	Literary Publications and Events
1562	First slave-trading expedition to Africa by John Hawkins	
1564	Births of William Shakespeare and Christopher Marlowe	
1565	The Turkish Siege of Malta	Arthur Golding's translation of Ovid's *Metamorphoses*
1566	James Stuart (later James VI of Scotland, James I of England) is born, son of Mary, Queen of Scots and Henry, Lord Darnley	William Painter, *The Palace of Pleasure*; Isabella Whitney, *The Copy of a Letter* (1566–7)
1567	Lord Darnley is murdered (allegedly by James Hepburn, Earl of Bothwell); Mary, Queen of Scots marries the Earl of Bothwell; abdication of Mary, Queen of Scots; Revolt in the Netherlands against Spanish rule; Defeat of Irish rebellion	Geoffrey Fenton, *Certain Tragicall Discourses of Bandello*; Opening of the Red Lion playhouse
1568	Mary, Queen of Scots flees to England	
1569	Unsuccessful rebellion of the Northern Earls (1569–70); Munster rebellion in Ireland (1569–73)	

Date	Historical and Cultural Events	Literary Publications and Events
1570	Elizabeth I is excommunicated by Pope	William Baldwin, *Beware the Cat*
1571	Ridolfi plot to place Mary, Queen of Scots on the English throne; Defeat of the Turks at the Battle of Lepanto	
1572	St Bartholomew's Day Massacre of protestants in Paris	
1573		George Gascoigne, *The Adventures of Master F. J.*; Isabella Whitney, *A Sweet Nosegay*
1575		Gascoigne, *The Poesies of Gascoigne*; Creation of St Paul's theatre
1576	The Spanish sack Antwerp; the Dutch provinces unite against Spain; Martin Frobisher makes his first voyage to find the North-West passage (1576–8)	Opening of the Theatre
1577	Sir Francis Drake begins his circumnavigation of the globe	Opening of the first Blackfriars theatre and the Curtain theatre
1578	Elizabeth I considers the marriage proposal of Francis, Duke of Alençon	John Lyly, *Euphues. The Anatomy of Wit*; Margaret Tyler (trans.), *A Mirror of Princely Deeds and Knighthood*

Date	Historical and Cultural Events	Literary Publications and Events
1579	Desmond rebellion in Ireland (1579–83)	Edmund Spenser, *The Shepheardes Calender*
1580		Lyly, *Euphues and his England*
1582		Thomas Watson, *Hekatompathia*
1583	Discovery of the Throckmorton plot for the Spanish invasion of England	Robert Greene, *Mamillia*; Queen's Players are formed
1584	Assassination of William of Orange	Lyly, *Campaspe*
1585	Anglo-Dutch treaty; sending of English force to the Netherlands; Establishment of the first English colony in America at Roanoke, Virginia	
1586	Babington Plot to free Mary, Queen of Scots; trial of Mary for her part in the plot; Battle of Zutphen against Spanish forces in the Netherlands; death of Sir Philip Sidney after being wounded in the battle	

Date	Historical and Cultural Events	Literary Publications and Events
1587	Execution of Mary, Queen of Scots	Philip Henslowe builds the Rose theatre; Performance of Marlowe's *Tamburlaine the Great* and Thomas Kyd's *The Spanish Tragedy* (?)
1588	Defeat of the Spanish Armada	Greene, *Pandosto*; Performance of Marlowe's *Dr Faustus* (1588–9?)
1589	Henri III of France assassinated	Greene, *Menaphon*; Thomas Lodge, *Scilla's Metamorphosis*; Performance of Marlowe's *The Jew of Malta*
1590		Lodge, *Rosalynde*; Marlowe, *Tamburlaine the Great, Parts I and II*; Sidney, *Arcadia* (New Arcadia); Spenser, *The Faerie Queene* (Books I–III); Shakespeare writes *The Two Gentlemen of Verona* (1590–1)
1591	Earl of Essex leads expedition to aid Henri of Navarre	Lyly, *Endymion*; Sidney, *Astrophil and Stella*; Shakespeare writes *Henry VI, Parts II* and *III* (1591–2)

Date	Historical and Cultural Events	Literary Publications and Events
1592	Plague in London closes the theatres	*Arden of Faversham*; Samuel Daniel, *Delia*; Lyly, *Gallathea*, *Midas*; Thomas Nashe, *Pierce Penniless*; Lady Mary Sidney, translation of Robert Garnier's *Marc Antoine*; Composition and/or performance of Marlowe's *Edward II*; Shakespeare's *Henry VI, Part I*, *Titus Andronicus*, *The Taming of the Shrew*, *Richard III* (1592–3)
1593	Plague in London continues; theatres remain closed; Henri of Navarre becomes Catholic	Barnabe Barnes, *Parthenophil and Pathenophe*; Giles Fletcher, *Licia*; Lodge, *Phillis*; Shakespeare, *Venus and Adonis*; Sidney, *The Countess of Pembroke's Arcadia* (conflating the Old and New *Arcadias*); Murder of Marlowe

Date	Historical and Cultural Events	Literary Publications and Events
1594	Start of the Nine Years War in Ireland, following the rebellion of Hugh O'Neill Henri of Navarre crowned Henri IV of France	Richard Barnfield, *The Affectionate Shepherd*; Michael Drayton, *Idea's Mirror*; Thomas Heywood, *Oenone and Paris*; Nashe, *The Unfortunate Traveller*; Shakespeare, *The Rape of Lucrece*, *Titus Andronicus*, *The First Part of the Contention of the Two Famous Houses of York and Lancaster* (*Henry VI, Part II*); Performance of Shakespeare's *The Comedy of Errors* (written 1592–4); Shakespeare writes *Love's Labour's Lost* (1594–5)
1595	Deaths of Sir Francis Drake and John Hawkins	George Chapman, *Ovid's Banquet of the Sense*; Drayton, *Endymion and Phoebe: Idea's Latmus*; Thomas Edwards, *Cephalus and Procris*; Sidney, *Defence of Poesy*; Shakespeare, *The True Tragedy of Richard Duke of York* (*Henry VI, Part III*); Shakespeare writes *A Midsummer Night's Dream* (1594–6), *Romeo and Juliet*, *Richard II*; Building of the Swan theatre

Date	Historical and Cultural Events	Literary Publications and Events
1596	Earl of Essex attacks Cadiz Food shortages and riots Peace with France	Sidney, *Works*; new edition of Spenser, *The Faerie Queene* (including Books IV–VI); Shakespeare writes *King John*, *The Merchant of Venice* (1596–7), *Henry IV, Part I* (1596–7)
1597	Failure of second Armada	Francis Bacon, *Essays*; Thomas Deloney, *Jack of Newbury*; Joseph Hall, *Virgidemiarum*; Shakespeare, *Romeo and Juliet*, *Richard II*, *Richard III*; Shakespeare writes *The Merry Wives of Windsor* (1597–8)
1598		Chapman/Marlowe, *Hero and Leander*; Everard Guilpin, *Skialethia*; John Marston, *Pygmalion's Image and Certain Satyres*; Shakespeare, *Love's Labour's Lost*, *Henry IV, Part I*; Composition and/or performance of William Haughton's *A Woman will have her Will*; Ben Jonson's *Every Man in His Humour*; Shakespeare's *Henry IV, Part II*, *Much Ado About Nothing*; Opening of Boar's Head theatre

Date	Historical and Cultural Events	Literary Publications and Events
1599	Bishops' Ban on satires	Chapman, *A Humorous Day's Mirth*; Performance of Thomas Dekker's *The Shoemaker's Holiday*; Jonson's *Every Man out of His Humour*; Shakespeare's *Henry V, Julius Caesar, As You Like It*; Opening of the Globe theatre
1600	Birth of Charles Stuart (later Charles I)	Shakespeare, *A Midsummer Night's Dream, The Merchant of Venice, Henry IV, Part II, Much Ado About Nothing, Henry V*; John Weever, *Faunus and Melliflora*; Shakespeare writes *Hamlet* (1600–1); Fortune theatre opened
1601	The Earl of Essex leads failed rebellion against the Queen, and is subsequently executed	Shakespeare, *The Phoenix and the Turtle*; Shakespeare writes *Twelfth Night, Troilus and Cressida* (1601–2)
1602		Francis Beaumont, *Salmacis and Hermaphroditis*; Marston, *Antonio and Mellida, Antonio's Revenge*; Shakespeare, *The Merry Wives of Windsor*

Date	Historical and Cultural Events	Literary Publications and Events
1603	Death of Elizabeth I; accession of James I; Surrender of Hugh O'Neill in Ireland	Florio's translation of Montaigne's *Essays*; Shakespeare, *Hamlet* (First Quarto); Shakespeare's acting company becomes the King's Men; Performance of Jonson's *Sejanus* (1603–4)
1604	Hampton Court Conference; peace treaty with Spain	Marlowe, *Dr Faustus* ('A' Text); Marston, *The Malcontent*; Shakespeare, *Hamlet* (Second Quarto); Performance of Chapman's *Bussy D'Ambois*; Shakespeare's *Measure for Measure*, *Othello*
1605	The Gunpowder Plot	Drayton, *Poems*; Composition/ Performance of Daniel's *Philotas*, *The Queen's Arcadia*; Jonson's *The Masque of Blackness*; Thomas Middleton's *A Mad World, My Masters*; Shakespeare's *All's Well That Ends Well*, *King Lear*
1606	Foundation of the Virginia Company	Performance of Jonson's *Volpone*; Middleton's *The Revenger's Tragedy*; Shakespeare's *Macbeth*, *Antony and Cleopatra* (1606–7)

Date	Historical and Cultural Events	Literary Publications and Events
1607	English colony founded in Jamestown, Virginia	Chapman, *Bussy D'Ambois*; Composition and/or performance of Beaumont's *The Knight of the Burning Pestle*; Shakespeare's *Pericles* (with George Wilkins) (1607–8); Opening of Red Bull and Whitefriars theatres
1608		Chapman, *The Conspiracy and Tragedy of Charles, Duke of Byron*; Hall, *Characters of Virtues and Vices*; Shakespeare, *King Lear*; Beaumont and John Fletcher write *Philaster* (1608–10); Shakespeare writes *Coriolanus*
1609		Shakespeare, *Sonnets*, *Troilus and Cressida*, *Pericles*; new edition of Spenser, *The Faerie Queene* (including Mutability Cantos); Performance of Jonson's *Epicoene* (1609–10); Shakespeare writes *Cymbeline* (1609–10), *The Winter's Tale* (1609–11); The King's Men start performing at the Second Blackfriars theatre

Date	Historical and Cultural Events	Literary Publications and Events
1610	Assassination of Henri IV of France	Fletcher, *The Faithful Shepherdess*; Performance of Jonson's *The Alchemist*
1611		King James Bible; Chapman, *The Iliad*; Aemilia Lanyer, *Salve Deus Rex Judaeorum*; Performance of Beaumont's and Fletcher's *A King and No King*; Dekker's and Middleton's *The Roaring Girl*; Jonson's *Catiline*; Shakespeare's *The Tempest* Beaumont and Fletcher write *The Maid's Tragedy*
1612	Death of Henry, Prince of Wales, eldest son of James I	Second edition of Bacon, *Essays*; John Webster, *The White Devil*
1613	Marriage of Princess Elizabeth to Frederick, the Elector Palatine	Elizabeth Carey, *The Tragedy of Mariam*; Performance of Middleton's *A Chaste Maid in Cheapside*; Shakespeare's *All is True (Henry VIII)* (with Fletcher); Shakespeare and Fletcher write *The Two Noble Kinsmen* (1613–14); First Globe theatre burns down

Date	Historical and Cultural Events	Literary Publications and Events
1614		Chapman, *The Odyssey*; Thomas Overbury, *Characters*; Performance of Jonson's *Bartholomew Fair*; Webster's *The Duchess of Malfi*; Second Globe theatre built; Hope theatre built
1615		Building of Porter's Hall theatre
1616	Trial of the Earl and Countess of Somerset for the murder of Sir Thomas Overbury	Chapman, *Whole Works of Homer*; James I, *Works*; Ben Jonson, *Works*; Marlowe, *Dr Faustus* ('B' Text); Death of Shakespeare; Jonson awarded a royal pension; Opening of Cockpit theatre
1617	Sir Walter Raleigh travels to Guiana	
1618	Start of the Thirty Years War in Europe	Performance of Jonson's *Pleasure Reconciled to Virtue*
1619	Death of Queen Anne; Frederick, Elector Palatine chosen King of Bohemia	Middleton writes *The Mayor of Queenborough* (1619–20)
1620	Elector Palatine loses Bohemia	Beaumont and Fletcher, *Philaster*

Date	Historical and Cultural Events	Literary Publications and Events
1621		Mary Wroth, *Urania*, Part I; Middleton writes *Women Beware Women*; Wroth writes *Love's Victory*
1622		Shakespeare, *Othello*; Performance of Fletcher's *The Spanish Curate*; Middleton's and William Rowley's *The Changeling*
1623	Prince Charles and the Duke of Buckingham visit Spain to negotiate a marriage with the Spanish Infanta	Daniel, *Whole Works*; Shakespeare, First Folio; Webster, *The Duchess of Malfi*
1624		John Donne, *Devotions*; Performance of Middleton's *A Game at Chess*
1625	Death of James I; accession of Charles I; Charles I marries French Princess Henrietta Maria; War with Spain	Final edition of Bacon, *Essays*
1626	Parliament attempts to impeach the Duke of Buckingham	Performance of Jonson's *The Staple of News*
1628	Assassination of the Duke of Buckingham; Publication of William Harvey's work on the circulation of the blood	Performance of John Ford's *Lover's Melancholy*

Date	Historical and Cultural Events	Literary Publications and Events
1629	Charles I suspends parliament and does not recall it until 1640	Composition/Performance of Jonson's *The New Inn*; Philip Massinger's *The Roman Actor*; Salisbury Court theatre built (1629–30)
1630	Birth of Prince Charles (future Charles II); Treaty of Madrid ends conflict with Spain	
1632		Donne, *Death's Duel*; Cockpit-in-Court converted for plays
1633		Donne, *Poems*; Ford, *'Tis Pity She's a Whore*, *The Broken Heart*, *Love's Sacrifice*; Sir Fulke Greville, *Works*; George Herbert, *The Temple*; Massinger, *A New Way to Pay Old Debts*
1634		Ford, *Perkin Warbeck*; Shakespeare and Fletcher, *The Two Noble Kinsmen*
1638		*Justa Edouardo King Naufrago* (including John Milton's 'Lycidas')
1639	First Bishops' War with Scotland	

Date	Historical and Cultural Events	Literary Publications and Events
1640	Charles recalls parliament; Second Bishops' War with Scotland ends with Treaty of Ripon	Thomas Carew, *Poems*; Donne, *LXXX Sermons*; Izaak Walton, *Life of Donne*
1642	Outbreak of Civil War; the public playhouses are closed by order of parliament	Thomas Browne, *Religio Medici*
1646	Presbyterian church system established by parliament; Charles surrenders to Scots	Richard Crashaw, *Steps to the Temple*; Milton, *Poems*; Henry Vaughan, *Poems*
1648	Second Civil War End of Thirty Years War	Robert Herrick, *Hesperides*
1649	Execution of Charles I; England declared a Commonwealth	Donne, *Fifty Sermons*; Richard Lovelace, *Lucasta*

Introduction

This century, like a golden age, has restored to light the liberal arts ... achieving what had been honoured among the ancients, but almost forgotten since. (Marsilio Ficino, 1482)[1]

THE HISTORICAL CONTEXT

The 'Renaissance' (meaning 'rebirth') describes the movement which saw renewed European interest in classical culture between the late fourteenth and mid-seventeenth centuries. Having initially sought to emulate the achievements of the Greek and Roman empires, Renaissance scholars and artists later sought to out-do their ancient predecessors, and therefore engaged in fresh intellectual and artistic exploration. The origins of the 'Renaissance' have been hotly debated but most scholars agree that it originated in late fourteenth-century Italy, where it was fostered by a new generation of humanist scholars. Its influence was gradually felt all across Europe, reaching England by the early sixteenth century. The specific term 'Renaissance' (or *rinascita*) was first used by Italian art historian Giorgio Vasari in his *Lives of the Most Eminent Painters* (1550) to describe the achievements of recent artists; achievements he saw as marking a revival in the arts, after a period of long decay following the fall of the Roman Empire. Not until the nineteenth century was the term used more broadly to describe the period and culture of early modern Europe (1500–1700); and only in the twentieth century did the term come to be a standard label for the era.

Some modern scholars have questioned the use of the term 'Renaissance', arguing that it overstates the break with the past and downplays Medieval knowledge of classical learning. Other critics argue that it is only relevant to the experiences of the classically educated, male elite. Such scholars often prefer to describe the period as 'early modern'; but this label has its drawbacks, too, potentially overemphasising the similarities between Renaissance and modern culture. The more traditional term 'Renaissance' is favoured for the title of this guide, but appears alongside the phrase 'early modern' in the text. Although Elizabethan and Stuart writers did not refer to their era as the 'Renaissance' it was a concept they understood, and highlights the fact that it was an era of new advances in European knowledge, akin to those associated with the great classical civilisations.

Religion

Religion was central to life in Renaissance England. Officially, everyone was Christian. The possibility that God did not exist was barely acknowledged and those who dared to express atheist views faced harsh penalties. In such a culture religion was not simply an ideology it was a way of life, and to write about any aspect of life was almost inevitably to touch on religion. The importance of Christianity in early Renaissance Europe was reinforced by the strength of the Catholic Church (led by the Pope). In 1500 all the major Western European states and their people belonged to it; but there had long been discontent within the Catholic community about perceived clerical corruption. In 1517 a new campaign for ecclesiastical reform came to a head when Martin Luther (an ex-monk), nailed ninety-five theses to the door of the church in Wittenberg that questioned the authority and doctrines of the Catholic Church. Initially, Luther and his fellow campaigners sought the reformation of the Church from within, but, faced with intransigence, criticism soon hardened into opposition and the reformers came to believe that the only way to re-establish God's 'true' church was to break away and found their own 'Protestant' Church. This movement became known as the Protestant Reformation.

At first Protestantism was a fringe religion but it grew in power as a number of Northern European states became Protestant. In 1534 the Protestant cause gained an unlikely ally in England when Henry VIII (1509–47) declared himself 'Supreme Head' of the Church of England. Henry's reasons for challenging the authority of the Pope and the Catholic Church were political and personal, rather than doctrinal. Little more than a decade earlier the Pope had awarded him the title of Defender of the Faith after he attacked Luther's views (1521); but by 1527 Henry was considering divorcing his first wife, Catherine of Aragon, so that he might marry Anne Boleyn. Officially, Henry sought the divorce on the grounds that Catherine was initially betrothed to his brother Arthur and that the match was, therefore, incestuous; but Henry's desire for Anne Boleyn and a male heir were equally powerful motives. Only the Pope could annul Henry's first marriage but, under pressure from the current emperor (Charles V), he refused to do so. By making himself Head of the Church of England Henry was able to circumvent the Pope's authority. His ally Thomas Cranmer became Archbishop of Canterbury and promptly declared Henry's union with Catherine invalid.

Given the reasons behind Henry's conflict with Rome, it is perhaps not surprising that the English Church did not alter substantially during his reign. The boldest change came with the dissolution of the monasteries and the holy orders associated with them (1536, 1539). While the suppression of the monastic orders could be justified as a way of dealing with their perceived corruption, the sale of monastic property was a way of generating money and buying support for the new regime: those nobles and gentlemen who profited from the sale had a vested interest in supporting Henry's rule and the independence of the English Church.

Henry's more spiritually zealous son Edward VI (1547–53) sought to reform the English Church along more explicitly Protestant lines but died after only a short rule to be replaced by his ardently Catholic sister, Mary (1553–58) (daughter of Catherine of Aragon). Mary could not re-establish the monasteries but she reintroduced the celibate religious orders, re-allied the English Church with Rome, and systematically persecuted Protestants; but the Marian counter-Reformation proved similarly brief, as Mary died of a tumour in 1558. She was succeeded by Elizabeth I, daughter of Henry VIII and Anne Boleyn.

Like her brother Edward, Elizabeth was Protestant, and was declared Head of the Church of England, but she claimed to have no wish to 'open windows into men's souls' and was ready to be more tolerant of Catholics, providing they were loyal and conformed outwardly. The Elizabethan Church Settlement ushered in a period of general stability, but religious dissent remained a problem. As well as facing the persistent threat of a Catholic invasion or assassination, the Queen faced calls for further religious reform from more advanced Protestants. Such would-be reformers came to be known as 'Puritans' because of their desire to further 'purify' the Church and their favouring of an ascetic religious culture.

Similar tensions characterised religious culture in Stuart England (1603–49). As well as facing periodic threats from Catholic dissidents (as exemplified by the Catholic Gunpowder Plot to assassinate James I in 1605), both James I and Charles I had to deal with Puritan calls for reform. Shortly after his accession James held a conference at Hampton Court Palace (1604) to consider one such petition; but he soon made it clear that he was completely opposed to the idea of the English Church becoming Presbyterian (that is, a church in which there was no clerical hierarchy). In his view the removal of church leaders was akin to an attack on his own position; as he put it, 'No Bishop, no King'.[2] On the other hand, James did not grant Catholics greater tolerance, as some Puritans had feared he might, and encouraged the preparation of a new English translation of the Bible (published in 1611 as the influential *King James Authorised Bible*).

Charles I shared his father's distaste for advanced Protestantism. More worryingly for Puritan reformers, Charles's sympathies appeared to be Anglo-Catholic. As well as marrying a French Catholic Princess (Henrietta Maria) and allowing her and her entourage to practice their religion at court, Charles promoted clerics such as William Laud, who were perceived to be sympathetic to Catholicism. Charles's religious conservatism was, likewise, demonstrated by his unpopular attempt to impose episcopacy in Scotland, where the Protestant Church had long been Presbyterian.

As well as leading to the so-called Bishops' wars with the Scots (in the 1630s), Charles's perceived sympathy for Catholicism contributed to the breakdown of his relationship with Parliament, a body increasingly dominated by Puritan sympathisers from the 1620s.

Catholicism and Protestantism

As Christians, Catholics and Protestants shared important beliefs (including the conviction that Jesus Christ was God's son and died on the cross to redeem man's sins), but contemporaries were more sensitive to the differences between them. Perhaps the most significant of these concerned their understanding of the individual's relationship to God. Catholics regarded the priest as an essential mediator between God and the individual, acting as the interpreter of God's Word and interceding with God on the behalf of his congregation. By contrast, Protestants encouraged individuals to forge their own relationship with God and preached the importance of direct access to God's Word and individual Bible reading.

Just as they challenged the authority of priests, so Protestants challenged the Pope's authority to rule over the Church and his claim to be God's chief representative on earth, insisting that he was no more than the 'Bishop of Rome'. Later, as antagonisms hardened, he came to be identified with the devil and Antichrist. Many Protestants became convinced that they were engaged in a religious war predicted in the Biblical Book of Revelation and its story of the conflict between a woman clothed with sun (who they identified with Protestantism) and the Scarlet Whore of Babylon (who they saw as a figure for Catholicism). In figuring the Catholic Church as a richly dressed whore, Protestant writers were pointing to the perceived corruption of Catholicism and its association with lavish visual display. Catholic churches were traditionally richly decorated; and icon worship (the practice of praying before images of Christ, Mary and the Saints) was a central part of worship. Protestants claimed that the focus should be on God's Word and that visual displays were a distraction. For this reason many reformers campaigned for the removal of images from churches (a movement known as 'iconoclasm').

Catholics and Protestants disagreed about matters of Christian doctrine, as well as modes of worship. One of the most serious disputes concerned the question of how God determined whether individuals were saved or damned. Catholic theology suggested that salvation was potentially open to everyone, right up until the last moment of life, and could be achieved through repentance for one's sins and 'good works'. By contrast most of the early Protestant churches adopted the theory of predestination, developed by John Calvin, which argued that men and women had no control over whether they were saved or damned because their fate was predestined by God before they were born.

Judaism and Islam

Western Europeans were generally Christian but recognised the existence of at least two other religions: Judaism and Islam. The followers of both faiths are conventionally stigmatised in the period's literature. Jews are associated with avarice and usury, while Islamic figures are stereotyped as barbaric, untrustworthy, lustful pagans. Yet most English people would have had little knowledge of either religion. This was especially true of Islam. Although Christians were accustomed to regard Islam as a false faith, most had to rely on second-hand accounts for their knowledge of it because the only Europeans who had much contact with the Islamic East were traders and diplomats. Opposition to Islam and the countries associated with it was deep-rooted, finding its origins in the Medieval Crusades to recover the Holy Land from the Muslims, but Western antipathy was fuelled in the sixteenth century by the growing power of the Ottoman (or Turkish) Empire and its extension westwards with the Turks laying 'claim to pivotal territory in the eastern Mediterranean and North Africa, including Cyprus in 1571 and Tunis in 1574'.[3] Such was the perceived threat that the Spanish, the Venetians and the Pope formed a league to fight against the Turks, famously defeating them in the Battle of Lepanto (1571).

The Jews had long been persecuted in Europe but were a more familiar religious minority than Muslims, living within (as well as beyond) Europe. Jews were expelled from England in 1290 but returned in small numbers during subsequent centuries. By the late sixteenth century there were small Jewish communities in London and Bristol, although those involved were obliged to conform outwardly to Protestantism, both because other religions were not tolerated and because of the strength of contemporary anti-Jewish feeling. Such antipathy had a long history: the association of the Jews with the death of Jesus and with money lending (which the Bible condemned) had long encouraged European Christians to look down on the Jews as an ungodly sect, while their status as an 'alien', homeless people made them a perennial object of suspicion. The curiosity and anxiety aroused by religious and cultural 'aliens' in the period is reflected in the ambivalent representation of Jews in late sixteenth-century plays such as Christopher Marlowe's *The Jew of Malta* and Shakespeare's *The Merchant of Venice*.

Magic

In Renaissance Europe faith in Christianity co-existed with a widespread belief in magic. Even monarchs and religious leaders took magic seriously. Elizabeth I famously consulted contemporary magus John Dee for advice about the most auspicious date for her coronation, while her successor, James I participated in a series of witchcraft trials and published his own study of the subject, *Demonology* (1597). The extent of popular interest in magic is reflected in the proliferation of texts about magic in the late sixteenth and early seventeenth centuries. In England such literature included non-fiction books about witchcraft, accounts of witchcraft trials, and a large body of poems, plays and prose romances featuring magicians and witches. Such literature appears to have proved especially popular in the Jacobean period, when the accession of James I generated fresh interest in the subject. One of the best known examples of Jacobean 'witchcraft' literature, William Shakespeare's *Macbeth* (performed c. 1606) (which features a chorus of witches who predict the future) is thought to have been written to cater for this fashion.

Perceptions of what constituted magic varied. Some contemporaries distinguished between 'black' and 'white' magic, categorising magic used to hurt or injure people, animals or property as 'black' and magic used to help or heal as 'white'. Contemporaries, likewise, distinguished between different types of magician, such as witches, magi, and cunning men and women. Witches were generally understood to be people 'who either by open or secret league, wittingly and willingly, consenteth to vse the aide and assistance of the Deuill, in the working of wonders'; while a magus was believed to be a 'great magician who by dint of deep learning, ascetic discipline, and patient skill could command the secret forces of the natural and supernatural world' (like Shakespeare's Prospero).[4] Far humbler was the figure of the 'cunning' man or woman, who was believed to possess knowledge that allowed him or her to heal animals and people.[5] Some contemporaries, including James I, condemned all kinds of magic as demonic, but anecdotal evidence suggests that others were not opposed to those who practiced 'white' magic; and the witchcraft laws, first introduced in the sixteenth century, focused on those who practised 'black' magic.

Politics

Renaissance England was ruled over by a monarch who inherited the crown by succession. Many people believed that the monarch was divinely appointed and derived his or her authority from God (a theory known as the 'divine right of rule'); others argued that the monarch ruled in parliament through the will of the people. On these grounds theorists such as George Buchanan argued that it was acceptable for subjects to depose a ruler who acted tyrannically. The question of when subjects might have the right to rebel was a subject taken up by a number of political thinkers, and was an especially pressing concern amongst early Protestants many of whom found their faith at odds with that of their rulers. Out of this concern arose what has become known as 'resistance theory': the theory that it was justifiable for individuals to resist the rule of any state that attempted to prevent them from practising their faith.[6]

Bolder theorists subjected monarchy itself to critical examination. As well as weighing up the respective merits of hereditary and elective monarchies, contemporary writers compared and contrasted the different types of government found in contemporary Europe with the imperial and republican governments associated with the Greek and Roman empires. In many cases, the effect of these comparisons was to suggest the superior merits of a republican political system in which rule was collective and determined by elected individuals. Some contemporaries, such as Thomas Hobbes, blamed the rise of republicanism and the English Civil War on the popular study of classical histories 'in which books the popular government was extolled by that glorious name of liberty, and monarchy disgraced by the name of tyranny'.[7]

English Parliamentarians may have been ready to rule without the monarch by the late 1640s but for most of the Tudor and Stuart periods this was unimaginable, not least because it was customary to identify the monarch with the state. Contemporary political theory taught people that the monarch had two bodies: a 'body politic' and a 'body natural'. The 'body natural' was the monarch's mortal, personal self, and the 'body politic' was the state, headed by the monarch, 'consisting of Policy and Government'.[8] The monarch was not expected to rule over the 'body politic' alone. By the sixteenth century it was customary for the monarch to take advice from a body of specially chosen counsellors known as the Privy Council and to consult periodically with parliament which consisted then (as now) of two houses of representatives of the people: the House of Lords and the House of Commons. The monarch was responsible for summoning parliament, and usually did so when she or he needed to raise money (for example, for wars). In return, the monarch was expected to listen to his or her subjects' grievances, and to act on them as seemed appropriate. But the relationship between monarch and parliament became increasingly strained in the Renaissance as they came into conflict on issues such as the royal succession and foreign policy, and disagreed about parliament's right to have a say on such issues. The Tudor and Stuart monarchs generally took the view that these were matters for the ruler to determine, whereas parliament argued for its right to influence royal decision-making.

It was not only privy councillors or their European equivalents that sought to give advice to Renaissance rulers. Contemporary writers, likewise, proffered them counsel. Two of the best known princely advice books are Erasmus's *The Education of a Christian Prince* (written 1516) and Machiavelli's *The Prince* (written 1513). The advice they offer is very different. Erasmus is concerned with how to become a model Christian prince, at the heart of which ideal is a belief in the importance of justice. Indeed, Erasmus argues that 'if you cannot defend your kingdom without violating justice, without much human bloodshed, or without great damage to the cause of religion' you should abdicate and 'prefer to be a just man than an unjust prince'.[9] Machiavelli, by contrast, describes what he regards as the most effective methods for achieving and maintaining power. This includes arguing that a Prince must be ready to be immoral, cruel and ready to break his word, advice totally at odds with Erasmus's emphasis on Christian virtue and justice.[10]

Machiavelli's readiness to advocate immoral actions meant that *The Prince* quickly became notorious when it was printed in 1536; and, by the end of the sixteenth century, Machiavelli's name had become synonymous with diabolical cunning and ruthless political manipulation. *The Prince* was not translated into English until 1640 but it is clear that many English Renaissance writers were familiar with Machiavelli's theories. Not only do they allude to him by name, and echo ideas from *The Prince*, but the stage 'Machiavel' (a cunning politician-cum-manipulator) became a stock role in the English Renaissance drama. Christopher Marlowe's 'Machevil', who reads the prologue to *The Jew of Malta*, is an obvious example of this, but many other Renaissance villains can be seen as variations on the Machiavellian type, including Edmund in *King Lear* and Iago in *Othello*.

The Court

The court was not simply home to the monarch, it housed the royal administration, played host to visiting ambassadors and dignitaries, and served as the chief distributor of government offices, privileges and honours. As the country's chief hub of power it attracted those ambitious for advancement. Succeeding at court was partly a matter of who you knew, and whose favour you could win, but to cultivate powerful patrons you also needed to impress. In a culture in which lavish display and conspicuous consumption were important markers of status and power, courtiers were expected to be richly dressed and to be generous patrons. Great men and women were, likewise, expected to be 'courtly' in their conduct and accomplishments. Expectations of both were high, as contemporary guides to courtliness reveal. In his *Book of the Courtier* (translated by Sir Thomas Hoby, 1561), Italian writer Baldassare Castiglione describes how the model Renaissance courtier was expected be a talented all-rounder, skilful in courtly conversation, sports, dancing and the arts. According to Castiglione, these accomplishments were ideally combined with an air of easy grace or 'recklessness' (*sprezzatura*) that made them seem effortless and spontaneous. To some extent what Castiglione praises is simply an extension of the Renaissance admiration for art which conceals itself, but it also suggests, as Julia Briggs notes, 'that self-consciousness, insincerity, and even dissimulation may be part of the courtier's skills', and helps to explain why the representation of courtiers is often ambiguous in Renaissance literature.[11]

Elizabeth I

Elizabeth I was the daughter of Henry VIII and Anne Boleyn. She succeeded to the English throne in 1558 and became the longest reigning Tudor monarch. It was an achievement that few contemporaries would have predicted at a time when women were generally deemed inferior to men and some people doubted women's ability to rule, including Protestant John Knox. In *The First Blast of the Trumpet Against the Monstrous Regiment of Women* (1558) he argued that: 'To promote a woman to bear rule, superiority, dominion or empire above any realm, nation, or city is repugnant to nature, contumely to God, a thing most contrarious to his revealed will and approved ordinance'.[12] Just as Elizabeth's gender informed reactions to her accession, so it shaped Elizabethan politics. Throughout her reign she was under pressure to marry and provide England with an heir. It was an expectation that she used to her advantage at home and abroad. While the possibility of a union with a European prince provided a way of encouraging England's continental rivals to compete for an alliance with the English, at home Elizabeth fostered a cult of chivalry, which cast her predominantly male courtiers in the role of lovers keen to serve and win the favour of their virgin mistress.

The early years of Elizabeth's reign were largely successful. While the Elizabethan Church Settlement saw the peaceful re-establishment of Protestantism, Elizabeth's political shrewdness, and her avoidance of marriage, prevented any serious conflicts between rival court factions and saved England from direct military conflict with the powers of Catholic Europe. The second half of her reign was to be more troubled, partly because the strategies Elizabeth had previously employed so successfully were no longer as effective. In both cases, Elizabeth's growing age was a problem. Internationally, it meant that the possibility of a marriage with the Queen was no longer the powerful bargaining tool that it had once been; and at home it made the artificiality of the courtly cult of chivalry increasingly apparent. Growing numbers of male courtiers became discontent with a culture which required them to 'woo' the Queen as if she were their lover, while the fact that she was past child-bearing age led to increasing anxiety about the royal succession. Elizabeth's difficulties were heightened by new political problems, several of which stemmed from Philip II of Spain's intensification of his campaign against continental Protestantism. This came to a head in the Netherlands. Theoretically a Spanish possession, the spread of Protestantism in the Netherlands led to a Dutch campaign for independence, and the outbreak of war between Dutch and Spanish troops. Elizabeth was generally reluctant to engage in military action, but felt obliged to act after the assassination of the Protestant leader, William of Orange (1584): she signed an Anglo-Dutch treaty (1585) and sent an English force to help the Dutch.

Philip of Spain's desire to attack England was increased after the execution of Catholic monarch, Mary, Queen of Scots in 1587. Elizabeth had been holding Mary prisoner from around 1569 after the Scots Queen fled to England having been implicated in the murder of her second husband and forced to abdicate the Scottish throne (1567). In England Mary became the focus for a number of Catholic plots to overthrow Elizabeth I and was directly implicated in the Babington plot (1586). Despite her reluctance to execute a fellow prince Elizabeth finally agreed to the death sentence. For the Spaniards and the Catholic Church it was a step too far and they launched a joint military crusade against the English.

A fleet was assembled and set sail from Lisbon in May 1588; but the Spanish 'Armada' failed. Some ships were destroyed off Calais; others were wrecked or dispersed by strong winds off the Scottish and Irish coasts. The defeat of the Spanish fleet was heralded in England as a sign that God had protected England and its 'true' church.

Problems with Catholic Spain gave way in the 1590s to troubles in Ireland. In theory Ireland was an English colony, but it remained predominantly Catholic and a series of rebellions against English rule provoked fears that it would be used to launch a Spanish invasion of England. For this reason, Elizabeth's government was especially concerned by the rebellion led by Hugh O'Neill, Earl of Tyrone (1594–1603). The English force sent to quell the uprising was headed by the Queen's glamorous young favourite, Robert Devereux, Earl of Essex, but the mission proved a fiasco. Essex ended up agreeing a truce with Tyrone and returned home to England without the Queen's permission (1599).

Elizabeth's problems in Ireland were compounded by fresh domestic difficulties, caused by rising inflation, growing unemployment, and a series of harvest failures and plague epidemics. Poverty and crime were on the increase and the country was experiencing a nationwide economic depression. Disaffection with the Queen's rule was intensified at court amongst younger male courtiers by Elizabeth's perceived parsimony and her distaste for military intervention in Europe. These men included a number of those associated with the dashing Earl of Essex who was to lead an ill-fated rebellion against the Queen on 8 February 1601. It is perhaps no coincidence that the same men were known to be interested in Roman republican history and to have drawn parallels between Elizabeth and her infamously weak predecessor, Richard II (1367–1400). While Roman history presented such men with alternative models of rule, the deposition of Richard II by Henry Bolingbroke (later Henry IV) provided a precedent for the overthrow of an unpopular monarch. Essex claimed that the uprising was on Elizabeth's behalf but it failed to generate public support and the ring-leaders were quickly caught and sentenced. Essex was executed on 25 February 1601. The remainder of Elizabeth's reign passed in comparative peace. By the time she died on 24 March

1603, Elizabeth I had overseen nearly half a century of civil peace and England's transformation into a leading Protestant state.

James I

On Elizabeth I's death the English crown passed to her nephew King James VI of Scotland, who became James I of England. James Stuart was the son of Mary, Queen of Scots and had been King in Scotland since 1567. His accession to the English throne was greeted with a mixture of anticipation and anxiety. Many people were suspicious of a man they perceived to be an outsider but the fact that James was married and had three children (Henry, Charles and Elizabeth) meant there were no immediate anxieties about the royal succession.

At court the cult of chivalry fostered by Elizabeth gave way to a new royal mythology which alternately presented James as a god-like emperor, and a wise, learned father to his people and husband to his land. This transformation was in keeping with James's patri-archal view of monarchy, which he explored in works such as *The True Law of Free Monarchies* (1598) and *Basilikon Doron* (1599). Like Charles I after him, James believed in absolute monarchy (that is, that his authority was not subject to the law or the will of others); a fact which brought him into conflict with parliament. Shortfalls in royal income obliged him to turn to parliament to raise money, particularly for England's military involvement in the religious wars in early seventeenth-century Europe, but James was not ready to allow parliament to offer advice on his policies.

James had his own distinctive political agenda, too. As King of England and Scotland, he wanted to unite his realms as 'Britain'. He was equally keen to be a peace-maker in Europe, signing a peace treaty with the Spanish (1604) and a trade deal with the French. In similar fashion, he hoped to create long term alliances on both sides of the European religious divide through the marriage of his chil-dren into Protestant and Catholic royal families: his daughter Elizabeth married Frederick V, the Protestant Elector Palatine of the Rhine (1613) and Charles married the French Catholic Princess, Henrietta Maria (1625). James was not to fulfil either of his politi-cal ambitions in the long term. Although he referred to himself as

King of 'Britain' he did not persuade the English parliament to agree to an English-Scottish union and he was forced to abandon his pacific foreign policy following the outbreak of the Thirty Years War in Europe.

James's disillusion with European politics was matched at home by growing disaffection with his rule. While parliament found him high-handed in his demands for money, military-minded Protestants objected to his pacific tendencies. There were concerns, too, about James's court. There had been complaints about corruption in the Elizabethan era but there was a general feeling that the court had become more immoral under James. As well as complaints about favouritism, and James's susceptibility to flattery, there were rumours that the court was sexually debauched. The ill reputation of the court was not helped by a series of scandals such as the trial and sentencing of Lady Frances Howard and Robert Carr, Earl of Somerset for the murder of Sir Thomas Overbury (1616).

Charles I

Charles I succeeded to the English throne in 1625. Like his father, he believed in absolute monarchy, but thought that it was the king's duty to lead his people by example and was therefore determined to rid the court of its perceived corruption. For similar reasons, and inspired by his increasing devotion to his wife, Henrietta Maria, Charles fostered a courtly cult of platonic love, encouraging contemporaries to see his loving marriage as a figure for his relationship with his people and his realm.

Charles's reformation of courtly conduct was generally welcomed but it did not prevent him from facing some of the same criticisms as his father. His close friendship with the Duke of Buckingham (once his father's friend) showed that he, too, was susceptible to favourites, while his sympathy for Anglo-Catholicism, and his insistence on his right to absolute authority led to similar conflicts with Puritan church reformers and parliament. The latter conflicts were to prove especially damaging. Like James, Charles was unable to fund his rule without recourse to parliament and its money-raising powers; and, like his father, he regarded it as parliament's duty to accede to such requests. Although it was customary for the monarch to listen to parliament, Charles did not believe it had the right to dictate the political agenda. Increasingly, members of parliament disagreed and conflict ensued. While Charles was insulted by parliament's refusal to grant him the money he needed to honour his military commitments in Europe and, later at home (against the Scots) Charles's parliaments complained about his 'forced loans, monopolies and arbitrary imprisonments' and his seeming 'disregard' for the law and the rights of his subjects.[13] Increasingly disillusioned, Charles ruled without any parliaments for more than a decade (a period known as the 'Personal Rule', 1629–40). Continued friction thereafter eventually led to the outbreak of the English Civil War (1642) in which Parliamentarians fought against Royalists for control of the state. Charles and his supporters were defeated and he was executed in 1649.

Society and Home

Renaissance society was hierarchical and patriarchal. At the top of the hierarchy was the monarch. The remainder of society was divided into four main groups of descending social status: nobles, gentry, citizens (such as merchants and tradesmen), and peasants or servants. Women were generally defined in terms of their relationships with men, and society as a whole was dominated by male power. This hierarchy was thought by many to be part of a larger divine order or great 'chain of being', presided over by God.[14] This helps to explain why at least some contemporaries thought that it was important to maintain social differences. On the other hand, the humanist emphasis upon self-improvement (see below) and the increasing wealth and power of the citizen classes encouraged greater social mobility.

Those born into the trading classes discovered that it was possible to improve their social status through education and hard work. Not only could such people potentially earn enough money to afford a good home and a comfortable lifestyle of the kind traditionally associated with the gentry and noble classes, but those wealthy enough had the chance to buy noble titles (in James's reign) or to marry their children into noble families, many of whom found themselves in increasing financial difficulties in the early modern period. Over the course of the Renaissance this led to a gradual transition from a social order 'based on rank and status to one based more directly on wealth and property'.[15]

The flourishing of the merchant classes, and the social changes it encouraged, was partly the result of a gradual transformation in the English economy. In the Medieval era England's economy was largely rural and based on wool and cloth. In the sixteenth century the growth of merchant adventurism, international trade and speculative financial activity led to the gradual institutionalisation of a market economy and encouraged urban immigration, especially to London. The capital was already far larger than any other city in England, but its population expanded massively in the Renaissance, growing from around 180,000 in 1576 to around 350,000 in 1642.[16]

As well as leading to problems with housing shortages and disease, the high levels of urban immigration and population growth put considerable strains on the Elizabethan social system. Fears that social problems would lead to disorder and crime encouraged the Elizabethan government to introduce the first national Poor Law in 1572 which required parishioners in every community to contribute a sum of money to be used to support the locally impoverished. Concerns about the social pressures created by immigration, likewise, encouraged tighter controls on people's movements. Immigration was generally discouraged; and travelling professionals, such as peddlers and players were required to carry a licence from the 1570s.

Contemporary attitudes to the social and economic changes witnessed in the Renaissance were mixed. The country's citizen classes generally embraced them; but others were concerned about the sudden influx of wealth and people into cities like London. Some feared that social mobility was a threat to order and there were concerns that the new market economy encouraged selfishness and materialism. Such anxieties are reflected in the period's literature, where satire of social climbers and urban materialism is common.

Home

At the heart of Renaissance society and its economy was the household and the nuclear family (of husband, wife and children), but families fluctuated in size and make-up. Life expectancy was generally much lower in the Renaissance so that it was not unusual for husbands and wives to outlive partners, and to marry several times, although widows were generally discouraged from doing so, as is illustrated by the story of the Duchess in John Webster's *The Duchess of Malfi* (see Chapter 1). In an age before effective contraception couples could expect to have many children, too, although not all were likely to survive until adulthood, as infant mortality rates were high. In his ground-breaking study of early modern life, Lawrence Stone suggested that low life expectancy figures and high infant mortality rates prevented people from forming close affective bonds with marriage partners and children; but more recent research has challenged this thesis, suggesting that deep attachments and grief about the death of partners and children was not unusual.[17]

Within the household men were expected to rule over their wives, children and servants as the king did over his subjects. The connection between royal and household rule was reinforced by the contemporary custom of describing the home as a 'little commonwealth' or state, 'by the good gouernment wherof, Gods glorie may bee aduanced, the common-wealthe, which standeth of seueral families, benefited, and all that liue in the familie may receiue much comfort and commoditie'.[18] The analogies drawn between household and state invested private life with importance, suggesting that the social order was partly dependent on order at the microcosmic level of the household.

Gender, Marriage and Sexuality

Gender

In the Renaissance gender difference was accepted. Men were expected to be active in the public sphere and to provide for, and protect their families, and women were encouraged to remain at home, nurturing and serving their loved ones. In practice, the distinction between the two genders was sometimes less clear-cut, especially in the trading and working classes. This caused anxiety. Some contemporaries feared that the blurring of traditional gender roles would lead to social breakdown.

In line with Biblical teaching, women were conventionally understood to be the 'weaker vessel'. This was one of the explanations given for women's traditional subjection to male authority. Support for the supposed inferiority of women was found in the teachings of Aristotelian (384–322 BC) and Galenic (2nd century) medicine. Galen, for example, argued that women were imperfect men, grounding his theory on his study of men's and women's sexual organs, which he believed were essentially the same (for this reason his theory is often referred to as the 'one-sex model'). According to Galen, women's sexual organs were an inverted version of those found in men, having failed to project outwards as a result of a defect of heat in the foetus.[19]

As the supposedly 'weaker' sex Renaissance women received extensive male advice about appropriate conduct. The model woman was expected to be chaste, silent and obedient. In practice, few women appear to have conformed straightforwardly to this 'ideal', but those who aggressively defied it faced social stigmatisation and punishment. Talkative or argumentative women faced condemnation as 'scolds' or 'shrews' and could be ducked under water on a 'cucking stool' or gagged with a 'scold's bridle', while unchaste women faced whipping as 'whores'.

Women punished in these ways were paying the price for not conforming to contemporary 'feminine' ideals. If the period's male writers are to be believed such women were not unusual. Although there are positive representations of women in Renaissance literature, negative stereotyping is much more common. According to women's detractors, they were fickle, lusty, vain, irrational, and not to be trusted, especially in matters of sexual fidelity and honour. The popularity of Joseph Swetnam's *Arraignment of Lewde, Idle, Froward, and Vnconstant Women* (1615) is a testimony to the currency of such female stereotypes.

In a society based on various forms of patriarchal inheritance (that is, inheritance from fathers and through men), the assumption that women were 'naturally' lusty was especially troubling and seems to have contributed to a virtual paranoia about female adultery. The same paranoia helps to explain why female chastity was so highly prized and why adulterous women were stigmatised: the only way that men could be sure that they were passing on wealth to their own children was if their wives were sexually faithful. 'Cuckolds' (husbands whose wives had been unfaithful) were mocked, too: jokes about such men having 'horns' (the traditional sign for a cuckolded man) were especially common and occur in a variety of Renaissance texts.

Social historians have struggled to account for this pronounced anxiety about female infidelity and the wide-spread demonising of women in the late sixteenth and early seventeenth centuries. Julia Briggs sees it as 'perhaps reflecting the recognition that women could never fully render the obedience or self-effacement called for by the patriarchal ideal'.[20] Others, such as Lisa Hopkins and Matthew Steggle, have suggested that it is 'rooted in the rise of cap-italism, and the concentration of property within a nuclear family', but it may also be connected to perceived changes in the relation-ship between the genders.[21] Contemporary literature makes it clear that at least some people feared that women were becoming more 'masculine'. Such fears find vivid expression in contemporary anecdotes about women being transformed into men, and the brief vogue for women wearing male attire in early seventeenth-century London.[22] The political and ecclesiastical authorities were quick to condemn the fashion. As well as transgressing the Biblical injunc-tion against cross-dressing (Deuteronomy 22:5) and blurring the visible difference between men and women, the fashion led to fears that women aimed to usurp male power. The anonymous author of *Hic Mulier: or, The man-woman* (1620), a pamphlet which attacks female cross-dressing, gives the impression that this usurpation is well under way, complaining that 'since the daies of Adam women were neuer so Masculine' and that they not only dress as men but ape traditionally masculine behaviour.[23]

Anxieties about women becoming masculine were all the greater because there were similar fears about men becoming 'feminine'. In *Haec-vir: Or, The womanish-man* (1620) the pamphlet which answers *Hic Mulier*, the female speaker alleges that women have only begun to assume 'masculine' dress and behaviour because of the effeminacy of contemporary men. As this suggests, manliness (like 'femininity') was understood to be 'a quality' that could be 'main-tained only through constant vigilance' and careful cultivation of manly qualities.[24] Contemporary worries about male effeminacy, like those about female adultery, reflect a pervasive anxiety about masculinity and the preservation of patriarchal authority in English Renaissance culture.

Marriage

Marriage was the institution at the heart of the Renaissance household. The legal age for marriage was lower than in modern Britain and different for men and women – girls might marry at 12 and boys at 14 – but most people did not marry until they were in their late twenties. In modern Western society marriages are generally expected to be based on love. This was not true in the same way in the Renaissance. Although love was desirable it was not in itself a sufficient justification for marriage. At the start of the sixteenth century marriages were more often social and economic alliances than romantic unions: men and women married to protect and consolidate family property and wealth, to achieve financial security, and to honour traditional family friendships, as often as they did out of love. For this reason, it was not unusual for relations to have a part in arranging marriages. People could not be married against their will, but, equally, they were expected to honour their family's wishes, and were not supposed to marry without parental consent. Romantic elopements are popular subjects in Renaissance literature, where they are usually sympathetically handled, but such unions were generally frowned on in contemporary communities.

Those who wished to marry had the option of two kinds of marriage promise: *sponsalia per verba de praesenti* ('spousals through words of the present') and *sponsalia per verba de futuro* ('spousals through words of the future').[25] The first type of promise occurs in *The Duchess of Malfi* when the Duchess and Antonio agree to take each other as man and wife in the present tense. This type of promise was instantly binding and meant that the man and woman who made the promise to each other were married. People were encouraged to have a church wedding but such a service was not essential. The second type of vow indicated a wish to be married in the future. A man and woman who took such a vow were engaged to marry but could change their minds, unless they consummated the relationship.

Like most Renaissance institutions, marriage was conventionally patriarchal. Biblical tradition taught that the husband was the head of the couple and that the wife was subject to his authority, as she was to the authority of the monarch and God. While husbands were expected to love and 'keep' their wives, wives were instructed to 'submit' themselves to the will of their husbands, in accordance with the teachings of St Paul in the Bible (Ephesians 5:22–24). The assumed superiority of husbands was reinforced legally. Under the Common Law a married woman had no independent legal identity or rights: husband and wife were recognised as one person, governed by the husband and a wife's possessions technically became his property. In practice, Renaissance marriages were not necessarily so unequal. The Catholic Church idealised celibacy and regarded marriage as a necessary evil, but Protestants argued for the moral and social value of marriage, and emphasised its function to provide mutual society. The Reformers never went so far as to suggest that husbands and wives were equals but their emphasis on mutual comfort suggested that husbands should see their wives as companions and appears to have contributed to the rise of what Lawrence Stone dubbed 'companionate marriage'.[26]

Whatever kind of marriage Renaissance couples formed it was binding, and could only be dissolved by the death of one of the partners. Divorce was theoretically possible, but in practice was rare: it required an Act of Parliament and was only granted in exceptional circumstances (such as the proven impotence of the husband). Mutual incompatibility, unhappiness and even domestic violence were not accepted as grounds for divorce.[27]

Sexuality

In the Renaissance people were not defined in terms of their sexual preferences, and the only acceptable form of sex, according to the Church, was chaste heterosexual sex between married men and women. Heterosexual sex before or outside of marriage was frowned on; but women's sexual 'honour' (or chastity) defined their social value and status in a way that men's did not; and writers and moralists paid much more attention to female sexuality. Women were commonly stereotyped as 'lusty' (as noted above), which led to persistent anxieties in the period about the possibility of female promiscuity, and a culture-wide demonisation of female sexuality.

Same-sex sexual activity was known to occur, particularly between men, but whether homosexuality existed (as a recognised sexual identity) is more contentious. Some scholars argue that there is evidence of men consciously expressing homosexual desire; others believe that contemporaries 'were far less certain about the distinction between hetero- and homosexuality and often had sexual relations with both sexes without regarding their behaviour as contradictory or strange'.[28] Evidence of male homosexual activity has been related to the strongly 'homosocial' nature of Renaissance society (see Glossary). As James Knowles notes: 'All the major institutions were entirely male, the social structure was built around systems of patronage and clientage between men, and many institutions, such as schools and universities, required men to share domestic space, and especially beds'.[29]

Like other forms of unorthodox sexual activity, sex between men was officially condemned and legally prohibited as a form of 'sodomy' (for which the penalty was execution). However, as recent research has shown, prosecutions were rare and buggery only appears to have faced punishment if it was accompanied by other perceived crimes against the social order such as rape (of the under-age) or religious and political dissent. Desire between women was occasionally acknowledged by contemporary writers but is gener-ally far less well-documented, partly because it was ignored officially and because people were more concerned about women having unlawful sex with men.

Humanism and Education

Renaissance humanism was an intellectual movement originating in Italy that encouraged the fresh study of classical learning. The movement was inspired by the rediscovery of lost Greek and Latin manuscripts following the fall of Constantinople (1453). Humanists believed that a fuller knowledge of the ancients and a thorough classical education was 'indispensable to civilized man'.[30] They, likewise, emphasised the importance of learning as a means of improving one's self, believing that man was unique amongst God's creations in his ability to transform himself through learning. It was their celebration of humanity that led to such scholars being known as humanists. For similar reasons the same name was adopted to describe the modern movement 'for the advancement of humanity without reliance on supernatural beliefs'.[31] But, unlike modern 'humanists', Renaissance humanists did not study humanity 'at the expense of God', seeing the careful improvement of one's self as a way of becoming closer to God.[32]

Humanist scholars were great advocates of education. In England the influence of early humanists such as Sir Thomas More led to the founding of new grammar schools up and down the country in the early sixteenth century, schools which made education available to a wide range of boys, including the sons of citizens and farmers as well as members of the gentry and nobility. England's two universities (Oxford and Cambridge) flourished in the Renaissance, too. The sixteenth and seventeenth centuries saw the founding of new colleges in both towns and an expansion in their student bodies.

At the heart of the school and university curriculum was the study of classical literature and Latin, the language of international scholarship and diplomacy. School boys and undergraduates studied a variety of classical authors and the art of 'rhetoric' (see Glossary). Among the most commonly studied authors were writers such as Cicero (for his style), Aristotle and Horace (for their theories on poetry), Ovid (for his use of myth), and Virgil and Quintillian (for their use of rhetorical figures).[33] As well as translating extracts from classical authors, students were set exercises which invited them to imitate classical styles, genres and rhetorical figures. In many schools boys studied and performed classical dramas, too, usually Seneca's tragedies and the Roman comedies of Plautus and Terence. Performing such plays was seen as a way of improving boys' fluency in Latin and developing their skills in public speaking. For similar reasons a number of university colleges encouraged student performances. Usually the dramas were in Latin but there are occasional examples of playwrights producing plays in English, as in 1566 when Richard Edwardes wrote a two-part English play (now lost) (*Palamon and Arcite*) for Elizabeth I's visit to Oxford University.

Elizabeth I was a talented scholar, trained in Latin, modern languages, rhetoric and the classics. Few women outside of the country's elites enjoyed the same kind of education. At the lower levels of society, girls were sometimes taught to read but not necessarily to write, and were more likely to receive instruction in practical skills such as needlework. Comparatively few women had access to the classical learning, new discoveries, and spirit of enquiry which characterises the humanist 'Renaissance'. This, combined with women's circumscribed rights in the period, led feminist historian Joan Kelly to conclude that for most women there was no Renaissance.[34] Kelly probably over-states her case but it is clearly true that the humanist revolution in education did not affect women or other politically marginalised groups in the same way that it did men from the middling and upper social classes.

The English Language

The type of English written and spoken in the Renaissance is known as early modern English. There are many similarities between early modern and modern English but significant differences, too. There was no standardised form of early modern English and it underwent important changes during the Renaissance. The modern grammatical system had yet to be fully established (so that dialect variations and the use of forms such as double negatives remained common); and it was usual to find words spelt in a variety of ways. Perhaps even more significantly, early modern English included words which are now obsolete and words whose meanings have changed since the sixteenth century (such as 'luxury' which then meant 'lechery').

The fact that early modern English was not standardised was one of the reasons that it and the other European vernacular languages were conventionally regarded as inferior to Latin. The comparatively low status of English was reinforced in the fifteenth century by the fact that it was considered too 'symple and rude' to be used for sophisticated artistic or intellectual expression.[35] The perceived deficiency of the vernacular was felt especially keenly by some of the period's writers and led to a growing desire to improve English during the sixteenth century. Richard Mulcaster wrote of his wish to develop 'the verie same treasur in our own tung' that was found in Latin, adding: 'I honor the *Latin* but I worship the *English*'.[36] As Mulcaster's comments suggest, the mission to improve English was partly nationalistic, and derived some of its intensity from England's increased isolation following the Reformation. Authors set about improving the language in different ways. Some encouraged the imitation of classical syntax, and the borrowing of words from Latin and other European languages; others such as Edmund Spenser preferred to expand the resources of the language by reviving archaic native words and borrowing from English dialects.

By the end of the sixteenth century English had been transformed. Most striking of all was the massive expansion in its vocabulary, a process which peaked around 1600. As N. F. Blake notes, the 'effect of this expansion was to produce a language with a very rich vocabulary and which often had more than one word for the same thing'.[37] Although there were some who worried about the speed with which the language had grown, its expansion made it a wonderfully versatile medium for writers, providing them with a host of ways of expressing their ideas and an armoury of new rhyme words. Without this linguistic 'revolution' English Renaissance literature would have been neither so rich nor so diverse.

Science

The Renaissance was an age of great scientific discoveries. Initially inspired to imitate the achievements of ancient scholars, Renaissance scientists increasingly realised that there was more to be learned about the world than their predecessors had discovered. In being ready to question classical wisdom Renaissance scientists were rejecting a tradition known as 'scholasticism' which asserted the unquestionable authority of ancient and canonical texts. Instead they adopted an empirical approach based on experimentation and direct observation of the world.

Fresh study of the universe led to important breakthroughs in scientific knowledge, but it was some time before the most radical discoveries were widely accepted. In the medical world, for example, the pioneering anatomical dissections performed by Andreas Vesalius, illustrated in his *The Structure of the Human Body* (1543), revealed significant errors in Galen's account of the body and showed that it was not made up of four humours, as had been previously supposed (see below). His research was confirmed and supplemented by William Harvey's description of the circulation of the blood (published in 1628).

Similarly transformative discoveries were made in the world of astronomy. Up until the mid-sixteenth century it was usual to accept the Ptolemaic model of the universe which suggested that the earth was a globe encased by a series of rotating, transparent spheres, each set with different planets and constellations; but in 1542 Nicolaus Copernicus published his *De Revolutionibus Orbium Coelestium* which argued that the solar system was heliocentric (that is, centred on the sun). Initially, there was considerable resistance to Copernicus's theory: it undermined Ptolemy's model and symbolically displaced man from the centre of the created universe; but confirmation of its accuracy was afforded when Galileo Galilei invented the telescope (1608).

Despite such advances credence continued to be lent to a number of ancient scientific theories, sometimes even after they had been discredited. The persistence of the theory of humours is a good example of this. According to this ancient theory the human body was made up of four humours: black bile, phlegm, blood and yellow bile. These were thought to correspond to the four elements that made up the world: earth (cold and dry), water (cold and moist), air (hot and moist) and fire (hot and dry). Ideally, the humours were evenly balanced but most people were believed to have a slightly different combination of the four, which dictated their personality (for instance, someone with a preponderance of black bile was expected to be melancholic). Vesalius's research in the early sixteenth century had conclusively disproved that that the body consisted of four liquids but humour theory continued to influence popular thinking about character as late as the end of the century when Ben Jonson wrote his parodic humours comedies, *Every Man in His Humour* (performed 1598) and *Every Man out of His Humour* (performed 1599).

Exploration, New Worlds and Race

The Renaissance spirit of enquiry encouraged voyages of geographical exploration which led to the discovery of new lands and trading routes. Probably most momentous of all was Christopher Columbus's discovery of the 'New World' (1492), an event which inspired an age of intense geographical exploration and colonisation. The American continent (or New World) had previously been unknown to Europeans and was not mentioned in the Bible. Its discovery had a profound impact on European views of the world. As well as raising troubling questions about the accuracy of the Bible, European encounters with America's native people 'with their different languages, cultures, religions and social organizations, challenged assumptions – ultimately derived from Aristotle – that human life everywhere was governed by certain universal laws'.[38] On the contrary, they suggested that there was no 'natural' society. This recognition was both unsettling and potentially revolutionary for it revealed that there was nothing inevitable about the given social order in Western Europe. This encouraged Renaissance thinkers to reflect on European society and to consider whether changes or alternatives were desirable. One of the most imaginative and playful examples of this is Sir Thomas More's *Utopia* (written 1515–16) which describes a fictitious country, supposedly somewhere near the New World. More uses his detailed account of Utopian society to encourage critical reflection on the social status quo in Henrician England. As this example suggests, the countries of the New World served partly as what Julia Briggs calls 'imaginative spaces' onto which Europeans could project their concerns and desires about their own societies.[39]

The discovery of the Americas suggested the possible existence of other unknown lands and spurred on the European race to explore the globe. At the forefront of this race were the Spanish. As well as being able to claim credit for Columbus's discovery of America they conquered Mexico (1519–21), Peru (1539–5), and sponsored Ferdinand Magellan's circumnavigation of the globe (1519–22). Other European nations including the Portuguese, French, Dutch and English were keen to follow their example. In England, the 'push' to explore the globe and open up new markets for merchants began in earnest in the Elizabethan period and intensified in the Stuart era. The first wave of explorations was led by adventurers such as Martin Frobisher, Sir Francis Drake, Sir Walter Raleigh and Richard Hakluyt the younger, and mainly focused on the New World. In concentrating their efforts on the Americas Elizabethan explorers were motivated by rumours of untold riches and rivalry with the Spanish, who, it was feared, would convert the New World to Catholicism if their colonisation of it went uncontested. Interest in voyages of exploration was fostered by the publication of travellers' accounts and histories of English exploration which gave recent English voyages prominent attention, such as Richard Hakluyt's *The Principal Navigations, Voyages, Traffics and Discoveries of the English Nation* (1589).

The first English colony in America was Sir Walter Raleigh's failed 1580s settlement on Roanoke Island, Virginia. This was followed in 1607 by the founding of Jamestown, the first permanent English settlement in America. The town was founded by Captain John Smith on behalf of the newly formed Virginia Company (1606). Similar companies were established with the intention of founding further American plantations, including the Bermuda Company (1615), the Plymouth Company (1620), and the Massachusetts Bay Company (1629).[40]

Like their European peers, English adventurers did not confine themselves to the New World. The Elizabethan period also saw important voyages to the northern hemisphere, and a series of expeditions on the African continent. At the same time, English merchants were cultivating new trade links which stretched beyond Europe into the East. Special companies were formed to oversee their development, including the Muscovy Company (1555), which aimed to develop trade with Russia, Persia and Greenland; the Levant Company (1592), focused on the Middle East, and the East India Company (1600).[41]

Otherness

The rise of global exploration and international trade, combined with the flourishing of travel literature, meant that Renaissance Europeans were increasingly conscious that the world was inhabited by racially and culturally diverse people; but few Englishmen or women would have sampled this diversity personally. There were overseas immigrants in England but most lived in London and the largest immigrant communities were European Protestants.

Ambassadors and traders from Africa and the East were occasional visitors, and there is some evidence of Jews and Africans living in England, but their numbers were small and their immigration was restricted. Openly practising Jews were not permitted, having been banished in 1290; and fears about the growing number of African natives in the country led Elizabeth I to draft an edict banishing 'Negroes' in 1601.[42]

The other way in which contemporaries might encounter people of different nations was through travel; but travel was expensive and difficult, and you needed government permission to travel abroad. Most English people (including many Renaissance authors) never left the country, and therefore relied on second-hand information for their knowledge of other countries and cultures. This probably accounts for authors' reliance on stereotypes when writing about those who were racial or cultural others and may help to explain the mixture of fascination and fear provoked by such 'strangers'.

Often those perceived to be 'other' are demonised. This is especially true of Jews and Muslims. Such characters are typically stigmatised as non-Christians (see Religion, above). For similar reasons, Protestants often satirise and demonise Catholics and vice versa. The handling of racial difference is more complex, as is demonstrated by the treatment of blackness. Renaissance authors were not sure what caused blackness – some thought it was the result of being too much in the sun, others believed 'it was an act of God (a curse against one of the sons of Noah)' – but they generally agreed that whiteness was superior.[43] This assumption was reinforced by the western association of blackness with sin and ugliness, and of whiteness with purity and beauty. Negative stereotypes presented blacks as wicked, unattractive and prone to vice and lust. Such negative stereotypes are vividly embodied in Shakespeare's villainous Moor, Aaron, in *Titus Andronicus*. Some of the same traits characterise his more famous black protagonist Othello, although Othello's representation is both more complex and sympathetic. Driven to jealousy and the murder of his wife by the wicked machinations of Iago, Othello in some respects fulfils the negative stereotype of the passionate black savage, but elsewhere in the play Shakespeare makes it clear that Othello is a charismatic lover and noble soldier. In doing so he draws on the period's more positive associations of blackness with virility and strength. Similar contradictions characterise European representations of American Indians. While some writers stigmatised them and their tribal customs as primitive and barbaric, others such as Michel de Montaigne praised them as 'noble' savages, leading a purer life than Europeans.[44]

Today, race is usually associated with skin colour but in the Renaissance it could refer to one's family ancestry and to one's national identity, too.[45] National stereotyping, like black stereotyping, is common in English literature. The representation of neighbouring Catholic countries such as France and Italy is especially fascinating. The countries are often admired for their literature, but their people are usually represented negatively. The French are stereotyped as fickle, vain and untrustworthy, and Italians are caricatured as devious, corrupt, vengeful and lecherous. The well-known antagonism between England and Catholic Spain informs the similarly negative representation of the Spanish and their frequent caricature as hot-blooded religious extremists. By contrast, the representation of the Dutch and the Germans (who were fellow Protestants) is generally benign, though comic: Dutch characters usually have funny accents, and Germans are conventionally presented as hard-drinkers.[46]

The representation of England's more immediate neighbours (Wales, Scotland, Ireland) is similarly politicised. England's nearest and closest neighbour was Wales: the principality had been part of the English realm since the 1535 Act of Union and had caused England few problems. This is probably why the representation of the Welsh is largely positive. Although they are sometimes mocked for their accents and their alleged taste for leeks and toasted cheese, Welsh characters are generally presented as loyal and good-natured, as in Shakespeare's *Henry V*, where Fluellen is one of the king's most devoted supporters.[47]

England's relationship with Ireland was more troubled, and contemporary representations of the Irish are often negative. Like Wales, Ireland was theoretically part of the English empire, but it was more resistant to English rule, especially following the Reformation, when its people remained predominantly Catholic. Like American Indians and Africans, the Irish, and their traditional tribal customs, are often stigmatised by contemporary English authors such as Edmund Spenser as primitive, threatening and in need of 'civilisation'.

England's relationship with sixteenth-century Scotland was similarly difficult. It was an independent country and a traditional enemy of England. The scandals surrounding Mary, Queen of Scots and her implication in a plot against Elizabeth I's life (1586) did little to ease English suspicions of the Scots. In this context it is not surprising that although there are some positive representations of individual Scots they are more often presented in terms akin to the Irish; that is, as primitive, barbarous and dangerous. Contemporary ambivalence about James I meant that negative stereotyping of the Scots remained common even after the accession of the Scottish monarch.

Writing

Patronage

In a culture in which generosity was a marker of status, monarchs and their richest nobles often chose to act as patrons (or sponsors) of the arts, offering support to a variety of painters, sculptors, musicians, players and writers. Some patrons, like Lady Mary Sidney, took an even livelier interest in artists and writers, inviting them to stay with them for prolonged periods. In return for patronage writers traditionally dedicated their works to the patrons who had supported them. Sometimes dedications took the form of a brief preface or dedicatory letter; in other cases the writer composed a dedicatory poem (or poems). Dedicating works to patrons could also be a way of eliciting the patronage and protection of the men or women honoured.

At a time when the literary status of living writers was not high and the opportunities for earning money through publication were limited, royal or noble patronage was a potentially valuable way of generating income and of lending one's work prestige and protection. This helps to explain the assiduity with which aspiring writers courted patrons and the rancour such competition occasionally produced. Frustrations were not unusual either: several contemporaries complained about the difficulties of securing patronage and their distaste for a system which forced them to be flatterers.

Ben Jonson wrestled with the problem of reconciling the demands of patrons, the literary market and his artistic integrity throughout his career; but he became one of the first English writers to make a career from his writing, partly through his work for the professional London stage and because of the generous patronage that he received from nobles such as Lord Aubigny and James I. Few of his peers managed to do likewise. Fiction writing was not generally regarded as a career in the Renaissance and there were few writing jobs. Selling one's fictions to the newly established printing presses was an option but there was little money to be made from it as there were no copyright laws and authors were not entitled to 'royalties' on the sale of their work; all they received was a one-off payment. Most of the period's published authors were people who were independently wealthy or who wrote in their spare time, earning their living from another career.

Publication

There were two main forms of publication in Renaissance England: manuscript and print. Manuscript publication involved the circulation of texts in handwritten manuscripts, transcribed in ink on paper or parchment. These might be written by the author, a professional scribe, or the owner of the text. Prior to the invention of print technology this was the way in which most written texts were recorded and disseminated.

The invention of moveable-type printing was to revolutionise the circulation of texts, making it possible to produce multiple copies of texts quickly and cheaply. The new form of printing was developed by Johannes Gutenberg in the mid-fifteenth century and pioneered in England by William Caxton, when he set up a printing press in the precincts of Westminster Abbey (1476). Caxton published a variety of Latin and English works, including literature by Medieval authors such as Chaucer and Gower. Other entrepreneurs soon followed his example. Most of the new presses were set up in London, which became the centre of the English book trade. In the mid-sixteenth century, the city's printers came together to form the

Stationers' Company (1557), a trade guild which was to be responsible for overseeing the activity of all printers. From 1586 printing presses were only allowed in London and the two university towns (Oxford and Cambridge), and all had to be registered. Like Caxton, many of England's early printers published a combination of learned and popular works in English. Cheaper books (such as individual plays) tended to be published in 'quarto' format, whereas more prestigious or learned books were published in the larger, more expensive 'folio' format (see Glossary).

Most living authors continued to circulate their fiction in manuscript. Not until the late sixteenth century was it to become usual to print the work of contemporary authors, and even then women and gentlemen writers often circulated their writing in manuscript instead. Part of the explanation for this lies in the comparatively low status of living writers in the first half of the sixteenth century and the early stigma attached to print publication. In the eyes of many elite male authors print was vulgar because of its association with the market and a public audience. The same stigma may have been a factor in women writers' favouring of manuscript circulation, although their generally limited access to printers offers a more pragmatic explanation for the scarcity of female published texts.

Manuscript circulation continued to be particularly attractive to elite writers because it was a more efficient way of circulating shorter texts and works 'directed at specialised readerships'.[48] The fact that manuscripts were not subject to contemporary censorship laws (see below) also meant that those working in manuscript had greater freedom to address contentious issues. It is no coincidence that manuscript writing was important amongst those who found themselves at odds with England's ruling regimes, such as Elizabethan and Stuart Catholics.

By the 1590s attitudes to print had begun to change and it was becoming increasingly common to publish literature by living authors. Many of the first Elizabethan writers to venture into print were non-courtiers but the posthumous publication of Sir Philip Sidney's sonnet collection, *Astrophil and Stella* (1591) and a collection of his works (1598) was to make print publication more acceptable even for elite writers and set a precedent for printing single-author collections, paving the way for the publication of Ben

Jonson's *Works* (1616), the Shakespeare First Folio (1623) and John Donne's *Poems* (1633).

Censorship

In 1559 new legislation was introduced which specified that all books to be printed had to be approved first 'by either six Privy Councillors or the Archbishop of Canterbury and the Bishop of London, or the Vice Chancellors of Oxford or Cambridge, if this was their place of publication'.[49] In 1586 this system was simplified by a Star Chamber decree which concentrated responsibility for licensing books in the hands of the Archbishop of Canterbury and the Bishop of London. Later their ecclesiastical subordinates were also permitted this authority. Texts licensed for publication would usually be recorded in the Stationers' Register.

The press licensers were also censors and had the right to ban or ask for corrections to any work they examined, if it was deemed offensive, libellous, seditious or in any other way unacceptable. When texts were censored it was generally because they dealt too overtly with contentious issues (such as religion or foreign policy) or because they alluded too directly to contemporary individuals. The punishments for printing unlicensed works and for breaching the censorship laws were potentially harsh including cutting off the right hand of the offender and hanging, but prosecutions were rare.

THE CRITICAL CONTEXT

The Renaissance

The flourishing of English literature and its rising status in the late sixteenth century was matched by growing critical interest in vernacular fiction and a fashion for books offering advice about writing. Most were written by practising writers. As well as identifying exemplary forms of writing, such early commentators were often concerned to establish the value of fiction. Sir Philip Sidney's *Defence of Poesy* (1595) is typical in this respect. According to Sidney many contemporaries were inclined to condemn the writing of poetry (their term for all fiction) for three main reasons: 'First, that there being many other more fruitful knowledges, a man might better spend his time in them than in this. Secondly, that it is the mother of lies. Thirdly, that it is the nurse of abuse, infecting us with many pestilent desires'. Sidney refutes each view and argues that the chief end of poetry is 'to teach and delight'.[50]

Most Renaissance writers defended fiction in similar terms. In making the case for the educational and recreational value of literature, they borrowed from classical literary theory and analogous statements by ancient authors such as Horace and Aristotle. Like the classical commentators, Renaissance authors such as Sidney believed that fiction writers were especially well-placed to teach their audiences because they made their instruction 'delightful'. For this reason Sidney argued that fiction was more instructive than history or philosophy. In similar fashion, poet and dramatist Ben Jonson argued for the potentially unique social role of the poet, famously observing in his commonplace book that 'he which can faine a *Common-wealth* (which is the *Poet*) can governe it with *Counsels*, strengthen it with *Lawes*, correct it with *Iudgements*, informe it with *Religion*, and *Morals*'.[51] In practice, poets never seem to have exercised the kind of power Jonson aspired to; and not all were as overtly or consistently concerned with instructing their audiences (as their detractors were quick to note).

There were similar debates about the nature of the writer's art and the relationship between fiction and reality. Classical literary theory taught writers to see fiction as an art of imitation. It was a view many Renaissance authors echoed. On these grounds, Ben Jonson was critical of fiction that he regarded as unnatural or unrealistic, arguing that: 'The true Artificer will not run away from nature, as hee were afraid of her; or depart from life, and the likenesse of Truth; but speake to the capacity of his hearers.'[52] On the other hand, authors such as Sidney suggested a more complex relationship between fiction and reality. According to Sidney, nature was the writer's starting point but he or she was 'not enclosed within the narrow warrant of her gifts, . . . freely ranging only within the zodiac of his own wit'. Indeed, Sidney suggested that the poet's god-like powers of creation allowed him or her to evoke a 'golden' world superior to that encountered in reality.[53]

Another recurrent feature of Renaissance books about fiction is their description of the key literary genres (most of them inherited from classical tradition). Much of their commentary on the genres is the same. There was rather less consistency between writers in practice and some specific points on which critics disagreed. Most of the early critics tended to frown, for example, on the mixing of genres (such as tragedy and comedy) and argued that comic and tragic playwrights should observe what were known as the classical 'unities' (see Glossary); but very few contemporary playwrights worried about the 'unities', and new and mixed genres were increasingly popular on the late Elizabethan and Jacobean stage. There were similar disagreements within the world of poetry about whether English poets should use rhyme. Rhyme was not used in classical poetry and some writers, such as Thomas Campion, were opposed to its use in English verse, but others such as Sidney and Samuel Daniel disagreed and argued for the virtues of rhyming poetry.[54]

As well as reflecting on the art of poetry and offering advice about how to write, several of the contemporary books on Renaissance fiction allude to current English writers, affording an insight into which were most highly regarded. Thus Sir Philip Sidney's *Defence of Poesy* singles out the author of *The Shepheardes Calender* (Edmund Spenser) for praise, while George Puttenham's *Art of English Poesie* (1589) illustrates many of the poetic devices it describes with examples from Sidney's work, and includes a chapter about 'Who in any age haue bene the most commended writers in our English Poesie'. As well as praising Medieval and early Renaissance authors such as Chaucer, Lydgate, Gower, Wyatt and Surrey, Puttenham offers a list of the men he regards as the leading Elizabethan court writers. This includes authors still studied today such as Sidney, Spenser and Sir Walter Raleigh, and men whose works are less well known such as Edward, Earl of Oxford and Thomas, Lord Buckhurst.[55]

Other authors, such as Francis Meres, compared past and present English writers with those of the ancient world. In Meres's *Palladis Tamia* (1598) Sidney, Spenser, Samuel Daniel, Michael Drayton, William Shakespeare, Christopher Marlowe and George Chapman are singled out for special commendation; and Shakespeare is identified as the period's best comic and tragic playwright.[56] In comparing English writers with the great poets of the ancient world

authors like Meres point to the growing status of vernacular literature and an emerging sense of an English literary tradition. At the
same time Meres's listing of key English authors is an early example
of canon-making (or the identification of a core set of authors as being
of high quality). In this context it is interesting that Shakespeare features so prominently in Meres's account, especially as a dramatist. It
suggests that even in his own time, Shakespeare was regarded by some
as the leading playwright of the English language. A similar assumption underpins Ben Jonson's famous assertion that Shakespeare was
'not of an age, but for all time'. In reality, Shakespeare's reputation as
a dramatist did not prove quite so timeless. Like the literature of most
of his peers, Shakespeare's dramas fell out of fashion in the late seventeenth century and his canonisation as England's leading playwright did not begin until the late eighteenth century. Many other
Renaissance authors remained neglected until the late nineteenth
century when there was a revival of interest in Renaissance literature.

Modern Criticism

Scholarly criticism of Renaissance literature is largely a modern
phenomenon, only becoming firmly established in the early twentieth century, when the study of English literature was introduced
at university. Specific interest in Renaissance literature was fuelled
by the publication of a number of collected editions of Renaissance
authors and texts in the late nineteenth and early twentieth centuries, which made the period's works more readily available for
study. Early criticism tended to focus on Shakespeare, Renaissance
drama and a small group of poets, but included important work on
Renaissance textual transmission by scholars known as the New
Bibliographers (including R. B. McKerrow, A. W. Pollard and
W. W. Greg) and ground-breaking research on the Renaissance
stage by authors such as E. K. Chambers. Other scholars studied
Renaissance literature for the information it was thought to provide
about Elizabethan and Stuart England and/or the lives and characters of its authors, while Sigmund Freud famously read Shakespeare
in psychoanalytical terms, using his work on *Hamlet* to help him
with the formulation of his theory of the 'Oedipal complex'
(describing sons who feel sexual desire for their mothers).

Freud's psychoanalytical approach to Shakespeare and the work of fellow psychoanalyst Carl Jung was to feed into later archetypal interpretations of Renaissance literature popularised in the mid-century by critics such as Northrop Frye, but the period from the 1920s to the 1960s was dominated by formalist criticism (which offers close readings of the formal aspects of texts, such as style, verse form, narrative structure, imagery and characterisation).[57] There were critics interested in the relationship between Renaissance literature and its historical context, such as L. C. Knights, but the majority favoured close-reading and were not concerned with factors external to the text.[58] Close-reading of this kind was popularised in English studies by I. A. Richards and by a group of American scholars known as the New Critics.

Since the 1960s, Renaissance scholarship (like literary criticism more generally) has diversified and become more theoretical, as scholars have reacted against formalism and early twentieth-century assumptions about the stability of textual meaning and the timelessness of great literature. Perhaps most significantly, there has been a general movement towards historicised readings which consider texts in relation to their contexts. This is reflected in Renaissance studies by the rise of New Historicism and Cultural Materialism, schools of criticism which share a commitment to historicised readings of Renaissance literature (see Critical Paradigms, below) and which have, together, put the business of contextualising Renaissance literature at the centre of scholarship on the period. In this respect, they have, arguably, been the most influential schools of criticism in late twentieth-century Renaissance studies, but they are not the only critical movements to have changed the study of Renaissance literature in significant ways. Feminism, queer studies and postcolonial theory have each generated important new work on gender, sexuality, race and nationhood in Renaissance literature (see Critical Paradigms, below).

The late twentieth and early twenty-first centuries have also seen important new work in the field of psychoanalysis and textual studies. While recent psychoanalytical critics have read Renaissance texts in terms of manifest and hidden content (and therefore as working in ways thought to be analogous to the human mind), new work on manuscript and print culture has transformed our understanding of textual transmission in the period and prompted lively debates about textual editing. This has been an especially heated topic in the field of Renaissance drama where there is sometimes a choice between using an authorial version of a play and a 'theatrical' version (that is, one prepared for performance). The preference of the New Bibliographers was for authorial texts but a growing number of recent scholars have made the case for printing performance texts. The new Oxford edition of Shakespeare which appeared in 1986 caused particular controversy when its editors opted 'when possible, to print the more theatrical version of each play'.[59] As this preference suggests, there has been growing interest in performance since the 1970s. This has led to the thriving of performance criticism, which analyses and contextualises past and present performance interpretations of Renaissance plays. Much of this criticism is concerned with theatre performance but the growing number of television and film adaptations of Renaissance plays, and Shakespeare in particular, has led to the emergence of a large body of criticism on screen adaptations. Although a comparatively recent development, performance criticism has become firmly established as a branch of Shakespeare and Renaissance studies and has its own dedicated journal, *Shakespeare Bulletin*.

Theatre history is another area of Renaissance scholarship that has been the subject of renewed interest in the past thirty years. As well as seeing important new work on contemporary playing practices, the theatre business, and the London playhouses, the establishment of the Records of Early English Drama project at the University of Toronto in Canada, which aims to catalogue and publish all records of drama in Britain up until 1642, has helped to foster interest in regional theatre and touring acting companies.

More recent years have seen the flourishing of another type of contextual criticism, known as 'Presentism'. Like Cultural Materialism, 'Presentist' criticism generally focuses on Renaissance drama but is concerned not with the significance of Renaissance literature in its own time, but with what it means in the present. The preoccupation of such critics with the present distinguishes them from late twentieth-century New Historicists such as Stephen Greenblatt who famously wrote of his desire to 'speak with the dead'. It is a distinction Terence Hawkes, one of the movement's leading proponents, makes explicit when he observes that Presentist Shakespeare criticism 'will not yearn to speak with the dead. It will aim, in the end, to talk to the living.'[60]

The Renaissance Canon

As well as witnessing important changes in the ways that scholars have read Renaissance literature, the last thirty years have seen significant changes in the canon of texts Renaissance scholars and students commonly study. Early twentieth-century Renaissance criticism concentrated on a small number of male authors (led by Shakespeare); but there was a widespread reaction against the traditional 'canon' of great English works in the 1970s, especially amongst feminist critics and those interested in the literature of ethnic minorities and other traditionally marginalised social groups. The fact that the recognised canon consisted almost exclusively of works by educated white male authors led such scholars to argue that it was sexist, racist and elitist. Some scholars wished to do away with the canon entirely; others sought to widen it so that it included a greater diversity of authors and works.

In Renaissance criticism this has led to a steady expansion of the authors studied by scholars and students and growing interest in Renaissance prose genres, popular forms of literature, manuscript writing, and regional literary and dramatic culture. There have been even more significant developments in the study of Renaissance women's writing. As well as encouraging new work on known female authors, the archival research of feminist critics has uncovered previously unknown authors and drawn attention to previously neglected forms of women's writing such as prayers, mothers' legacies (letters of advice to their children), and women's manuscript miscellanies. The desire to make women's writing more widely available has, likewise, led to the preparation of new editions of women's works, and a series of anthologies of Renaissance women's writing, such as *The Paradise of Women: Writings by English Women of the Renaissance*, edited by Betty Travitsky (1980), *Kissing the Rod: An Anthology of Seventeenth-Century Women's Verse*, edited by Germaine Greer, Jeslyn Medoff, Melinda Sansome and Susan Hastings (1988), *Renaissance Drama by Women: Texts and Documents*, edited by S. P.

Cerasano and Marion Wynne-Davies (1996), *Early Modern Women Poets: An Anthology*, edited by Jane Stevenson and Peter Davidson (2001), and *Women's Writing of the Early Modern Period, 1588–1688*, edited by Stephanie Hodgson-Wright (2002).

The expansion of the canon of Renaissance literature these scholarly developments have effected is reflected in the increased diversity of texts commonly included in the most recent editions of student anthologies (such as the popular *Norton Anthology of English Literature*) and taught on undergraduate and graduate Renaissance courses. Canonical authors such as Shakespeare continue to be widely studied, but students are increasingly likely to be exposed to the work of other dramatists, women writers and less traditional literary genres as well.

Critical Paradigms

New Historicism / Cultural Materialism

New Historicism and Cultural Materialism both emerged in the 1980s. They share a commitment to studying literary texts in relation to their historical context, and agree with pioneering Marxist scholar, Raymond Williams, that it is not possible to 'separate literature and art from other kinds of social practice, in such a way as to make them subject to quite special and distinct laws'.[61] On the contrary they see literature as closely linked to other forms of cultural discourse, and, therefore, do not believe literary and non-literary texts can be separated. Similarly, New Historicists and Cultural Materialists reject the idea of a timeless 'inalterable human nature', arguing that concepts of human nature are socially conditioned.[62]

New Historicism originated in North America, where it was pioneered and named by Stephen Greenblatt. Greenblatt's thinking about literature was informed not only by Marx's theories about society but by the work of Michel Foucault on power and Louis Althusser on ideology. In works such as *Shakespearean Negotiations* (1988), Greenblatt argues for understanding literary texts not simply as works 'marked by the creative intelligence and private obsessions of individuals' but as 'the products of collective negotiation and exchange'. Through historicised close readings of works by authors such as Shakespeare, Greenblatt aimed to reveal more about these 'collective' practices and to establish what he termed 'a poetics of culture'.[63]

Underpinning Greenblatt's work, and that of later New Historicists, is a preoccupation with what fellow historicist Louis Montrose describes as the 'Historicity of Texts, and the Textuality of History'.[64] This dual concern is reflected in historicists' characteristic reading of literary texts alongside non-literary works, and their focus on the close reading of both. In Stephen Greenblatt's essay on Shakespeare's *Henry IV* plays and *Henry V*, for example, he analyses the representation of power and authority in Shakespeare's histories alongside Thomas Harriot's *A Brief and True Report of the New Found Land of Virginia* (1588), which describes colonists' early encounters with native American Indians. Greenblatt argues that both sets of texts are concerned with subversion and the containment of disorder, and can 'be seen to confirm the Machiavellian hypothesis of the origin of princely power in force and fraud'.[65] A similar preoccupation with subversion and the workings of power is characteristic of New Historicist criticism, as is Greenblatt's assumption that the subversion found in Renaissance texts is contained.

Cultural Materialism, the British counterpart of New Historicism, was given its name by Jonathan Dollimore and Alan Sinfield.[66] Although the movement has much in common with New Historicism, it is more specifically concerned with the material conditions in which literary texts are produced, both in their own time and subsequently. Thus Dollimore's and Sinfield's *Political Shakespeare* (1985) volume not only includes essays which relate Shakespeare's plays to their original historical context but ones which consider how they have been appropriated and reinterpreted over time (this includes essays on Shakespeare on screen, and Shakespeare's place in the modern school curriculum). The Cultural Materialists' preoccupation with the present function of Renaissance literature is matched by a more overt political agenda. Its leading proponents are open about their 'commitment to the transformation of a social order which exploits people on grounds of race, gender and class', and are therefore especially keen to register politically dissident and marginalised voices in their literary analyses.[67]

Their political agenda leads Dollimore and Sinfield to read Shakespeare plays such as *Henry V* in terms of what they expose about class inequalities and the historical workings of power and ideology. Similarly, feminist Cultural Materialists such as Kathleen McLuskie analyse plays such as *King Lear* and *Measure for Measure* in terms of what they reveal about the material conditions underpinning Renaissance patriarchal ideology, and thus about the 'historicity' (rather than timelessness) of patriarchal thinking and Shakespeare.[68] Unlike the New Historicists, many Cultural Materialists see the subversion found in Renaissance texts as a potential agent for social change.

The renewed sensitivity to history and context encouraged by historicist and materialist critics has been welcomed by most scholars and has led to some exciting and highly original research, but neither school of interpretation has escaped criticism. While Cultural Materialists have been accused of offering reductive readings of playwrights such as Shakespeare, New Historicists have faced complaints about the arbitrariness of the comparisons they draw between literary and non-literary works, the narrowness of some of their close readings, their selective use of evidence, their insensitivity to matters of genre and bibliography, their over-statement of the power of the state, and their early failure to historicise their own methodology and assumptions.[69] Both schools of interpretation have, likewise, faced criticism for their narrow preoccupation with power, and their focus on canonical authors and male-centred texts.[70]

Feminism

Feminist literary criticism emerged out of the feminist movement of the 1960s but has developed into a varied school of interpretation. Some critics focus on the representation of women and gender in literature; others concentrate on women's writing and the female literary tradition. In Renaissance studies much of the early feminist scholarship was of the first kind, concentrating on the representation of women in Shakespeare. In many cases this involved championing female characters and arguing for or against the misogyny of Renaissance literature. Among the pioneering works was Juliet Dusinberre's *Shakespeare and the Nature of Women* (1975), which explored the representation of women in Shakespearean drama and concluded that Shakespeare was a proto-feminist because his plays are implicitly sceptical about the concept of women's nature. In similar fashion, *The Woman's Part: Feminist Criticism of Shakespeare*, edited by Carolyn Ruth Swift Lenz, Gayle Greene and Carol Thomas Neely (1980) brought together a collection of feminist essays which focus on the depiction of women and gender in Shakespeare, many of which suggest that his plays are amenable to appropriation for the feminist cause. Other scholars such as Coppélia Kahn and Janet Adelman used psychoanalytic theory to think about the central role of women in the definition of male identity within Shakespearean drama.[71] At the same time, feminist literary historians such as Betty Travitsky and Germaine Greer were working to recover and draw attention to Renaissance women's writing.

Most Renaissance scholars welcomed the new attention to women and women's writing, acknowledging that both subjects had been neglected by earlier critics, but there were debates about some of the approaches taken. Like psychoanalytical critics, many of the first feminists faced criticism for treating the female characters in Renaissance literature as real people. Other scholars questioned the value of studies which concentrated exclusively on the representation of female characters, or that considered the works of playwrights such as Shakespeare in isolation. There were also complaints about feminist scholars' failure to historicise their studies. Lisa Jardine was amongst those who reacted most strongly against early studies arguing that 'concentrating on the female characters, or protesting as political feminists at the sexist views expressed by the male characters, will not get us very far with a feminist Shakespeare criticism appropriate to the 1980s'.[72] In her view what was needed, and what she aimed to offer, was a more carefully historicised account of Renaissance drama and its treatment of women. Such research suggested to her that the apparent interest in women exhibited by such texts was not evidence of women's improving social status or playwrights' enlightened views but of 'patriarchy's unexpressed worry about the great social changes which characterised the period – worries which could be made conveniently concrete in the voluminous and endemic debates about "the woman question"'.[73] The same desire to offer a more historical account of women's representation underpinned Linda Woodbridge's *Women and the English Renaissance: Literature and the Nature of Womankind, 1540–1620* (1984). Kathleen McLuskie offered another alternative to 'special pleading on behalf of female characters', arguing that feminist criticism was 'equally well served by making a text reveal the conditions in which a particular ideology of femininity functions and by both revealing and subverting the hold which such an ideology has for readers both female and male'.[74]

Since the 1990s feminist criticism has moved away from an exclusive focus on women to a broader interest in the handling of gender and sexuality in Renaissance literature, and has seen a shift from championing or castigating characters and authors to studies concerned with what Renaissance texts reveal about the construction of gender identity. Thus in a fascinating study of Ophelia, Elaine Showalter offers not an account or defence of Ophelia's role in *Hamlet* but an analysis of 'the *history* of her representation': an analysis which reveals that the representation of Ophelia has varied over time, not as a result of changing 'theories of the meaning of the play or the Prince' but in accordance with 'attitudes towards women', madness and female sexuality.[75]

The 1990s and the early twenty-first century have also witnessed the growth of work on early modern women authors. This has resulted in a series of new studies of Renaissance women's literature and the publication of new editions and anthologies of women's writing (see above). Much of the new work on women's writing is historicist and has benefited from significant advances in our knowledge of early modern women's lives as a result of pioneering research by feminist historians such as Sara Mendelson and Patricia Crawford.[76]

Like early feminist studies of male Renaissance authors, some of the first scholars of early modern women's writing have faced criticism for their preoccupation with defending women authors and their tendency to treat them as the same. As more recent feminists have emphasised, there are significant social and cultural differences between the period's women writers, patrons and readers. For similar reasons, it has been argued that the most fruitful literary contexts for discussing women's works are not always those afforded by other women writers, as earlier feminist scholars sometimes assumed. Ann Baynes Coiro, for example, argues that Aemilia Lanyer has more in common with an ambitious middle-class male poet such as Ben Jonson than with many of the aristocratic women writers with whom she has usually been compared (see Chapter 2).[77]

A similar sensitivity to 'difference' characterises one of the most recent developments in feminist criticism: 'difference feminism'. Difference feminists are interested in studying gender in relation to other categories of cultural 'difference', such as social class and race. Renaissance scholars working in this area are often especially interested in the way that attitudes to gender, social and racial 'difference' parallel each other. As recent research has shown, lower-class people, non-whites and women all faced stigmatisation as social inferiors in early modern English culture.[78]

Queer Theory

Queer theory describes a school of literary criticism that emerged in the 1980s which is concerned with exploring the representation and marginalisation of gays and lesbians in literature. One of the first studies to be published in the field was Eve Kosofsky Sedgwick's *Between Men: English Literature and Male Homosocial Desire* (1985). Since its publication studies of homosexuality in literature have multiplied, as have histories of homosexuality. One of the important questions raised by these studies has been whether homosexuality existed in earlier societies as an identity-defining sexual preference. The modern terms used to describe human sexuality (including 'homosexuality' and 'heterosexuality') were invented in the nineteenth century. This has led at least some scholars to argue that the terms describe modern concepts and that sexuality in the pre-modern world was not conceived of in the same way.

In his pioneering history of *Homosexuality in Renaissance England* (1982) Alan Bray makes much this point, arguing that to 'talk of an individual in this period as being or not being "a homosexual" is an anachronism and ruinously misleading'.[79] As Bray's research shows, homosexual activity between men was known to occur and could be punished as sodomy, but it was seen as a common 'sin' not a sexual preference or identity specific to some men (or women). Most

Renaissance queer theorists accept that 'homosexuality' did not exist in the early modern period (in the sense understood today) but in his influential study of *Homosexual Desire in Shakespeare's England* (1991) Bruce Smith argues that there are signs in some contemporary works, such as Shakespeare's sonnets to the 'Young Man', of the emergence of a 'specifically homosexual subjectivity'.[80]

More generally, Renaissance queer theorists have drawn attention to the widespread interest in same-sex desire within the period's literature. As well as encouraging fresh attention to works which incorporate same-sex desire this has led to fascinating research on cross-dressing and homoeroticism on the Renaissance stage. Cross-dressing was customary in the professional theatre because its performers were all-male, but contemporary playwrights also incorporate cross-dressing and flirt with same-sex desire in their romantic comedies, where cross-dressing often leads to men temporarily desiring men and women temporarily desiring women.

Female same-sex desire is less commonly depicted in Renaissance literature. This is perhaps because much of the surviving literature is written by men and because it was not a source of cultural anxiety in the same way that sex between men was. Although it was known that women sometimes desired each other, lesbian sex was not thought to be possible and was therefore ignored by most contemporary writers and the law. In some respects this makes it all the more intriguing that lesbian desire is explored by at least some of the period's writers. Growing attention is now being paid to this aspect of Renaissance literature, following the pioneering work of feminist scholars such as Valerie Traub.[81] As Traub's research suggests, there are important overlaps between modern feminist and queer studies: many feminists share with queer theorists an interest in sexual difference, and related issues such as gender identity, and constructions of masculinity and femininity. Collectively, their research has contributed to sexuality and gender studies becoming a thriving area of early modern research.

Postcolonialism

Postcolonial criticism emerged in the 1970s and studies the representation and marginalisation of the racial 'other' in the literature produced by one-time colonial powers such as Britain. Renaissance postcolonial criticism explores how the representation of race and ethnicity in early modern English literature relates to conventional views and definitions of racial and religious otherness in the period. Another strand of postcolonial criticism looks at the place of Shakespeare in the culture of ex-colonial countries, such as in Africa and India. This has included fascinating research on the use of plays like *Othello* in the late twentieth-century battle over apartheid in South Africa.[82] More recently, Renaissance postcolonialism has expanded to include work on the representation of England's relationship with its closest sixteenth-century colony, Ireland. This has led to fresh attention to works which consciously address the 'Irish problem' (such as Book V of Edmund Spenser's *The Faerie Queene*) and to literature which glances at the difficulties in Ireland more subtly.

Critical interest in postcolonial studies was fostered by the 1960s campaign for greater racial equality in the developed world, and the 'de-colonisation movements in Africa, Asia, the Caribbean, and Latin America'.[83] The latter movements saw a series of one-time British and European colonies gain political independence and assert the value of their native cultures. Like New Historicist criticism, postcolonial studies of race in Renaissance literature often look at literary texts through, or in relation to, contemporary non-fictional sources, such as travel narratives, accounts of voyages and international histories. Such intertextual analysis is used to contextualise literary representations of race and to think more generally about the ways in which Renaissance culture constructed racial difference. In some cases this work has overlapped with that of feminists writing about gender difference.[84]

One of the texts that has been at the heart of Renaissance postcolonial criticism is Shakespeare's *The Tempest* (see Chapter 1). The play tells the story of exiled Italian duke-cum-magician Prospero and his daughter Miranda who have been stranded for many years on an unknown Mediterranean island inhabited only by a native called Caliban. Having initially befriended and enjoyed the help of Caliban, the native's alleged attempt to rape Miranda leads Prospero to enslave Caliban and seize control of the island. Up until the late twentieth century it was usual to read the play as 'an allegory about artistic creation', and to see Prospero as a figure for Shakespeare as artist.[85] As a consequence, it was, likewise, usual to accept Prospero's negative view of Caliban. However, the rise of postcolonialism has encouraged scholars to reconsider the relationship of Prospero and Caliban in terms of colonialism and racial oppression. In such readings Caliban becomes a figure for the various native people subjected to European colonial rule at home and abroad.

Such analyses have produced reinterpretations of works such as *The Tempest*; but analysing Renaissance literature in terms of colonialist discourse is not without its problems. As Meredith Skura points out, colonialist discourse was only just beginning to emerge in the early seventeenth century. For this reason, some scholars argue that it is more appropriate to analyse Renaissance literature in terms of its part in the formulation of colonialist discourse.[86]

SUMMARY OF KEY POINTS

- **Religion:** The Reformation split the Christian Church into Roman Catholic and Protestant churches. Late sixteenth-century England was officially Protestant.
- **Politics:** England was ruled over by a monarch, who was generally accepted had the 'divine right to rule' and derived his or her authority from God.
- **Society:** Society was hierarchical and patriarchal, although social mobility was increasing as a result of economic growth and the rise of the merchant classes.
- **Gender:** Women were conventionally deemed inferior to men but there is evidence of anxiety about changing gender roles and masculinity in the period.
- **Marriage:** Some historians argue that the early modern period saw the rise of 'companionate marriage'.
- **Sexuality:** Sexuality was not regarded as a defining feature of identity and the modern concepts of heterosexuality and homosexuality had yet to be formulated; sex outside of marriage or between people of the same sex was condemned.
- **Humanism:** Humanists encouraged the study of classical learning and self-improvement through education.

- **Language**: Early modern English was not standardised and underwent significant changes in the sixteenth century, including a massive expansion in vocabulary, which contributed to its gradual rise in status.
- **Science**: The Renaissance was an era of significant scientific discoveries, but belief in a variety of older theories persisted.
- **Exploration and Race**: The Renaissance witnessed the discovery of the New World, the first wave of European colonialism, and the flourishing of international trade; negative stereotyping of racial 'others' was common.
- **Writing**: Most Renaissance writers were amateurs; many sought the patronage of powerful noblemen and women, but only a few authors were able to make a career out of writing.
- **Publication**: The invention of moveable-type printing made printed literature much more common but manuscript circulation of literature continued to be important, especially amongst gentlemen and women authors.
- **Renaissance Literary Criticism**: The status of English literature gradually increased during the sixteenth century and the period witnessed some of the first literary criticism about native literature. Some authors began to identify a 'canon' of leading English writers.
- **Modern Literary Criticism**: Scholarly criticism of Renaissance literature is largely a twentieth-century phenomenon. Early twentieth-century criticism was mainly formalist. The late twentieth century saw more emphasis on historicised and theoretical readings, and a move to expand the accepted canon of Renaissance texts to include more popular genres, prose texts and women's writing.

NOTES

1. Cited in *Bloomsbury Guides to English Literature – The Renaissance: From 1500 to 1660*, ed. Marion Wynne-Davies (London: Bloomsbury, 1994), p. 3.
2. Cited in William Barlow, *The Summe and Substance of the Conference, which, it pleased his Excellent Maiestie to have with*

the Lords Bishops, and other of his Cleargie, (at which the most of the Lords of the Councell were present) in his Maiesties Privie-Chamber, at Hampton Court, January 14 1603 (London: Mathew Law, 1605), p. 36.

3. Emily C. Bartels, 'Shakespeare's view of the world', in *Shakespeare: An Oxford Guide*, ed. Stanley Wells and Lena Cowen Orlin (Oxford: Oxford University Press, 2003), pp. 151–64 (p. 193).

4. William Perkins, *A Discourse of the Damned Art of Witchcraft* (Cambridge: Cantrel Legge, 1608), p. 167; Stephen Greenblatt, *The Norton Shakespeare*, ed. Stephen Greenblatt et al. (London: Norton, 1997), p. 3048.

5. Alan MacFarlane, *Witchcraft in Tudor and Stuart England*, 2nd edn (London: Routledge, 1999), p. xxxiii.

6. Among the most influential works which argued for subjects' right to resist rulers were those produced by continental Protestants, Theodore Beza (*De jure magistratuum*, 1576) and Philippe de Mornay (*Vindiciae contra tyrannos*, 1579).

7. Thomas Hobbes, *Behemoth*, in *The Collected Works of Thomas Hobbes*, 12 vols, ed. William Molesworth (London: Routledge, [1839–45] 1997), VI, p. 168.

8. Edmund Plowden, cited in Ernst Kantorowicz, *The King's Two Bodies: A Study in Medieval Political Theology* (Princeton, NJ: Princeton University Press, [1957] 1981), p. 7.

9. Erasmus, *The Education of A Christian Prince*, trans. Lisa Jardine (Cambridge: Cambridge University Press, 2002), pp. 19–20.

10. Machiavelli, *The Prince*, ed. Quentin Skinner and Russell Price (Cambridge: Cambridge University Press, 2007), p. 55, pp. 59–60, pp. 61–2.

11. Julia Briggs, *This Stage-Play World, Texts and Contexts, 1580–1625*, 2nd edn (Oxford: Oxford University Press, 1997), p. 211.

12. Kate Aughterson (ed.), *The English Renaissance: An Anthology of Sources and Documents* (London: Routledge, 1998), p. 89.

13. Martin Butler, 'Romans in Britain: *The Roman Actor* and the Early Stuart Classical Play', in *Philip Massinger: A Critical Reassessment*, ed. Douglas Howard (Cambridge: Cambridge University Press, 1985), pp. 139–70 (p. 154).

14. See E. M. W. Tillyard, *The Elizabethan World Picture* (London: Chatto & Windus, [1943] 1950), pp. 24–5.

15. Margot Heinemann, *Puritanism and Theatre: Thomas Middleton and Opposition Drama under the Early Stuarts* (Cambridge: Cambridge University Press, 1980), p. 3.

16. Douglas Bruster, *Drama and the Market in the Age of Shakespeare* (Cambridge: Cambridge University Press, 1992), p. 19.

17. Lawrence Stone, *The Family, Sex and Marriage in England, 1500–1800*, abridged edn (London: Penguin, 1990), p. 50, p. 66, pp. 81–2, p. 88. For counter-evidence see Michael MacDonald, *Mystical Bedlam: Madness, Anxiety and Healing in Seventeenth-Century England* (Cambridge: Cambridge University Press, 1981), p. 82, pp. 103–4.

18. Robert Cleaver, *A Godly Form of Household Government* (London: Thomas Man, 1598), sig. B.

19. See Kate Aughterson (ed.), *Renaissance Woman: A Sourcebook* (London: Routledge, 1995), pp. 47–8.

20. Briggs, pp. 67–8.

21. Lisa Hopkins and Matthew Steggle, *Renaissance Literature and Culture* (London: Continuum, 2006), p. 54.

22. See Stephen Greenblatt, *Shakespearean Negotiations: The Circulation of Social Energy in Renaissance England* (Oxford: Clarendon, 1990), p. 81 for an anecdote about a woman who reputedly turned into a man.

23. Anonymous, *Hic Mulier: or, The man-woman* (London: I. T., 1620), sig. A3.

24. Stephen Orgel, *Impersonations: The Performance of Gender in Shakespeare's England* (Cambridge: Cambridge University Press, 1996), p. 19.

25. Hopkins and Steggle, p. 50.

26. Stone, p. 149.

27. Briggs, p. 53.

28. Andrew Hadfield, *The English Renaissance, 1500–1620* (Oxford: Blackwell, 2001), p. 255.

29. James Knowles, 'Sexuality: A Renaissance Category?', in *A Companion to English Renaissance Literature and Culture*, ed. Michael Hattaway (Oxford: Blackwell, 2003), pp. 674–89 (p. 681).

30. Wynne-Davies, p. 164.
31. Ibid., p. 163.
32. Hadfield, p. 241.
33. Ibid., p. 242.
34. 'Did Women Have a Renaissance?' (1977), in *Women, History and Theory: The Essays of Joan Kelly* (Chicago, IL: University of Chicago Press, 1984), pp. 19–50.
35. William Caxton, cited in Gary Waller, *English Poetry of the Sixteenth Century* (London: Longman, 1986), p. 60.
36. Richard Mulcaster, *The First Part of the Elementarie* (London: Thomas Vautrollier, 1582), p. 254.
37. N. F. Blake, 'The English Language of the Early Modern Period', in *A Companion to English Renaissance Literature and Culture*, ed. Michael Hattaway (Oxford: Blackwell, 2003), pp. 71–80 (p. 79).
38. Briggs, p. 79.
39. Ibid., p. 79.
40. William H. Sherman, 'Travel and Trade', in *A Companion to Renaissance Drama*, ed. Arthur F. Kinney (Oxford: Blackwell, 2004), pp. 109–20 (p. 116).
41. Ibid., p. 116.
42. *Tudor Royal Proclamations: III, 1588–1603*, ed. James F. Larkin and Paul L. Hughes (New Haven, CT: Yale University Press, 1969), p. 221.
43. Bartels, p. 159.
44. See Michel de Montaigne, 'On the Cannibals', in *The Complete Essays*, trans. M. A. Screech (London: Penguin, 1991), pp. 232–3.
45. Margo Hendricks, 'Race: A Renaissance Category?', in *A Companion to English Renaissance Literature and Culture*, ed. Michael Hattaway (Oxford: Blackwell, 2003), pp. 690–8 (p. 693, p. 697).
46. Hadfield, pp. 260–3.
47. Ibid., pp. 33–4.
48. Harold Love and Arthur F. Marotti, 'Manuscript Transmission and Circulation', in *The Cambridge History of Early Modern Literature*, ed. David Loewenstein and Janel

Mueller (Cambridge: Cambridge University Press, 2002), pp. 55–80 (p. 55).

49. Michelle O'Callaghan, 'Publication: Print and Manuscript', in *A Companion to English Renaissance Literature and Culture*, ed. Michael Hattaway (Oxford: Blackwell, 2003), pp. 81–94 (p. 90).

50. Sir Philip Sidney, *The Defence of Poesy*, in *The Major Works*, ed. Katherine Duncan-Jones (Oxford: Oxford University Press, 2002), p. 234, p. 217.

51. Ben Jonson, *Timber: Or Discoveries*, in *The Complete Works*, ed. C. H. Herford, Percy and Evelyn Simpson, 11 vols (Oxford: Clarendon, 1925–52), VIII ([1947], 1954), p. 595.

52. Ibid., p. 587.

53. Sidney, p. 216.

54. See Thomas Campion, *Obseruations in the Art of English Poesie* (London: Andrew Wise, 1602); Sidney, p. 248; Samuel Daniel, *A Defence of Ryme* (London: Edward Blount, 1603).

55. Sidney, p. 242; George Puttenham, *The Arte of English Poesie* (London: Richard Field, 1589), p. 51, p. 49.

56. Francis Meres, *Palladis Tamia. Wits Treasury* (London: Cuthbert Burbie, 1598), p. 280, p. 282.

57. See Northrop Frye, *A Natural Perspective: the Development of Shakespearean Comedy* (London: Columbia University Press, 1965).

58. See L. C. Knights, *Drama and Society in the Age of Jonson* (London: Chatto & Windus, 1937).

59. *The Oxford Shakespeare: The Complete Works*, ed. Stanley Wells and Gary Taylor, 2nd edn (Oxford: Clarendon Press, 2005), p. xxxix.

60. Terence Hawkes, *Shakespeare in the Present* (London: Routledge, 2002), p. 4.

61. Cited in Jonathan Dollimore, 'Introduction: Shakespeare, cultural materialism and the new historicism', in *Political Shakespeare: Essays in Cultural Materialism*, ed. Jonathan Dollimore and Alan Sinfield, 2nd edn (Manchester: Manchester University Press, 2003), pp. 2–17 (p. 4).

62. H. Aram Veeser, 'Introduction', in *The New Historicism*, ed. H. Aram Veeser (Berkeley, CA: University of California Press, 1989), pp. ix–xvi (p. xi).

63. Greenblatt, *Shakespearean Negotiations*, p. vii, p. 5.
64. Louis Montrose, 'Professing the Renaissance: The Politics and Poetics of Culture', in *The New Historicism*, ed. H. Aram Veeser (Berkeley, CA: University of California Press, 1989), pp. 15–36 (p. 23).
65. See Stephen Greenblatt, 'Invisible Bullets: Renaissance Authority and its Subversion, *Henry IV* and *Henry V*', in *Political Shakespeare: Essays in Cultural Materialism*, ed. Jonathan Dollimore and Alan Sinfield, 2nd edn (Manchester: Manchester University Press, 2003), pp. 18–47 (p. 20).
66. 'Foreword', in *Political Shakespeare: Essays in Cultural Materialism*, ed. Jonathan Dollimore and Alan Sinfield, 2nd edn (Manchester: Manchester University Press, 2003), pp. vii–viii (p. vii).
67. Ibid., p. viii.
68. See Jonathan Dollimore and Alan Sinfield, 'History and Ideology: the instance of *Henry V*', in *Alternative Shakespeares*, ed. John Drakakis (London: Methuen, [1985] 1996), pp. 206–27; Kathleen McLuskie, 'The patriarchal bard: feminist criticism of Shakespeare: *King Lear* and *Measure for Measure*', in *Political Shakespeare: Essays in Cultural Materialism*, ed. Jonathan Dollimore and Alan Sinfield, 2nd edn (Manchester: Manchester University Press, 2003), pp. 88–108.
69. See, for example, Graham Bradshaw, *Misrepresentations: Shakespeare and the Materialists* (Ithaca, NY: Cornell University Press, 1993); Walter Cohen, 'Political Criticism of Shakespeare', in *Shakespeare Reproduced*, ed. Jean Howard and Marion O'Connor (London: Methuen, 1987), pp. 18–46; and Jean Howard, 'The New Historicism in Renaissance Studies', *ELR*, 16 (1986), 13–43 (38–40, 42–3).
70. See Edward Pechter, 'The New Historicism and its Discontents: Politicizing Renaissance Drama', *PMLA*, 102 (1987), 292–303; and Carol Thomas Neely, 'Constructing the Subject: Feminist Practice and the New Renaissance Discourses', *ELR*, 18 (1988), 5–18.
71. Coppélia Kahn, *Man's Estate: Masculine Identity in Shakespeare* (Berkeley, CA: University of California Press,

1980); Janet Adelman, *Suffocating Mothers: Fantasies of Maternal Origin in Shakespeare's Plays, 'Hamlet' to 'The Tempest'* (London: Routledge, 1992).

72. Lisa Jardine, *Still Harping on Daughters: Women and Drama in the Age of Shakespeare* (Hemel Hempstead: Harvester Wheatsheaf, 1983), p. 1.

73. Ibid., p. 6.

74. McLuskie, p. 106.

75. Elaine Showalter, 'Representing Ophelia: Women, Madness and the Responsibilities of Feminist Criticism', in *Shakespeare and the Question of Theory*, ed. Patricia Parker and Geoffrey Hartman (London: Routledge, [1985] 1993), pp. 77–94 (p. 79, p. 80, p. 92).

76. Sara Mendelson and Patricia Crawford, *Women in Early Modern England: 1550–1720* (Oxford: Oxford University Press, 1998).

77. Ann Baynes Coiro, 'Writing in Service: Sexual Politics and Class Position in the Poetry of Aemilia Lanyer and Ben Jonson', *Criticism*, 35 (1993), 357–76 (359).

78. See, for example, Kim F. Hall, *Things of Darkness: Economies of Race and Gender in Early Modern England* (Ithaca, NY: Cornell University Press, 1996).

79. Alan Bray, *Homosexuality in Renaissance England* (London: Gay Men's Press, 1982), p. 16.

80. Bruce Smith, *Homosexual Desire in Shakespeare's England: A Cultural Poetics* (Chicago, IL: University of Chicago Press, 1991), p. 23.

81. See Valerie Traub, *Desire and Anxiety: Circulations of Sexuality in Shakespearean Drama* (London: Routledge, 1992) and *The Renaissance of Lesbianism in Early Modern England* (Cambridge: Cambridge University Press, 2002).

82. See Martin Orkin, *Shakespeare Against Apartheid* (Craighall: Ad. Donker, 1987).

83. Jyotsna Singh, 'Post-colonial criticism', in *Shakespeare: An Oxford Guide*, ed. Stanley Wells and Lena Cowen Orlin (Oxford: Oxford University Press, 2003), pp. 492–500 (p. 492).

84. See Ania Loomba, *Gender, Race, Renaissance Drama* (Manchester: Manchester University Press, 1989).

85. Singh, p. 501.
86. Meredith Anne Skura, 'Discourse and the Individual: The Case of Colonialism in *The Tempest*', *SQ*, 40 (1989), 42–69 (57, 47, 58).

Drama

All the world's a stage
And all the men and women merely players
(William Shakespeare, *As You Like It*, II, vii, 138–9)

When Jacques likens the world to a stage in his famous speech from *As You Like It* he rehearses what would have been a familiar trope: the metaphorical identification of life with theatre was commonplace in the Renaissance. There were good reasons for contemporaries to draw such parallels. Not only was human identity increasingly perceived in terms of role-playing but many of the rituals associated with the exercise of power in Renaissance England were theatrical. A good example of this is afforded by the judicial system and the practice of executing felons on public scaffolds, a show of power that drew large audiences. The same culture of theatrically displayed power is found in the pageantry and drama associated with the court. In the absence of a standing army or national police force England's monarchs depended on ritualised displays of power to reinforce their authority and ensure the obedience of their subjects. The pervasive theatricality of Renaissance culture helps to explain the special currency of the 'life as theatre' metaphor in the period and, perhaps, informed the contemporary fascination with drama.

THE PROFESSIONAL STAGE

The Red Lion theatre, built by grocer John Brayne, is the earliest known permanent playhouse in London. Its opening in 1567 marked the beginning of a seminal era in English theatre history. By 1642 when the outbreak of Civil War led parliament to ban public stage plays, English theatrical culture had changed profoundly. Prior to the Elizabethan era acting companies were accustomed to performing in a variety of spaces, ranging from inns and churches to private houses. As a consequence plays needed to be adaptable for different venues. This tended to mean relying on a minimalist staging style. The development of permanent playhouses made it possible for acting companies to build up larger stocks of playing gear and to experiment with increasingly sophisticated stage machinery, while the regular, controlled access theatres provided to large audiences made playing more profitable than it had been previously. For the first time it became possible to make a living from the stage. This led to the gradual professionalising of the theatre world. At the same time increasing restrictions upon the performance of religious plays of the kind which had dominated the Medieval theatre world led to the secularisation of English drama.

Playing Companies

English Renaissance theatre was company-based and male-dominated (as women were not allowed to act publicly until the Restoration). By the late sixteenth century, there were two main types of troupe: adult and boy companies.

Adult Companies

Most adult companies had a royal or noble patron, under whose name they would travel and perform. Shakespeare, for example, belonged from 1594 to the Lord Chamberlain's Men, and after 1603 was one of the King's Men (after King James I assumed patronage of the troupe). For elite men and women patronage of players was one way of displaying their power and wealth, while such patronage lent players status and protection and could procure them generous rewards.

By the 1590s most adult acting companies consisted of between twelve and fifteen players. Although most of the actors were adults it was usual for companies to include two or more boys as apprentice players. Most plays from the period include many more characters than there would be actors in a company, so 'doubling' (or the playing of more than one role) was a common practice. But it was not unusual for players to specialise in certain kinds of role. Some actors (such as Will Kemp and Robert Armin) were known for playing 'clowns'. Others, such as Edward Alleyn and Richard Burbage, specialised in playing 'heroic' leading roles. While Alleyn was renowned for his barn-storming performance of larger-than-life characters such as Marlowe's Tamburlaine, Burbage was admired for his Protean ability to play a variety of characters, ranging from Shakespeare's Richard III to Hamlet and Othello.

Female roles were another specialism, generally being assigned to the company's boy players. It is a convention Shakespeare's Cleopatra alludes to when she complains (anachronistically) about the fact that 'some squeaking Cleopatra' will 'boy [her] greatness' when the Romans stage plays about her (V, ii, 215). In other plays, such as Shakespeare's *Twelfth Night*, cross-dressing is written into the plot. Playwrights drew attention to the theatrical convention of cross-dressing in order to create comic complications and to raise playful questions about gender identity and sexuality. Not all contemporaries approved of the custom, believing that it was at odds with Biblical injunctions against cross-dressing, and a threat to conventional sexual and gender boundaries.

Boy Companies

The professional boy companies emerged from the Renaissance tradition of performing plays in grammar and choral schools (see Academic Drama, below). The reputation that some schoolboys gained for skilful performance led to their invitation to perform at the Tudor court. Before such performances the boys would usually stage a rehearsal at their school or chapel which would be attended by a number of courtiers (as a way of screening the intended performance). Over time the number of courtiers attending these preview performances increased and the custom of offering a monetary gift became all but obligatory. The commercial opportunity this presented did not go long unnoticed. In the 1570s the choristers of St Paul's Cathedral and the Chapel Royal began to perform plays regularly in specially converted theatres to paying audiences. The commercial activities of neither company lasted long – by 1590 both troupes appear to have been suppressed following their staging of dangerously topical plays – but they had set a precedent for commercial boy playing and were to resume professional performing in the early seventeenth century. During this second period of activity (1599–1608) they briefly rivalled the adult companies in reputation and success; and several new boy troupes were established in their wake in the seventeenth century.

Like the schoolboys who performed on an occasional basis, the commercial companies mainly consisted of boys aged between eleven and sixteen, managed by their school or choral master. The high reputation of the boy performers and their prestigious association with the world of academia perhaps explains why many of the period's leading playwrights were keen to write for them. Most of the boys' plays were courtly in theme and satirical in tone, and many included music and songs, providing opportunities for the most talented choristers to show-off their skills. Courtly subjects suited their generally elite audiences, while the visual tension between the boys' youth and the adult roles they played appears to have invested their performance with a pervasive air of mockery which invited their use as satirical mirrors of their elders. It was a high risk mode of theatre and the scandal their topical comedies courted eventually led to their suppression for a second time: the St Paul's playhouse was closed by 1606 and royal patronage was withdrawn from the Blackfriars boys in 1608.

Space to Play

Up until the 1560s there were no buildings specifically designed for acting in England. When John Brayne built the Red Lion theatre this was to change. Following his example, a series of playhouses was opened in the capital. The new theatres (or 'playhouses' as they were often known) were of two types: open-air or amphitheatre playhouses and indoor or hall playhouses.

Open-air Playhouses

The Red Lion was the first of the open-air playhouses, but by autumn 1568 John Brayne appears to have abandoned his pioneering theatrical venture. His brother-in-law, James Burbage was to show more stamina. In 1576 he built the Theatre: it was London's second open-air playhouse and Burbage had high hopes for it. His choice of name (English for the Latin word *theatrum*) reflects his ambitions, inviting audiences to draw parallels between his playhouse and the theatres of antiquity. The Theatre remained in regular use until the early 1590s when a dispute between Burbage and his landlord over the lease for the plot of ground on which it was built led to its closure (1598). Fearing they would lose the building, Burbage's sons and a group of others dismantled the playhouse over Christmas and arranged for the removal of its timbers to the Bankside. There they were to be re-used for the period's most famous playhouse, the Globe (1599).

By the beginning of the Civil War at least eight open-air playhouses had been purpose-built in London: the Red Lion (1567); the Theatre (1576); the Curtain (1577); the Rose (1587); the Swan (1596); the Globe (1599); the Fortune (1600); and the Hope (1614). Other buildings were adapted to serve as open-air playhouses, as at the Boar's Head (1598) and the Red Bull (1607). All of the purpose-built playhouses were erected on the outskirts of London. Serious overcrowding within the city walls meant that it was all but impossible to get land for development in the city centre. At the same time, by building in the 'Liberties' (suburban districts beyond the immediate control of the city council) the players enjoyed more freedom. Other entertainment industries and illicit businesses clustered in the 'Liberties' for similar reasons. The Bankside where the Globe was erected was famous not only for its new playhouses but for its bear-baiting arenas and brothels: all vied for Londoners' pennies.

None of the open-air theatres of Renaissance London survives intact but legal documents, visitor accounts, contemporary

illustrations and the information yielded by archaeological inves-
tigations at the foundations of the Globe, Rose and Hope playhouses have taught us a great deal about them. Most were
polygonal timber-framed buildings, made up of three tiers of galleries around an open yard. From the outside they appeared
roughly circular. Some of the playhouses were much bigger than
others but their design was essentially similar. The roofed galleries
were fitted with seating, with the most comfortable furnishings
reserved for the rooms nearest the stage (the "Lords' Rooms").
Other spectators stood in the open central area known as the
'yard'. The stage jutted into the yard and was usually square or
rectangular, and might be fitted with a trap door which could be
used for the entry and exit of characters such as the ghost in
Hamlet. The symbolic association of the below stage area with
'hell' made the trap door an especially appropriate entry point for
devils.

At the rear of the stage stood a tiring-house where the actors
dressed. The lower level was usually fitted with two side doors and,
in some cases, with a central opening covered by a painted cloth. On
the upper level there was a gallery, part of which could be used for
action above, such as the balcony scene in *Romeo and Juliet*. At the
later open-air playhouses it was usual for the stage to be fitted with
a stage-cover known as the 'heavens'. This was often decorated to
look like a night-sky and was sometimes fitted with a trap door for
divine descents.

Plays were staged daily in the afternoon and the playhouses were
generally open all year round (with the exception of Sundays and
Lent). In the Elizabethan era you could see a play for as little as one
pence, a comparatively small fee even then. Given this, it is perhaps
not surprising that large numbers of people were drawn to the playhouses. By 1595 it is estimated that the two leading acting companies were attracting audiences of around 15,000 people every week.[1]
Information about who went to see the plays is less plentiful, but
suggests that audiences could be socially diverse, including men,
women and children of all ages, and a mix of social groups, ranging
from apprentices and servants to merchants, lawyers, nobles and
visiting ambassadors.

Indoor Playhouses

The earliest indoor theatres were established around the same time as the Theatre. The first was created by Sebastian Westcott, master of the choristers of St Paul's, and was used by the choristers periodically between 1575–89 and 1599–1606. The hall which the boys adopted as their theatre appears to have been 'on an upper floor in the almonry' of the cathedral.[2] The second indoor playhouse was founded by Richard Farrant, master of the Children of the Chapel Royal. Farrant created his theatre in the buttery of the former Blackfriars monastery (1576). It continued to be used by his boys until 1584. In both cases the theatres the masters established were officially rehearsal spaces for the boys' regular court performances. In practice, they became commercial playing venues and set a precedent for professional indoor theatres.

In 1596 James Burbage followed their lead, purchasing the Upper Frater of the Blackfriars complex with the intention of creating an indoor playhouse for his son's acting company, the Lord Chamberlain's Men. Unfortunately, Burbage could not get permission to use the playhouse, so his sons sub-let the property to Henry Evans who used it as a theatre for the Children of the Chapel Royal (1600–8). In 1609 Richard Burbage's company (now the King's Men) began using the theatre as their winter venue (they continued to play at the Globe in the summer).

The King's Men's success with the second Blackfriars theatre started a fashion for indoor playhouses. Among the new indoor theatres were the Whitefriars (1607), the Cockpit (1616), and the Salisbury Court theatre (1629–30). Most were conversions of existing buildings; and were based within the city walls or the wealthy north-western suburbs of London. The indoor theatres varied in size but were generally much smaller than the open-air playhouses. As at the open-air theatres there were galleries (around the sides of the hall) and a 'yard' area in the centre filled with benches. At the side of the stage there were special 'boxes' (the equivalent of the Lords' rooms), but if you were especially keen to show off new clothes, good looks, or wit (in mischievous asides to the actors) you could hire a stool and sit on the stage. Like the buildings, the stages of the indoor theatres were typically much smaller than those at the open-air theatres, but might be fitted with a stage trap and were backed in similar fashion by a tiring house. Unlike at the open-air playhouses, artificial lighting was used for all performances.

Performances at the indoor theatres were less regular, and entry was more expensive. At the second Blackfriars even the cheapest seats cost six pence, six times the price of the cheapest tickets at the Globe. For this reason audiences at the indoor theatres are likely to have been more privileged, mainly consisting of members of the nobility, the gentry or the wealthy merchant classes. Over time the slightly different make-up of the audiences appears to have influenced the kinds of play performed. At the open-air Red Bull, for example, the players reportedly specialised in heroic ('drum and trumpet') plays, while at indoor theatres like Salisbury Court the emphasis was on courtly plays. The result was a growing rivalry and snobbery between troupes based at the open-air and indoor theatres.

Playwriting, Regulation, Publication

Playwriting

Whereas touring players were able to rely on a relatively small repertory of plays, the regular performances staged at the permanent playhouses created a consistent demand for new plays in the late sixteenth century. This demand fostered the talents of a new generation of playwrights and led to an unprecedented surge in playwriting of which the surviving corpus of Renaissance plays is only a small part. While some of these new writers were university educated, many others (including Shakespeare) were products of the grammar-school system (see Introduction). For both sets of men, the theatre provided an alternative arena in which to employ their learning and wit to the traditional educated and craft-based professions. In many cases, they chose to work collaboratively, sharing the writing of individual plays between them.

Once a play was completed the playwright(s) submitted a copy of it to the acting company or playhouse manager. Having purchased the play it became their property and the preparations for performance would begin. This would include having at least two copies of the play made: one for sending to the Master of the Revels for licensing (see below) and one that could be divided into 'parts' for the actors. The latter were collected on individual scrolls, with each speech preceded by a cue. At least one copy of the play would also be marked up as a prompt-book. This might include adding details about props, correcting and enlarging stage directions, and regularising characters' names.

The collaborative nature of much Renaissance playwriting facilitated the rapid production of plays, as did dramatists' regular use of existing stories for the plots. Shakespeare frequently borrowed from the work of others, sometimes word for word.[3] Renaissance audiences did not share the post-Romantic preoccupation with originality. Instead writers were judged according to the skill with which they used their sources. The sixteenth-century flourishing of the printing press provided playwrights with a rich storehouse of material. The racy Italian novellas of writers such as Matteo Bandello and Gerald Cinthio with their tales of violence and lust proved especially popular, but playwrights also ransacked classical literature, Spanish and Italian chivalric romances, contemporary continental comedies, and the wave of new history chronicles published in the late sixteenth century.[4]

The style and genre of the plays written for the Renaissance stage was also influenced by earlier dramatic traditions. The episodic organisation of many early Elizabethan romances and history plays finds its model in the diffuse structure of the Medieval 'miracle' or 'mystery' plays (which dramatised episodes from the Bible), while the earlier era's 'saints' plays (with their tales of suffering, miracles and redemption) afforded a model for the romances of the Jacobean stage. The influence of Medieval 'morality' plays (see Glossary) was even more extensive. Although few Renaissance plays adopted their allegorical mode, the concept of a battle between good and evil for the soul of a representative man underlies many Renaissance tragedies, and the mischievous 'Vice' figure of the moralities (a servant of the devil known for his playful asides to the audience) can be seen behind the witty anarchic clowns of Elizabethan comedy and the artful villains of Renaissance tragedy with their penchant for confiding their villainous plans in the audience.

Classical dramatic traditions were, likewise, to have a bearing on the development of English Renaissance drama. While scholars were fascinated by the classical dramatic theories of Aristotle, playwrights appear to have been more directly influenced by the classical plays themselves. The Roman comedies of Terence and Plautus and the Roman revenge tragedies of Seneca were especially popular models.

Early English plays were usually written in short rhyming couplets; Elizabethan and Stuart dramatic writing was to be far more varied. The late 1580s saw the introduction of a new kind of verse: unrhymed iambic pentameter, or 'blank verse' (see Glossary). Although now synonymous with Shakespeare the first use of blank verse in a play was in *Gorboduc*, a neo-classical tragedy written by Thomas Norton and Thomas Sackville for private performance (1561–2). Blank verse was popularised on the public stage (1587–8) by Christopher Marlowe's *Tamburlaine the Great* plays. In the prologue to *Tamburlaine, Part I* the classically trained Marlowe explicitly rejected the traditions of English rhyming verse: 'From jigging veins of rhyming mother wits / And such conceits as clownage keeps in pay, / We'll lead you to the stately tent of war, / Where you shall hear the Scythian Tamburlaine / Threat'ning the world with high astounding terms'.[5] In this mini-manifesto Marlowe proclaimed blank verse to be a more elevated, serious verse form; and it soon became the favoured form for tragedies.

In the late sixteenth and early seventeenth centuries an increasing number of playwrights experimented with prose, too. John Lyly developed a conspicuously artificial prose style, involving the use of parallelism, antithesis and elaborate figures of speech. Other playwrights, such as Shakespeare, mixed verse and prose. In these cases it became common to use verse for noble characters and prose for commoners, although playwrights sometimes used a shift from verse to prose (or vice versa) simply as a way of marking a change in mood or focus in a scene. Prose is spoken occasionally, therefore, by high-class characters, and verse by lower-class figures.

In classical and Medieval drama characters are often personifications of abstract concepts or 'types'. 'Typed' characters feature in Renaissance drama, too, but there was an increasing tendency to individualise characters, especially through language. At the same time, the developing use of asides and soliloquies as devices for the revelation of characters' private thoughts became a way of suggesting that characters had an inner self.

Unlike classical dramas which typically begin 'the action near or at' a 'crisis', most English Renaissance plays 'embrace a long temporal period' and move between a series of different locations.[6] In doing so they do not observe the so-called dramatic 'unities' (see Glossary) outlined by Aristotle and were therefore criticised by contemporary authors such as Sir Philip Sidney. In similar fashion, most Renaissance plays incorporate multiple plots and styles. Often one plot is the main plot and others are sub-plots but their relationship to each other varies. Sometimes the plots intersect or are analogous in theme, as in *Hamlet* where the sub-plots involving Laertes and Fortinbras revolve around how to avenge a dead father, as does the main plot featuring Hamlet. In other cases the multiple plots contrast with each other, either in theme or style. In either case, it was common to alternate between different plots and styles in consecutive scenes.

The close player-audience relationship fostered by the proximity between actors and audiences in Renaissance playhouses also appears to have affected the style of the period's drama. Perhaps most significantly audiences were not asked to accept theatrical illusions as real. On the contrary, playwrights repeatedly emphasised the theatricality of what audiences were watching. Theatrical metaphors and jokes are common, as are devices such as prologues, epilogues, asides, soliloquies and plays-within-plays.

Regulation

English Renaissance drama was subject to two separate licensing systems: licensing for print, and licensing for performance. From 1559 all books to be printed had to be licensed (see Introduction). The press licensers were also censors and had the right to ban or ask for corrections to any work they examined. Direct evidence of plays being censored before or after publication is rare and generally indirect. Often it is the survival of different versions of a printed play that alerts us to the possibility of censorship. This is the case with William Shakespeare's *Richard II*. Scholars have long noted the absence of a key episode from the Elizabethan editions of the play (1597, 1598): the on-stage deposition of Richard II during which he is forced to hand over his crown to the usurper Henry Bolingbroke.

The episode is included for the first time in the new edition of the play published in 1608. It is possible that Shakespeare simply revised his play in the Jacobean era but the fact that parallels had been drawn between Elizabeth I and Richard II has led many scholars to conclude that the deposition scene was initially censored as being too provocative.

From 1581 responsibility for authorising plays for performance was placed in the hands of the Queen's Master of the Revels, Edmund Tilney. Initially, players were expected to present or perform their plays in person before the Master; later it became usual to present him with a copy of the play. If he was unhappy with any part of a script he could order the acting company to rewrite it or to cut it entirely. Required corrections were often made by the author.

The surviving evidence suggests that the Masters were 'scrupulous' censors but 'applied relatively broad criteria of what was permissible'.[7] As Richard Dutton notes, the Master's main function was 'to ensure, not exactly the innocence of a play, but that its fictional veiling was adequate, that serious offence might not be offered to members of the court or to friendly foreign dignitaries'.[8] One way of veiling topical commentary was to set plays in foreign countries or past historical periods which afforded parallels with contemporary England. Other playwrights sought to evade the censor's pen by cultivating what Annabel Patterson has described as a 'functional ambiguity' in their representation of potentially controversial subject matter.[9]

When plays were censored prior to performance it was generally because they dealt too directly with living individuals or politically sensitive subjects. On other occasions plays faced retrospective censorship because they caused offence when performed. In some cases, they were plays that had initially received a performance licence. In 1624 the King's Men caused a scandal when they satirised the Spanish ambassador, Conde de Gondomar, in their production of Thomas Middleton's *A Game at Chess*. The play capitalised on contemporary anti-Spanish feeling which was running high following King James's failed attempt to broker a marriage between his son Charles and the Spanish Infanta earlier that year. Despite its obvious topicality, the play had received a license from

Henry Herbert, then Master of the Revels. Herbert was no doubt aware of the play's anti-Spanish content, but would not have known from the text that Gondomar was to be personally satirised in the performance. The performers and playwright bore the brunt of James's subsequent ire: the King's Men were temporarily forbidden to play, and an arrest warrant was made out for Thomas Middleton.[10]

Publication

Most Renaissance plays were written for performance rather than for reading. As a consequence, many were never published. Those that were printed generally went through a series of processes. First, the publisher had to obtain a licence to print the play (see Introduction). The next step was to get permission to print the play from the Stationers' Company. Many publishers would also pay to have the details of their ownership of the text entered in the Stationers' Register. (Later this became obligatory). The latter were both ways of ensuring that no one else was allowed to publish the text. Having completed these preparations the publisher would arrange to have the play printed by a professional printer. When the printed plays were ready the publisher would sell them wholesale to booksellers, who would sell on individual copies to the public (for around six pence each).[11]

Most plays were printed as small 'quarto' editions (roughly A5-sized pamphlets) (see Glossary). Later collection editions of plays of the kind published by Ben Jonson (1616) and the friends of William Shakespeare (1623) were much grander affairs. They were printed as 'folios' (see Glossary). These were larger, often leather-bound, books. They were more expensive and traditionally associated with learned or prestigious works, such as the Bible. To use such a format for the publication of plays was to claim a higher status for popular drama than it had usually been accorded.

Printed versions of plays were not necessarily the same as those performed in the theatre. Variations between printed editions are not unusual either. These differences probably reflect the nature of the manuscript sold to, or used by, each publisher. Some play editions appear to have been based on a copy of the performance promptbook or a memorial re-construction by one of the actors. Others appear to have been based on authorial manuscripts. The latter tend to be longer than those based on performance texts, as it was not unusual for acting companies to adapt the texts they bought from writers and playwrights sometimes revised or restored material to their plays for printing. It used to be common to describe the surviving play texts as either 'good' (authorial-derived) quartos or 'bad' (performance-derived) quartos, but recent scholars have questioned the validity of these distinctions and the assumption that performance-derived texts are inferior.

Staging

One of the most distinctive features of Renaissance staging, from a modern perspective, is the absence of sets or scenery. Renaissance plays had to be adaptable for a variety of venues and therefore usually evoked settings through textual allusions. For much of the action the stage itself was bare but Renaissance staging was not without sophistication and visual spectacle was vitally important. Most acting companies owned a stock of playing gear and musical instruments, and made regular use of a variety of properties, ranging from small items such as swords and crowns to impressive pieces of stage furniture, such as the rock, cage, tomb and Hell mouth listed amongst Philip Henslowe's properties at the Rose theatre (1598).[12]

Costume played an even more significant part in the spectacle of performances. Players' outfits were often colourful and lavish and acting companies generally invested far more money in their wardrobes of playing apparel than their props. As with props, the costume wardrobe was generally an adaptable stock, although outfits were occasionally made for specific characters and plays. Thus a late sixteenth-century inventory of playing apparel prepared by Edward Alleyn lists a variety of cloaks, gowns, suits, jerkins and doublets, as well costumes for named characters such as a 'hary ye viii gowne' and 'faustus Jerkin his clok'.[13]

A great deal of symbolism was attached to clothing in the Renaissance, a fact which actors exploited in their costuming. The time and context of certain scenes, such as night-time or bedroom episodes could be indicated through characters' wearing of appropriate dress (such as night-shirts). Likewise, in a culture in which sumptuary laws restricted who could wear the richest materials and colours, apparel was used to indicate characters' social class. Audiences would expect lowly characters to be plainly dressed and elite figures to be the most finely and colourfully attired. They would probably have been sensitive to breaches of this code, too, as when playwrights call for elite characters to appear in humble apparel (as part of a disguise) or for socially aspirant characters to dress richly.

Renaissance plays frequently draw attention to their illusory nature, but this did not prevent acting companies from attempting a degree of realism in their staging. Musical instruments were used to provide music and a range of realistic sound effects, from on and off-stage battle noises to birdsong. Special devices were created to produce other sounds, such as thunder, too. Live weapons, including guns and cannons, were occasionally used to similarly dramatic effect, but were not without their risks. In 1613 the small cannons fired during a performance of Shakespeare's and Fletcher's *Henry VIII* at the Globe literally brought the house down, after setting the theatre's thatched roof on fire.

Stage directions indicate that plays sometimes incorporated striking visual effects as well, especially in the early seventeenth century. While trap doors in the stage and stage heavens were used to permit the emergence of characters (such as ghosts) from below, and the descent of divine figures from above, gunpowder and fireworks were used to create thrilling storm and lightning effects. Throughout the Renaissance players made great efforts to create convincing displays of on-stage gore, too, using sponges soaked with wine and bladders filled with animal blood to mimic bleeding effects. Sometimes even more bloody effects were called for, as in George Peele's *The Battle of Alcazar* (1594) in which three characters are disembowelled on-stage. The accompanying bookkeeper's direction indicates how the gruesome spectacle was to be created, calling for ' "3 violls of blood and a sheeps gather", that is, a bladder holding liver, heart, and lungs'.[14]

PRIVATE AND OCCASIONAL DRAMA

English Renaissance theatre was not confined to the public play-houses and performances of the professional acting companies. The Medieval tradition of civic and church-sponsored local drama persisted in some communities, and private, occasional drama thrived in schools and university colleges, the Inns of Court, elite households and at court. Although the latter 'comprises a small fraction of the period's output' the elite nature of the audiences meant that each form of private drama enjoyed a high profile in the period and attracted the involvement of most of the leading play-wrights of the day.[15]

Academic Drama

By the time Elizabeth I succeeded to the English throne there was an established tradition of performing plays in schools and university colleges, often at holiday times. Some school and college statutes even made such performances an annual requirement. Most of the plays performed were classical (or neoclassical) and written in Latin. The comedies of Roman authors Plautus and Terence, and the tragedies of Seneca were especially popular. The main motive for performing such plays was pedagogic: it was seen as a way of enhancing students' fluency in Latin, and of developing students' skills in oratory and rhetoric. Later it became customary for schoolboys to perform plays in English, too, many of them modelled on classical comedies. Plays in the vernacular were performed at the universities, too, but more rarely because they were held in lower esteem.

School and university plays were usually performed in school-rooms or halls, sometimes on specially erected wooden stages. Seating galleries were occasionally erected, too, so that the whole hall was turned into a temporary theatre, rather like the indoor play-houses of London. Scenery was not generally used but surviving records suggest that the staging of student productions could be lavish, especially at richer schools and colleges. Several schools and colleges maintained a stock of costumes and props specifically for their annual productions. There is also some evidence of scholars borrowing playing gear from the Court Revels Office, as did the professional London actors on occasion. In 1566 the expenses for the two plays performed by Westminster's scholars before the Queen included four pence spent on boat hire 'to bring apparel from the reuells' and ten shillings given to the 'yeoman of the reuells'.[16]

Despite the low esteem in which professional players were generally held in the academic world, some scholars were evidently interested in the popular stage, as is manifested occasionally in academic plays. In the anonymous *Second Part of the Return From Parnassus*, the last play of a trilogy performed at St John's College, Cambridge between 1598–1601, two characters discuss the merits of contemporary writers, including a number of professional playwrights; and Richard Burbage and Will Kemp, two of the period's most famous professional players, are brought on-stage to audition a pair of students for their acting company. The playwrights and players are satirised, but this satire is qualified by the author's evident fascination with both. In the audition scene one of the students even delivers a speech from Shakespeare's *Richard III*, after Burbage mischievously suggests that he would suit the part of Richard 'Humpback'.[17]

Inns of Court Drama

The four London Inns of Court (Middle Temple, Inner Temple, Gray's Inn and Lincoln's Inn) served as the country's law schools, but they were more than places for learning about the law. As Martin Butler notes, the Inns 'brought together a unique constituency of gentlemen and aristocrats, many of whom were in residence as much for the acquirement of social graces' and the forging of useful social or political connections 'as for a proficiency in the law'.[18] Such training was especially valuable for those with aspirations for a career at court or in politics.

By the late sixteenth century there was a tradition of performing plays and masques at the Inns. Like most private dramas, Inns of Court performances generally took place over Christmas and formed part of the lawyers' seasonal celebrations. These celebrations could be elaborate, not only including the performance of plays but extended feasting, dicing and the election of a Christmas Prince to preside over the festivities.

Sometimes professional players were commissioned to perform at the Inns. Shakespeare's company famously staged *The Comedy of Errors* at Gray's Inn (1594) and *Twelfth Night* at Middle Temple Hall (1602). In the Jacobean era it also became usual to invite professional players to perform the speaking parts in Inns of Court masques, but the shows were mostly written and performed by its members. Like the plays written for the public stage, most Inns of Court shows were in English. In keeping with the sharp-witted culture of the Inns, lawyers appear to have had a particular taste for dramatic satire, parody and topical commentary.

During the first half of Queen Elizabeth's reign the political scene was dominated by debates about the royal succession and the Queen's marriage. The same two issues recur in many Elizabethan Inns of Court entertainments. Under the Stuarts the political issues, and the themes of Inns of Court drama, were different. During the 1630s, for example, when there were growing anxieties about the personal rule of King Charles, the lawyers' entertainments showed a new preoccupation with the importance of rule by law.

On occasion, the lawyer-writers sought to offer the monarch or his/her advisors counsel. One of the best documented examples of this is afforded by Thomas Norton's and Thomas Sackville's *Gorboduc* which was performed at the Inner Temple and the court (Christmas 1561–2). Although superficially about the downfall of ancient British ruler, King Gorboduc, Norton and Sackville used Gorboduc's story to emphasise the importance of establishing the royal succession with the agreement of parliament, and to offer covert support to Lord Robert Dudley's suit to marry the Queen.

Plays at the Inns were usually staged in the evening in the dining hall. For the grander performances the hall was turned into a temporary theatre, complete with stage, seating scaffolds and artificial lighting. Visiting professionals routinely travelled with playing gear so their Inns of Court performances are likely to have been staged in costume, and accompanied by props, music and special effects. Surviving evidence suggests that the lawyers went to similar efforts to impress their audiences when mounting their own productions.

Pleasing a lawyer-dominated audience could be a challenge, especially if you were a troupe of visiting actors. Although many were avid theatre-goers, lawyers were sometimes aggressive critics and could be unruly spectators. In-house performers could probably expect a warmer welcome but still had to work hard to impress audiences possibly familiar not only with the drama of the public stage but with court and university theatre.

Court Drama

Dramatic entertainment was an integral part of English Renaissance court culture. Both Elizabeth and James were patrons of acting companies and regularly invited professional troupes to perform at court. Most of the plays the professional troupes performed were drawn from their playhouse repertories; others appear to have been written with court performance in mind. King James's well-known interest in witchcraft is thought to have been a factor, for instance, in Shakespeare's decision to write *Macbeth* (c.1606), a play which explores the pernicious effects of witchcraft and which looks forward to James's inheritance of the Scottish throne.

Plays were not the only form of dramatic entertainment enjoyed by the court. The Tudor and Stuart eras saw the thriving of the court masque, a multimedia form of entertainment combining music, dance and speech (see Court Masques, below) and Renaissance English monarchs were accustomed to being entertained with short dramatic 'pageants' both at court and when they visited provincial cities and noble houses on progress. Usually allegorical or mythical in style and content, these brief 'shows' or speeches were primarily intended to compliment the monarch but this did not prevent hosts from using their entertainments to offer advice about royal policy or to advance their cause(s) with the monarch. In 1575 the Earl of Leicester famously hoped to use his entertainment of Elizabeth I at Kenilworth Castle to advance his suit to marry her. Whether the Queen should marry, and who she should choose, were frequent themes of the courtly 'shows' staged in the first half of Elizabeth's reign. Later, when it became clear that Elizabeth was unlikely to marry, it became common for pageant writers to celebrate the Queen's virginity instead, often presenting her as a chaste goddess such as Diana or Astrea.

Household and Closet Drama

Many noblemen and women followed the example of their monarchs and patronised drama. Some lent their names to acting companies; others hosted performances by touring players. Nobles called on to host the monarch in the provinces often arranged for the performance of welcoming shows and/or a play or masque (as noted above); and some commissioned play and masque performances to celebrate important holidays and household events (such as weddings). Sir John Harington invited a troupe of London players to perform at his country estate, Burley-on-the-Hill, as part of the Christmas festivities he organised in 1595–6. The troupe (probably the Lord Chamberlain's Men) gave a performance of Shakespeare's *Titus Andronicus*.

Other nobles mounted their own amateur household productions. Sir Edward Dering of Surrenden Hall, Kent appears to have staged several plays at his home in 1623–4, including John Fletcher's *The Spanish Curate* and a conflated version of Shakespeare's *Henry IV, Parts I and II*.[19] On other occasions the plays or masques performed were the compositions of household members. Thus Sir John Harington's Christmas guests (1595–6) were entertained not only with *Titus Andronicus* but with a masque written by Harington's brother-in-law, Sir Edward Wingfield.

A number of noblemen and women wrote plays and masques in the Renaissance, including Sir William Percy, Lady Mary Sidney, Sir Fulke Greville, Elizabeth Carey, Viscountess Falkland and Lady Mary Wroth. Many of these appear to have been closet dramas: plays written to be read rather than performed, modelled in some cases on the plays of Seneca. Plays in the latter tradition usually observe the classical 'unities' and are divided into five acts separated by speeches spoken by a Chorus. The major characters tend to speak in long soliloquies and messengers are used to report off-stage action. Other noble works, such as Lady Mary Wroth's *Love's Victory* (written around 1621), include detailed stage directions which suggest that they were written with performance in mind and might therefore have been read aloud or performed within the households of their authors.

Most performances in elite houses appear to have been staged in the evening, in the dining hall or great chamber. Sometimes plays were performed on stages, as at court; other performances are likely to have been acted on the hall or chamber floor. The professional performances staged at private houses are likely to have been costumed and accompanied by props and stage furniture, as it was usual for companies to take a stock of playing gear on tour. Evidence about the staging of private amateur theatricals is scarcer. Some may have been 'readings' rather than full performances, but other entertainments appear to have been staged with costumes and props. In 1623 Sir Edward Dering paid seventeen shillings and six-pence 'ffor heades of haire and beardes', apparently for use in performances at Surrenden.[20]

The audiences for private household drama varied. Sometimes plays and masques were staged for the exclusive amusement of household members, but they were also a form of entertainment that might be shared with guests. The play performed at Lathom House (home of the Earl of Derby) during the New Year period in 1588–9 was given before Sir John Savage and the Earl's household council which included 'many of the leading gentry of Lancashire'.[21]

The private nature of household theatre allowed women to participate as actors as well as dancers, and provided more scope for politically and socially risqué drama. It is no coincidence that a number of the plays and masques written for private reading and performance incorporate potentially contentious topical allusions. Some offer extended commentary on current events, including *The Emperor's Favourite*, an early seventeenth-century manuscript play owned by the Newdigate family of Arbury Hall, Nuneaton. In this instance, it is clear that the play's unflattering story about Crispinus, favourite of Roman Emperor Nero, is a veiled representation of the career of Stuart court favourite, George Villiers, Duke of Buckingham.[22]

ATTITUDES TO DRAMA

Renaissance attitudes to drama were complex. The large audiences drawn to players' performances, and the thriving of the metropolitan playhouses, are testimony to a widespread taste for drama, but the theatre faced criticism from a number of quarters. The first wave of anti-theatrical feeling followed the opening of the first permanent playhouses. Many of the early critics, such as John Northbrooke, condemned contemporary plays as morally corrupting, arguing that they taught people to be wicked by presenting them with images of vice, subversion and profanity.[23] Some even equated plays with the Devil and described the playhouses as Satan's synagogues, places intended to entice spectators to their damnation.[24] Such complaints were fuelled by the anxiety that playing was drawing people away from church services. The cross-dressing used in the theatre was interpreted by some commentators as another proof of its wickedness. Opponents of the practice argued that it transgressed the biblical injunction against cross-dressing (Deuteronomy 22:5) and encouraged homosexual desire.[25]

Other contemporaries directed their complaints at the acting profession, arguing that it was not a proper trade, as actors did not 'make' anything. William Prynne is typical in this respect arguing that plays 'in their best acceptation are but vanities or idle creations, which have no price, no worth or value in them: they cannot therefore be vendible because they are not valuable'.[26] Other critics such as Stephen Gosson attacked players as deceivers, equating their dramatic illusions with lies.[27] There were concerns about the social effects of theatre, too. Opponents complained that plays distracted people from their trades and encouraged the poorest to spend money on recreation that they could ill afford. There was also anxiety about the large crowds drawn to the playhouses. In the eyes of the City Council the latter made the playhouses magnets for crime, disorder and the spread of disease.

Contemporary playwrights generally caricature opponents of the theatre as puritan killjoys, and, in some cases, it is clear that critics' opposition to theatre was informed by a puritan-inspired distrust of its illusions. However, not all puritans were opponents of theatre, nor were critics of the theatre always motivated by moral or religious concerns. The social and economic explanations given by the City Council for their opposition to public theatre have often been seen as 'mere excuses', but recent research suggests that their motives for curbing play performances were 'as much practical as doctrinal'.[28]

The opponents of the theatre were a small, if vocal, minority. This probably explains why there were comparatively few published 'defences' of the theatre. Two of the stage's most eloquent champions were Thomas Nashe and Thomas Heywood. In *Pierce Penniless his Supplication to the Devil* (1592) Nashe rejects the idea that contemporary plays teach people to be immoral, arguing that playwrights discourage vice by showing that it is always punished. In similar fashion, he argues for the positive didactic function of contemporary plays, describing them as 'a rare exercise of vertue', not least because many were based on 'English Chronicles' and celebrated 'our fore-fathers valiant actes'.[29]

In his *Apology for Actors* (1612) Thomas Heywood offers a fuller defence of the stage. This includes emphasising the antiquity of drama, its accepted place in academic culture, and asking that critics not censure all players simply because some are 'degenerate'.[30] At the same time, he addresses some of the common complaints about the public theatre, including its use of cross-dressing. In this case he argues for a distinction between theatre and life: 'But to see our youths attired in the habit of women, who knows not what their intents be? Who cannot distinguish them by their names, assuredly knowing, they are but to represent such a Lady, at such a time appointed?'[31] Heywood argues for the positive value of theatre, too, arguing that it is 'an ornament to the Citty', that playwrights have helped to refine the English language, and, finally (like Nashe) that plays have 'taught the vnlearned the knowledge of many famous histories'.[32]

COMEDY

The 1590s saw English drama diverge into three broad types: comedies, histories and tragedies. The first important developments were in comedy. John Lyly produced a series of pioneering comedies for the new boy companies, including *Campaspe* (1584) and *Endymion: The Man in the Moon* (1591). Whereas comedies had traditionally been written in verse, Lyly experimented with an ornate prose style akin to that he employed in his well-known prose works *Euphues. The Anatomy of Wit* (1578) and *Euphues and His*

England (1580). His plots are similarly intricate, with several of his plays incorporating multiple, thematically and structurally related stories. In *Endymion*, for example, the story of the moon goddess, Cynthia's initially unrequited love for the shepherd Endymion is mirrored by several other examples of frustrated passion, and is, itself, thought to have been an allegory for the relationship between Elizabeth and her one-time favourite, Robert Dudley, Earl of Leicester.

Lyly's elaborately rhetorical writing was later parodied, but his witty, courtly comedies proved influential, placing verbal play and 'love between the sexes' at the heart of English comic writing, as is reflected in the romantic comedies which flourished in the 1590s with Shakespeare as their leading author.[33] Typically, these comedies 'involve some frustration of true love, a journey by a lover, improbable or even magical events, and a resolution in marriage or the promise of marriage arising from some discovery about identity'.[34] Like classical comedies, Shakespeare's are defined as comic by their conventionally 'happy' endings, rather than their use of humour, although humour is a common aspect of the genre.

Shakespeare's romantic comedies were not as conspicuously political as Lyly's, but their concern with issues such as gender and marriage was topical in an era which saw extended debates on these subjects. The turn of the century saw the emergence of two new strands of comic writing which focused on contemporary life more directly: 'humours' comedy and 'city' comedy. Humours comedies are defined by their realistic modern settings, their focus on tales of sexual intrigue, and their characterisation of individuals in terms of a particular humour or eccentricity.[35] The pioneer of this comic sub-genre was George Chapman with *A Humorous Day's Mirth* (performed 1597). Ben Jonson followed soon after with his now better known humours comedies: *Every Man in His Humour* (performed 1598) and *Every Man out of His Humour* (performed 1599). Collectively, they opened up English comedy to new types of character and a wider range of social situations.

City comedies focus on contemporary urban life and real-life settings (usually in London). Many of the plays are concerned with the thriving commercial culture associated with the city, but love, sex and marriage are also important themes. The earliest surviving city comedy is William Haughton's *A Woman Will Have Her Will* (or *An Englishman for my Money*) (performed 1598), but the playwright who popularised the genre was Thomas Dekker with *The Shoemaker's Holiday* (performed 1599). The latter tells the story of London shoe-maker Simon Eyre and his rise to become Mayor of London. Like most of the early city comedies, its mood is festive and its perspective on the city is patriotic and romantic, celebrating London as a place ready to reward the efforts of hard-working Englishmen.

Jacobean city comedies are more cynical and ambivalent in their representation of city life. Arguably, this reflects the fact that there was growing concern that the emergent market economy was breeding selfishness and avarice. In the comedies of Ben Jonson and Thomas Middleton these fears appear to be realised for they are full of characters whose only concern is money. The biting satirical treatment such characters generally receive has led critics such as Brian Gibbons to argue that Jacobean city comedies offer a 'radical critique of their age' and mercantile culture.[36]

Although playwrights such as Shakespeare continued to write superficially romantic comedies in the early seventeenth century, more realistic settings became common and satire became the dom-inant comic mode (a development many scholars have linked to contemporary pessimism about the new reign of King James). In some cases the use of more scathing humour was matched by the incorporation of conventionally tragic themes or events. Shakespeare's *Measure for Measure* (performed 1604), for example, is overshadowed by a preoccupation with justice and death. Other playwrights were to take such experimentation further, writing tragicomedies (see below).

Twelfth Night, or What You Will (performed c. 1601)

Twelfth Night is thought to have been written by Shakespeare (1564–1616) around 1601. Its title alludes to the last of the twelve days of Christmas (January 6). In the Renaissance this night was traditionally celebrated with music, dancing and games, many of which involved festive disorder, disguise and the temporary sub-version of normal rules. A similar festive 'disorder' turns the world upside-down in Shakespeare's *Twelfth Night*.

The play's main plot centres on the love triangle between Duke Orsino, Countess Olivia, and Viola, the young woman who is shipwrecked and separated from her twin (Sebastian) off the coast of Illyria. Comic discord ensues when Viola disguises herself as a boy and joins the household of Orsino as a page (Cesario). Orsino sends the disguised Viola to woo Olivia on his behalf, but rather than being moved to care for Orsino, Olivia becomes infatuated with Cesario (Viola), and Viola admits to being in love with the Duke. Shakespeare reinforces the audience's awareness of the complex interconnection between the three characters by giving them names that look and sound similar, something not found in his source (Barnaby Rich's *Apollonius and Silla*).

Like most of Shakespeare's romantic comedies, the play ends with the pairing off of the main characters in marriage (Orsino with Viola, Olivia with Sebastian), and the apparent restoration of order as the misunderstandings generated by Viola's disguise are resolved by the revelation of her real identity; but other aspects of the play look forward to Shakespeare's darker Jacobean comedies. Feste's mournful songs about the transience of love and life tinge the play with melancholy, and death and sorrow haunt the play from its opening in a way unusual for romantic comedy. Some critics have argued that there are discordant elements in the play's ending, too. Perhaps most conspicuously, Malvolio leaves the stage swearing revenge on them all (V, i, 365), and Antonio's fate is left uncertain.

Much of the recent criticism of *Twelfth Night* has concerned its handling of gender and sexuality. This has included a growing interest in Viola's cross-dressing. On the Renaissance stage it was usual for female roles to be played by boys, but it was a controversial custom. In *Twelfth Night* the homoerotic possibilities (and dangers) of disguising one's gender are realised when Olivia becomes infatuated with Cesario/Viola. Olivia may not know it but she loves a woman. The play solves this problem by substituting a male version of Viola (Sebastian) at the crucial moment of marriage but this does not change the fact that Olivia's desires were homosexual. The homoerotic dimension of Olivia's attraction to Viola is reinforced by the attention the play draws to Viola's feminine appearance, even when in male attire. As Orsino notes, 'all is semblative a woman's part' (I, iv, 33).

Several critics have detected a similar homoerotic undercurrent in the relationships between Antonio and Sebastian, and Viola and Orsino. Antonio's passionate devotion to Sebastian is framed in terms of a 'love' that could be perceived as homoerotic, and the Duke's jealous attachment to his young servant and his acceptance of the play's heroine in her 'masculine usurped attire' (V, i, 243) suggest an attraction to Viola as Cesario.

Feminists have been similarly interested by the play's topical concern with gender roles. Contemporary orthodoxy taught that virtuous daughters and wives should be chaste, silent and obedient but the heroines of Shakespearean comedy rarely conform straight-forwardly to this 'ideal', as is demonstrated in *Twelfth Night*. Even before she appears in the play, Olivia's story and social position identify her as unconventional. As the head of her household she enjoys a power and independence unusual for Renaissance women, but akin to that enjoyed by Elizabeth I, to whom Olivia has been compared. Like Elizabeth, Olivia initially resists the prospect of marriage. For some critics Olivia's distaste for marriage suggests that she is reluctant to give up her independence. Olivia is similarly unconventional in her later courtship of Cesario and 'his' double, Sebastian. Rather than waiting to be wooed she takes the initiative as men were expected to do. Sebastian's fortuitous meeting with Olivia ensures that her desire has a socially conventional outcome. Not only is she married to a man rather than a woman, but he is revealed to be of good birth. In this way the potentially socially and sexually transgressive aspects of her desire for Cesario are neu-tralised. More than this, by marrying and taking a new 'master' Olivia assumes a more conventional female role. For some critics this, along with the embarrassing revelation that she, like Malvolio, has been tricked and foolish, is a form of comic punishment for Olivia's previously unconventional behaviour.[37] Others question the idea that Olivia's marriage sees her 'mastered', arguing that she chooses the biddable Sebastian because he is willing to let her command him.[38]

Whereas Olivia's social position renders her an unusual woman, Viola's circumstances force her into unconventional behaviour. Alone in a new land, she assumes a male disguise as a form of pro-tection. Once assumed, this disguise invites her to behave in ways conventionally deemed masculine. Perhaps most significantly, her disguise makes it acceptable for her to talk. She proves a talented, eloquent orator, capable of bantering wittily with Feste and of speaking movingly about love with Orsino and Olivia. It is her talent for the latter that first attracts the Countess and which fosters the intimate friendship which develops between herself and Orsino. Contemporaries such as Montaigne thought women were incapable of such friendship, and the intimacy which makes it possible would not usually have been possible for an unmarried woman. Viola's loyal and capable service challenges negative expectations about women in similar fashion.

Various clues are given to Viola's true gender but none of the characters suspects that she is a woman. This is dramatically necessary but also suggests that her performance of maleness is meant to be convincing, as were contemporary boys' performances of female roles such as Viola's. In both cases, the ability to impersonate the opposite gender successfully was potentially radical, drawing attention to the possibility that gender roles were not natural but 'a matter of performance'.[39]

For some critics Viola's planned change of clothes at the end of the play and her betrothal to Orsino signal her acceptance of a more conventional gender role and an end to the play's challenging of gender stereotypes. Others find the ending less conservative. For R. W. Maslen the fact that Viola remains in male dress seems 'to promise that their marriage will be an egalitarian one, based not on mastery and control . . . but on mutual confidence and respect like the Elizabethan ideal of same-sex friendship'.[40]

The Alchemist (performed 1610)

Ben Jonson's *The Alchemist* was probably first performed by the King's Men at their Blackfriars theatre in 1610. Like most Jacobean city comedies, the play is set in contemporary London and offers a satirical perspective on a cross-section of its people. Less common of the genre is Jonson's decision to observe the classical 'unities'. In keeping with the recommendations of Aristotle, the play's dramatic action all takes place in one day and one location (a house in the Blackfriars). At the heart of the play's tightly woven plot are

Jonson's three con-artists: Subtle (a quack doctor-cum-alchemist), Face (previously, Jeremy the butler), and Doll Common. In a parody of contemporary mercantile ventures, the trio style their scheme to con Londoners with false promises of alchemical gold as a business or 'venture tripartite'.[41]

Based in the Blackfriars home of Jeremy's gentleman master (Lovewit), the trio's alchemical scam proves lucrative, with the threesome using it to extort a large quantity of gold and money from the avaricious and foolish Londoners lured to the house by their desire for riches or the doctor's magical help. The greedy and the foolish are punished alike with the disappointment of their desires, and the unexpected return of Lovewit obliges the conspirators to abandon their scheme. Subtle and Doll are forced to flee empty-handed, while Face/Jeremy secures his Master's pardon by confessing all and helping him to marry the young and wealthy, Dame Pliant.

Like many Jacobean city comedies the play satirises the avarice increasingly associated with metropolitan culture, but Jonson's moralising is qualified by an implicit admiration for the wit of his villains and his generous treatment of them. Subtle and Doll are forced to leave the Blackfriars with nothing, but there is no formal punishment of the tricksters, and Face ends up pardoned and able to keep some of his 'pelf'. If the play has a moral to teach, therefore, it is an unconventional one about the value of wit as well as the evils of greed.

Alchemy, or the art of distilling precious metals from base ones, was officially illegal in Renaissance England, but this did not stop some contemporaries from engaging in alchemical projects. The dream of being able to create gold was a seductive one, especially in an emergent market economy in which power was increasingly based on wealth rather than social standing. At the same time, the association of alchemy with transformation and the pursuit of gold made it a potentially powerful metaphor for social and personal change and greed, as Jonson (1572–1637) demonstrates in *The Alchemist*.

Jonson invited original audiences to see *The Alchemist* as an extension of their own world and its vices by locating its action specifically in 1610 and a house 'in the Friars' (I, i, 17) (the year and location of its first performance). Most of the action in *The Alchemist* takes place in one room of Lovewit's Blackfriars house. By narrowing his setting in this way Jonson was also able to take advantage of the distinctive theatrical conditions at the Blackfriars. With its smaller indoor stage and covered auditorium, the second Blackfriars theatre was more confined and potentially claustrophobic than open-air theatres like the Globe. Jonson writes this claustrophobia into *The Alchemist*. The confined space in which the tricksters operate becomes a powerful way of building dramatic tension. Subtle, Face and Doll continually have to be careful that they are not overheard in their plotting, and that their various customers do not meet and, inadvertently, betray their differing scams. Managing all their 'victims' in this way calls for considerable ingenuity and an ability to think on their feet, especially in the second half of the play when their customers start arriving in quick succession, sometimes unexpectedly, as in Act Three scene Five. In this scene Subtle, Doll and Face are in the middle of tricking Dapper into thinking he is to meet the Fairy Queen when Sir Epicure Mammon arrives. As they have more to gain from Mammon they deem dealing with him more pressing and resort to hiding Dapper in the privy with a gag of gingerbread to keep him quiet; there he is temporarily forgotten.

Subtle, Face and Doll, and the Londoners drawn to their sham laboratory turn to alchemy in the hope of quick riches, self-transformation and the fulfilment of their fantasies. While their customers expect Subtle to make gold for them through his alchemical art, the con-artists use their duplicitous 'art' to extract 'gold' from their gullible visitors, and dream of transforming themselves from (social and economic) baseness to greatness. All end up disappointed and with little to show for their efforts. In similar fashion, Lovewit finds little evidence of the sophisticated alchemical laboratory Subtle claims to have presided over. The only signs of the 'scam' are a 'few cracked pots and glasses, and a furnace' (V, v, 40). Implicitly, the transformation of the house into an alchemical centre was as illusory as the promises the tricksters made their victims. As a temporary house of illusions, Lovewit's home invites comparison with the Blackfriars theatre, where the play was performed. Indeed, Ian Donaldson argues that the 'two houses of illusion are in fact *the same house*, and the charlatans who arouse and exploit the fantasies of their victims are (when all is said and done) members of the company of the King's Men, who use similar arts to somewhat similar ends'.[42] Jonson's consciousness of the analogies between alchemy, con-artistry and theatre might help to explain his ambivalent treatment of his villains. As potential figures for the dramatist and the actor, it would be difficult for a playwright to condemn them and their 'illusions' outright.

TRAGEDY

Tragedy is a genre that finds it roots in the drama of ancient Greece and Rome, but the first tragedies in English were not written until the Renaissance. Shakespeare and his contemporaries were not generally familiar with Greek tragedy but knew about Aristotle's poetic theory, according to which tragedy traces the fall from fortune of a great man as a consequence of pride or a fatal flaw or mistake in judgement (*hamartia*, in Greek). This reversal in fortune (*peripeteia*) is followed by a moment of recognition (*anagnorisis*). The play generally ends with the death of the protagonist, an event which is expected to have a cathartic affect, provoking fear and pity in audiences. Later theorists claimed that Aristotle argued for the observation of the 'unities' of time, place and action, too (see Glossary). Few English tragedies share this concern with the 'unities', but the reversals of fortune, fatal flaws and tragic recognitions associated with Aristotelian tragedy find parallels in many Elizabethan and Stuart plays. There are even closer parallels between the period's tragedies and those written by Roman poet, Seneca (c. 4 BC–AD 65). Seneca's dramas, which are typically concerned with revenge and feature supernatural phenomena, prophecies and bloody violence, provided the inspiration for the popular sub-genre of revenge tragedy (see below). English playwrights were also influenced by native stories about the rise and fall of great men (or *de casibus* literature). Such tales were popular in the Medieval era and continued to be well-read in the Renaissance: the fall of the protagonists warned readers about the uncertainty of human life, and the folly of worldly ambition.

Two of the earliest and most influential tragic playwrights were Christopher Marlowe and Thomas Kyd. Marlowe's first hit for the public stage, *Tamburlaine the Great, Part I* (performed 1587) invites audiences to view its protagonist in its 'tragic glass' (line 7) but rather than tracing the rise and fall of a great man it tells the story of the undefeated rise to power of a lowly-born shepherd. Marlowe's *Doctor Faustus* (performed 1588–9?) is similarly atypical of classical tragedy, telling the story of the rise and fall of a learned, but humbly-born, scholar. In other tragedies Marlowe did focus on 'great' individuals (such as Edward II) but plays such as *Faustus* and *Tamburlaine* suggested that people of modest rank could be the subjects of tragedy.

Thomas Kyd was to have a similarly profound influence, pioneering the sub-genre of revenge tragedy on the English stage with his neo-Senecan drama, *The Spanish Tragedy* (written c.1582–92). In this play the ghost of Don Andrea, a Spanish nobleman killed in battle with the Portuguese, returns from the underworld to watch the avenging of his death on its perpetrator, Balthazar, Prince of Portugal, but only after Balthazar and Lorenzo (nephew of the Spanish king) have killed Don Andrea's good friend Horatio in order that Balthazar might court Don Andrea's lover, Bel-Imperia. The revenge is finally enacted by Bel-Imperia and Hieronimo (the grief-crazed father of Horatio) during their performance of a court play. The tragedy was a huge success, and prompted many writers to produce revenge plays in the same mould.

In the 1580s and 1590s playwrights experimented with another new type of tragedy: 'domestic' tragedy. Whereas classical tragedy focused on the politically and socially elite, these plays concentrated on the private lives of men and women of less than noble status. One of the best known domestic tragedies is *Arden of Faversham* (1592) which tells the story of the real-life murder of Thomas Arden by his wife and her lover at his home in Faversham, Kent. Like *Arden*, the other plays today described as domestic tragedies are not only domestic in focus but contemporary and English in setting. At the heart of the tragedy there is usually a violation of household order and harmony. Often this is figured in terms of a literal violation of the domestic space, as in *Arden* when the protagonist is killed by his wife and her lover at his own table.

Tragedy did not become dominant on the English stage until the early seventeenth century. At the forefront of the Jacobean fashion for tragedy was Shakespeare who wrote a series of tragedies including *Hamlet* (in 1600–1), *Othello* (in 1603–4), *King Lear* (in 1605), *Macbeth* (in 1606), and *Antony and Cleopatra* (in 1606–7). While *Hamlet* was novel in its handling of the delayed revenge typical of revenge tragedies (see below), Shakespeare's other tragedies eschewed the explicit moralising of *de casibus* literature and raised questions about the inevitability of human suffering in a way atypical of classical tragedy. Cultural Materialists argue that this made tragedy a potentially 'radical' political genre. At least some Stuart writers (including Ben Jonson, George Chapman and Philip Massinger) exploited this potential, using tragedy to comment indirectly on current political concerns. It is no coincidence that Jacobean tragedies are often preoccupied with court corruption. The initial optimism which accompanied the accession of James I (1603) soon gave way to concerns about royal favouritism and courtly vice. Likewise, the recurrent concern with tyranny and the rights of subjects in Caroline tragedy is informed by contemporary anxieties about the absolute power claimed by Charles I.

As well as sharing a concern with corruption, Jacobean tragedies are distinguished by the growing importance of female characters within them. Women's assumed inferiority and their association with the domestic sphere meant that they were not usually regarded as 'heroic' subjects. John Webster's *The White Devil* (1612) and *The Duchess of Malfi* (performed 1614) challenged this assumption by focusing on female protagonists. At the same time, Webster's equation of sexual and political transgression mirrored the use of romantic and sexual intrigue as metaphors for, and symptoms of, political corruption in plays such as Francis Beaumont's and John Fletcher's *Philaster* (written 1608–10) and Philip Massinger's *The Roman Actor* (performed 1629). Other Stuart playwrights, such as Thomas Middleton, treated the disruptive effects of sexual desire as a tragic subject in its own right writing plays such as *Women Beware Women* (in 1621) and *The Changeling* (co-authored with William Rowley, 1622). John Ford added to the same tradition in the Caroline era with plays such as *'Tis Pity She's a Whore* (1633), a revenge drama about brother–sister incest.

Hamlet (performed c. 1600–1)

By the time Shakespeare came to write *Hamlet* English audiences were very familiar with the conventions of revenge tragedy. Some would have known Hamlet's story, too: it can be traced back at least as far as the twelfth-century *Danish History* of Saxo Grammaticus, and had been adapted previously in a (now lost) *Hamlet* play. Shakespeare's version of the tale differs from that found in Grammaticus. In Grammaticus's account there are no extended sub-plots, no ghost, no play performance; and Amleth (Hamlet) experiences no doubts about avenging his father. Some of these changes (like the introduction of Old Hamlet's ghost) are borrowings from the earlier *Hamlet* play; others appear to have been Shakespeare's invention and part of the way in which he sought to make his play distinctive at a time when revenge tragedies had largely fallen out of fashion.

Hamlet is similarly distinctive in its preoccupation with theatre and its treatment of Hamlet's delayed revenge. It was usual for revenge protagonists to delay their revenge but, characteristically, the delay is part of a calculated strategy or caused by practical obstacles. In Hamlet's case it is less clear why he does not act. The hero offers a number of possible explanations for his inaction, including 'thinking too precisely on th'event', and cowardice (IV, iv, 9.30); and critics have offered others, including melancholy (A. C. Bradley), immaturity (L. C. Knights), and Shakespeare's wish to make Hamlet a mystery and thus reinvigorate the revenge genre (William Empson).[43] Perhaps most controversially, Sigmund Freud suggested that Hamlet suffers from an Oedipal complex, which prevents him acting against Claudius because Claudius has done what he secretly wishes to do: that is, to take his father's place with his mother.[44] The play itself never settles the question of why Hamlet defers his revenge. Some regard this as an artistic flaw; others believe it is what makes Shakespeare's protagonist realistic and *Hamlet* fascinating.

More recent scholars have been interested in the play's relationship to its original political and cultural context. Written around the turn of the seventeenth century *Hamlet*'s concern with the accession of a new monarch and court corruption would have been topical. The troubled 1590s had seen growing disaffection with the

Elizabethan regime, and increasing political anxiety about who would succeed the ageing, childless monarch. The succession to the English crown was based on inheritance but there were debates about whether an alternative system would be preferable. In *Hamlet* Shakespeare explores an elective monarchy and shows that it might not protect states from misrule.

In his first scene, Claudius draws attention to the support he has received in his election and provides one of the first proofs of his political skill. Through his carefully crafted rhetoric Claudius attempts to smooth over the potential controversy surrounding his assumption of his brother's throne and wife by suggesting that mourning and celebration are not incompatible. This argument finds its most vivid illustration in the paradoxical images he uses when alluding to his marriage to Gertrude, describing how he has met it 'as 'twere with a defeated joy, / With one auspicious and one dropping eye' (I, ii, 9–10).

Whereas Old Hamlet's ghostly appearance in armour and his 'martial stalk' (1.1.65) are indicative of his reputation as a warrior king, Claudius is implicitly revealed to be a more modern ruler, a politician who uses Machiavellian cunning and manipulation, rather than direct force, to obtain his ends. His later actions confirm this distinction as the king consistently resorts to subterfuge as he struggles to conceal his guilt and defend himself against Hamlet. Polonius, Ophelia, Gertrude, Rosencrantz and Guildenstern, all find themselves used by Claudius as he attempts to 'pluck out the heart of' Hamlet's 'mystery' (III, ii, 336); and Claudius manipulates Laertes into attempting Hamlet's murder by underhand means during the closing duel. Implicitly, Claudius's habitual use of subterfuge corrupts the court, just as his original crime corrupts the legitimacy of his kingship. There were similar fears about the effects of dissimulation within the English court.

Hamlet is one of the few courtiers who recognises that something is 'rotten in the state of Denmark' (I, iv, 67), and that this stems from Claudius. Even before the ghost reveals the extent of Claudius's villainy Hamlet knows to distrust his uncle, instinctively recognising that he is a man that 'seems' other than he is. Hamlet rejects such dissimulation claiming that he knows 'not "seems"' (I, ii, 76), but his later actions show that he, too, is capable of

Machiavellian cunning. Not only does he assume an 'antic disposi-tion' (I, v, 174) in order to deceive Claudius about his intentions, but he uses the play-within-the-play as a trap for the king. In these actions Hamlet arguably has more in common with his politic uncle than the play's more conspicuously Medieval warrior princes, Old Hamlet and Fortinbras. It is perhaps significant that neither char-acter's cunning strategies are wholly successful: Claudius does not succeed in concealing his crime and retaining power, and Hamlet's revenge is eventually opportunistic, rather than facilitated by his subterfuges. In this respect the play may be suggesting that dissim-ulation has its limits when it comes to achieving one's political or personal goals, a potentially pointed 'lesson' at a time when courtiers were increasingly accused of Machiavellianism.

Hamlet's representation of women has been interpreted in simi-larly topical terms. Growing discontent with Elizabeth I's rule in the 1590s was matched by a resurgence of the political misogyny which characterised the early years of her reign. Some critics detect a similar misogyny in *Hamlet* and the views of its protagonist.[45] In the second scene of the play Gertrude's hasty marriage to Claudius prompts Hamlet to complain that 'frailty, thy name is woman' (I, ii, 146), thus interpreting Gertrude's fickleness as characteristic of her gender. In similar fashion, he accuses Ophelia, and women more generally, of being deceivers, citing their use of make-up as an example of their inherent falsehood (III, i, 142–3).

Whether the play endorses such gender stereotypes is more con-tentious. Some critics have argued that the play does support such thinking by stereotyping Gertrude and Ophelia. Gertrude's char-acter appears to be a variation on the Renaissance stereotype of the 'lusty widow', and Ophelia's descent into madness is in keeping with Renaissance assumptions about women's mental weakness. Other scholars have suggested that the play's handling of gender is more complex. Implicitly, Hamlet's misogyny stems from Gertrude's sudden marriage to Claudius and the questions it raises about her love for his father: blaming her gender is a way of explain-ing her behaviour. The discovery of Claudius's villainy appears to warp his view of men in similar fashion, prompting him to warn Ophelia that 'we / are arrant knaves all. Believe none of us' (III, i, 128–9). Audiences are not necessarily expected to share either perspective, especially as Hamlet does not consistently share them himself. His invectives against Gertrude and Ophelia are countered, for example, by his evident concern to redeem his mother and his grief for the dead Ophelia.

Hamlet's fears about his own masculinity provide another context for understanding his attacks on women. In a culture in which masculinity was equated with action, Hamlet's prolonged inaction leaves him in a potentially 'feminine' position, as he acknowledges when he berates himself for cursing like a 'whore' (II, ii, 564). Hamlet's castigation of women could be seen, partly, as a rejection of that which he sees as 'feminine' in himself, and therefore as one of the ways in which he seeks to stir himself to the 'masculine' action his father has commanded.[46] Anxieties about masculinity in Renaissance England appear to have fuelled contemporary misogyny in similar fashion (see Introduction).

The Duchess of Malfi (performed 1614)

Webster's *The Duchess of Malfi* was a pioneering play, eschewing tragedy's conventional focus on a male protagonist to dramatise the fall of a great woman. The Duchess is a young Italian widow and the ruler of her dead husband's state (Malfi). Her two brothers (The Cardinal and Ferdinand) do not wish her to remarry. Tragedy ensues when the Duchess ignores their warnings and secretly marries her household steward, Antonio. When the brothers learn of her illicit marriage to a social inferior they vow revenge, and contrive to have the Duchess and most of her children killed. They themselves are later killed by the assassin they used (Bosola) and the play ends with the Duchess's and Antonio's eldest son being declared the next Duke of Malfi. The play was based on the real story of Giovanna d'Aragona (born around 1478), as told in William Painter's *The Palace of Pleasure* (1566), although Webster (1580?–1625?) added and adapted his source and changed the ending (in reality, the Duchess's brothers survived). In a culture in which there was anxiety about female power and social mobility, and widows were discouraged from remarrying, Webster's focus on a female ruler and widow who remarries below herself socially was potentially controversial, as was the play's topical preoccupation with court corruption and its tragic social as well as personal consequences.

Most modern critical attention has focused on the Duchess and the way that audiences are invited to respond to her tragedy. In Webster's source the Duchess and her marriage are condemned as 'lusty' and degrading. Some critics, such as Lisa Jardine, argue that they are condemned in similar fashion in Webster's play. In her view the Duchess's marriage is based on sexual desire and is the 'initial base action' which precipitates her tragic fall.[47] In similar fashion, Joyce E. Peterson argues that the Duchess wrongly privileges her private desires before her public responsibilities and that the play insists 'inexorably on her culpability as a ruler, on her responsibility for her own fate, and, worse, for the disruption of her duchy'.[48]

Other scholars have challenged the idea that the Duchess is 'lusty' and culpable for her tragedy. Frank Whigham argues that the character of Julia (the Cardinal's mistress) 'deflects the judgmental charge of lasciviousness away from the Duchess', while Dympna Callaghan describes the Duchess as 'a completely innocent victim'.[49] William Empson went further, famously arguing that 'the moral of this play . . . is not that the Duchess was wanton but that her brothers were sinfully proud'.[50] In similar fashion critics such as Mary Beth Rose have argued that the marriage of the Duchess and Antonio is celebrated (rather than demonised) as a pioneering 'companionate' marriage (see Introduction).[51]

Part of the explanation for the divided nature of critics' responses is to be found in the contrasting perspectives the play offers on the Duchess and her marriage. The first act is indicative in this respect, incorporating two antithetical characterisations of the Duchess, one offered by Antonio and the other by her brothers. Antonio's description of the 'right noble Duchess' constructs her as an ideal chaste, virtuous woman.[52] By contrast, her brothers treat her as the archetypal 'lusty widow' (I, iii, 47).

Webster's portrayal of the Duchess does not appear to conform straightforwardly to either stereotype. The woman we finally meet in the play is witty, self-assured, and sexually knowing, as is demonstrated when she interrupts her brothers' lecture about not remarrying to observe that 'Diamonds are of most value, / They say, that have passed through most jewellers' hands' (I, iii, 8–9); but her desire to marry Antonio seems to be based on her admiration for his merits as well as sexual attraction. The unconventionality of the Duchess is illustrated more fully by her readiness to marry a social inferior, and the active part she plays in their courtship. Unequal marriages were not unknown in Renaissance England but were generally discouraged and tended to take contemporaries by surprise, as is the case in *The Duchess of Malfi*, where even the wily Bosola does not imagine that the Duchess's lover could be her steward.

Despite its unconventional nature, the marital relationship itself is portrayed in largely positive fashion. In keeping with the new Protestant emphasis on companionship in marriage, the Duchess and Antonio are presented as enjoying a loving, comparatively equal relationship. The play's handling of their sexual love is similarly positive. In the intimate scene in the Duchess's bedroom (III, ii) the Duchess is shown to be playful and assertive in her sexuality, as is Antonio, suggesting that his taste is not for the passive 'ideal' wife of traditional Renaissance wisdom, while the warm, mutually loving nature of their exchanges challenges the idea that their relationship is simply lustful.

The demonisation of the Duchess's brothers (the two main opponents of her marriage) also encourages sympathy for the Duchess, and qualifies the force of their attacks upon the match. Unlike his source, Webster has the brothers die, and in an inglorious manner that invites interpretation as a punishment for their mistreatment of their sister: Ferdinand goes mad with guilt and he and the Cardinal end up perishing at the hand of their hired assassin (Bosola).

The Duchess's representation changes in the second half of the play. Imprisoned and separated from Antonio and her children she becomes, superficially, the archetypal passive, suffering tragic heroine. Some critics see the change as a way of eliciting sympathy for a heroine whose unorthodox behaviour might otherwise diminish pity for her plight. Others have suggested that the Duchess's characterisation is more complex, even in these scenes, noting that she takes charge of her execution, faces death boldly, and retains a sense of wit, observing to Bosola that the manner of her death is inconsequential: 'What would it pleasure me to have my throat cut / With diamonds? Or to be smothered / With cassia? Or to be shot to death with pearls?' (IV, ii, 194–6). The dignity and bravery of her death is reinforced by the desperation with which her maid Cariola resists Bosola. There is no moralising conclusion which makes clear how audiences are expected to reflect on her actions or her marriage, but the Duchess's calm embracing of her end and her philosophical reflections on her life suggest that she is to be seen as 'heroic'.

HISTORY

'History' plays dramatised the stories of (reputedly) historical characters and events. Most focused on the male-dominated worlds of politics and rule. Some playwrights wrote dramas based on Roman, Eastern, or recent Western European events; many more wrote plays about Medieval English history. When modern critics discuss Renaissance history plays they are usually alluding to the latter. In many cases playwrights based their plays on the material they found in the historical chronicles produced in increasing numbers in the sixteenth and early-seventeenth centuries. For those concentrating on English history this included works such as Edward Hall's *The union of the two noble and illustre families of Lancaster and York* (1547), and Raphael Holinshed's *Chronicles of England, Scotland, and Ireland* (1577, 1587). Shakespeare found Holinshed an especially rich source, using the *Chronicles* for 'fully thirteen of the thirty-seven plays usually accepted as' his including the plays of his two tetralogies (see below).[53]

Like their chronicle sources, such plays catered for the widespread Renaissance interest in history, and the lessons it was believed to afford the present. Accounts or dramatisations of historical events could be used to comment on sensitive contemporary issues, too, such as the royal succession and subjects' right to resist bad rulers. Renaissance history plays are varied in style but many explore similar topical themes. Thus Elizabethan histories share a 'preoccupation with internecine strife and disputed succession which mirrors the anxieties of late Elizabethan politics', while Stuart history plays are more often concerned with absolute rule and the rights of subjects.[54]

History plays can be traced back to the early sixteenth century but enjoyed their greatest vogue at the end of the century. Christopher Marlowe played an important part in popularising the genre on the professional stage, but the playwright who contributed most to the 1590s vogue for histories was Shakespeare. Between 1591 and 1600 he wrote nine English history plays: *Henry VI, Part II* and *Henry VI, Part III* (in 1591); *Henry VI, Part I* (in 1592); *Richard III* (in 1592–3); *Richard II* (in 1595); *King John* (in 1596); *Henry IV, Part I* (in 1596–7); *Henry IV, Part 2* (in 1597–8); and *Henry V* (in 1599). Eight of the plays are commonly grouped into two cycles because of their historically chronological sequence: the three *Henry VI* plays and *Richard III* are usually described as the 'first tetralogy', and *Richard II*, the *Henry IV* plays, and *Henry V* are described as the 'second tetralogy'. The relationship between the assorted plays and the extent to which Shakespeare intended them to be seen as sequences have been hotly debated. Early twentieth-century critics tended to see the tetralogies as 'a unified, cohesive, organic totality of dramatic and historical writing', whereas late twentieth-century scholars have emphasised their diversity and the discontinuities between them.[55]

Although stylistically varied, Shakespeare's histories share common themes, including a preoccupation with succession and historical causation. Like the chroniclers he used as sources, Shakespeare sometimes interprets historical events in terms of divine providence and at others as being the result of human actions. The plays are also linked by their concentration on 'the workings of power at the highest level of the monarchic state' and 'the problematics of early modern kingship', a focus shared with many humanist historians but less common amongst his fellow historical dramatists who were 'more interested in the problematics of subjecthood'.[56] For some critics Shakespeare's histories demystify monarchical rule in a potentially radical way. Others argue that they 'reveal the workings of monarchy while showing also the desirability, indeed the necessity, of the institution'.[57]

The vogue for English history plays waned in the seventeenth century, as contemporary playwrights such as Shakespeare generally turned their attention to other genres. A late exception is John Ford's *Chronicle History of Perkin Warbeck* (1634) which tells the historical story of one of the pretenders to Henry VII's crown. Some critics argue that the genre had outlived its popularity. Others note that it was increasingly difficult to find new material to dramatise about recent English history, and that the peaceful accession of James diminished anxiety about some of the issues central to Elizabethan history plays (such as succession). The growing popularity of genres such as city comedy and romance are indicative of changing theatrical tastes, too, reflecting an increased interest in drama about the present, and romantic, rather than historically grounded, representations of the past. That history proper was increasingly perceived as the province of historians may have been another factor in the waning of historical drama.

Tamburlaine the Great (performed 1587–8)

Tamburlaine the Great was the play which launched Christopher Marlowe's short but spectacularly successful playwriting career. It proved so popular that Marlowe followed it up with a sequel the following year (1588). Part of the popularity of the *Tamburlaine* plays appears to have derived from the fact that they were innovative. Whereas Tudor historians and earlier dramatists tended to present history as divinely ordered, Marlowe (1564–93) followed the example of Italian humanists and focused on man's part in shaping historical events. There are allusions to divine power, and Tamburlaine styles himself the 'scourge of God', but the *Tamburlaine* plays never confirm that the Scythian's tyranny is divinely sanctioned and there is little evidence of godly intervention within them. In Part II the defeat of the Christians by the Turks and Tamburlaine's final illness are presented as possible examples of divine retribution but in both cases Marlowe is careful to suggest that the real explanation is mundane. Orcanes assumes God has punished the Christians for forswearing their oath of peace, but Gazellus attributes the Christians' defeat simply to 'the fortune of the wars' (*Tamburlaine, Part II*, II, iii, 31). Similarly, although the occurrence of Tamburlaine's illness shortly after his burning of the Koran could suggest Mahomet is punishing him, the Physician who examines him suggests the explanation of his malady is purely physical (*Tamburlaine, Part II*, V, iii, 82–99).

Marlowe is similarly original in his engagement with tragedy. In the Prologue to Part I he invites audiences to 'view' Tamburlaine's history in a 'tragic glass' (*Tamburlaine, Part I*, Prologue, 7), but rather than charting the tragic fall of a great man the play presents the rise to greatness of a humbly-born shepherd; and in place of the 'jigging' rhyme found in early Elizabethan plays, Marlowe uses blank verse and 'high astounding' rhetoric (*Tamburlaine, Part I*, Prologue, 5). Later writers would parody Marlowe's 'mighty' lines but the style was much imitated.

Contemporary allusions suggest that audiences found the plays similarly spectacular visually. Like Medieval drama, the *Tamburlaine* plays are emblematic in style, manifesting Tamburlaine's power through a series of symbolic shows. In Part I his ability to conquer emperors is demonstrated when he literalises his claim to 'tread on emperors' (*Tamburlaine, Part I*, IV, ii, 32) by using captured Turkish leader, Bajazeth, as his footstool. In similar fashion, he advertises his victory over the kings of Trebizon, Soria, Natolia and Jerusalem by forcing them to wear bridles and pull his chariot like beasts (*Tamburlaine, Part II*, IV, iii). The theatricality of these symbolic 'shows' highlights Tamburlaine's (and Marlowe's) recognition of the political power of spectacle.

At the heart of modern critical debates about the *Tamburlaine* plays has been the question of how audiences are to respond to the protagonist. Marlowe based the plays on the supposedly historical character, Timur the Lame, a fourteenth-century Mongol conqueror (1336–1405). By the late sixteenth century there were several accounts of Timur's life (including Petrus Perondinus's *Vita Magni Tamelames*, 1551 and George Whetstone's *The English Mirror*, 1586), but they represent Timur in conflicting ways. For some historians (such as Perondinus) he is a brutal tyrant deserving of condemnation; for others, such as Whetstone, he is a mighty prince 'who liberated his homeland "from the servitude of the Sarizens and kinges of Persia" '.[58]

Marlowe's treatment of Tamburlaine draws on both historical traditions but places distinctive emphasis on the Scythian's humble origins. Like later Marlovian heroes, Tamburlaine is a self-made man, driven to conquer the world by his dreams of power. For humbler members of the audience Tamburlaine's transformation from shepherd to world-conqueror was a potentially inspiring as well as exciting 'fantasy of power'.[59] For others, Tamburlaine's social mobility, his cultural 'otherness', and his succession to power through force, rather than birth or rank, are likely to have been troubling.

Like Marlowe's sources, his *Tamburlaine* plays offer different perspectives on the Scythian. In the opening scene of Part I Meander and Mycetes demonise Tamburlaine, condemning him as a 'Scythian thief' (I, i, 36), who 'robs' (I, i, 37) merchants and dreams of conquering the East with his 'lawless train' (I, i, 39). His actions, like his birth and race, are deemed base and his pursuit of power is characterised as illegal. Others complain of Tamburlaine's cruelty and tyranny. Indeed, so ruthless is he believed to be that foes such as Meander and Cosroe fear that 'he was never sprung of human race' (II, vi, 12).

Tamburlaine and his followers characterise the shepherd and his aspirations in very different fashion. While his loyal generals (Theridamas, Usumcasane and Techelles) admire Tamburlaine's natural 'majesty' (*Tamburlaine, Part I*, I, ii, 165), Tamburlaine claims his rise to power is predestined. When he first meets Theridamas he presents himself as favourite of the Gods, claiming that Jove is ready to 'stretch his hand from heaven' to protect him (*Tamburlaine, Part I*, I, ii, 175). Later he styles himself 'the scourge and wrath of God' (*Tamburlaine, Part I*, III, iii, 44), and in Part II cites this role as justification for his career of cruel conquest: 'these terrors and these tyrannies / (If tyrannies war's justice ye repute) / I execute, enjoined me from above, / To scourge the pride of such as heaven abhors' (*Tamburlaine, Part II*, IV, ii, 145–8).

Like Marlowe's characters, modern audiences and critics have been divided in their views of Tamburlaine. Some critics, such as Roy Battenhouse, argue that we are meant to condemn him and that the two plays 'offer one of the most grandly moral spectacles in the whole realm of English drama'.[60] Others claim that audiences are invited to admire rather than to judge or condemn Tamburlaine.[61] A third school of critics suggest that the plays were 'designed . . . to leave audiences painfully suspended between admiration and disgust for Marlowe's protagonist'.[62] But, if Marlowe's aim was to invite ambivalent responses or outright condemnation, contemporary accounts suggest that he was not wholly successful: most spectators appear to have been impressed by Tamburlaine.[63]

Henry V (performed 1599)

For many critics Henry V is Shakespeare's most sophisticated historical drama, showing a sensitive awareness of the interpretive nature of history and the difficulties inherent in any attempt to recreate the past. It tells the story of Henry V (1387–1422), one of the most famous kings of England, renowned for his successful war to claim the French crown and his victory over the French at the Battle of Agincourt (1415). Most Tudor histories celebrate Henry V's reign; Shakespeare's representation of the king is more complex. In its concern with succession and its representation of a king renowned for his aggressive foreign policy Shakespeare's play was more overtly topical, too. In 1599 rebellion in Ireland led Elizabeth I to launch a campaign against the Irish, headed by the young and dashing Earl of Essex (the man some contemporaries believed should become the ageing Queen's heir). Written prior to Essex's departure (and the failure of his expedition), some critics have seen the successful war against France as 'a re-presentation of the attempt to conquer Ireland and the hoped-for unity of Britain'.[64]

Critics and audiences have been divided in their responses to Henry V. While early twentieth-century critics tended to see the play as a patriotic chronicle, celebrating Henry V as 'the mirror of all Christian kings' (II, Prologue, 6), more recent historicist and materialist scholars have argued that the play demystifies the patriotic myth-making surrounding Henry, presenting him as a charismatic but Machiavellian ruler.[65] As Phyllis Rackin notes, 'both views can be supported by evidence from the play text, for it offers not only opposed interpretations but also opposed accounts of the action'.[66] In its double perspective on Henry, Norman Rabkin likens the play to pictures that show a duck when looked at from one direction and a rabbit from another and argues that the play's 'ultimate power is precisely the fact that it points in two opposite directions'.[67]

Much of the play's ambiguity relates to Shakespeare's handling of his famous hero. The Chorus presents Henry as a model king and he is praised in similar fashion by numerous characters within the play. When the Archbishop of Canterbury and the Bishop of Ely discuss the new king they praise him as an exemplary ruler; expert in 'divinity', 'commonwealth affairs', 'war' and 'policy' (I, i, 39, 42, 44, 46). Henry is admired in similarly warm terms by fellow soldiers, such as Gower and Fluellen. For them he is a 'gallant king' (IV, viii, 8) who bears comparison with the legendary Alexander the Great. Even Henry's old Cheapside friends commend him as 'a good king' (II, i, 114), despite his rejection of them upon his assumption of the crown. In similar fashion, the Chorus celebrates Henry's ability to inspire his men and his achievements against the French, praising him for his bravery and for leading by example.

Such overt celebration of Henry is tempered by the questions the play raises about the morality of the king's actions and the French campaign. The play opens with a scene of intrigue pertinent to the soon-to-be-announced war: the audience overhears Canterbury and Ely plotting to protect the Church's possessions from a Bill in the Commons by offering to help Henry financially if he chooses to war against France. Such a promise of money smacks of a 'bribe' and raises questions about the integrity of the war enterprise. Similar tensions underpin the discussion of Henry's claim to the French throne. Superficially, Henry appears to be the exemplary ruler the clerics have described. He is sober in his discussion of the possibility of war; he judicially seeks the advice of his counsellors; and he insists that Canterbury tell him truthfully whether his claim to the French throne is just. But the scene could be read as a carefully contrived performance intended to provide the necessary justification for a war Henry has already determined to undertake. We discover, for instance, that he has already made claim to 'certain dukedoms' in France (I, ii, 247), a pre-emptive claim which elicits the Dauphin's insulting gift of tennis balls; and we know Canterbury is predisposed to support a war.

The ambiguities surrounding Henry and the war are intensified by the contrasting perspectives offered on both through the play's sub-plots. In several cases sub-plot scenes parody the main action. During the battle of Harfleur, for example, Henry's famous rallying speech which begins 'Once more unto the breach, dear friends' (III, i, 1) is echoed moments later by Bardolph: 'On, on, on, on, on!

To the breach, to the breach! (III, ii, 1). Bardolph's invocation is a comic imitation of Henry's and could be seen as undercutting its heroic rhetoric, just as Bardolph, Pistol and Nym undermine Henry's heroic characterisation of the English, by proving cowardly.

Henry's views are challenged more directly when he talks to three common soldiers on the eve of Agincourt: Williams, Bates and Court. Disguised as Harry *Le Roi*, the men do not know that they are talking to the king and therefore offer their views of the war openly. Like his companions, Williams is ready to fight for the king, but is not convinced that Henry's cause is 'just and his quarrel honour / able' (IV, i, 121–2) and debunks the heroic rhetoric with which Henry and the Chorus describe battle, focusing instead on the king's responsibility for war, and the destruction and distress that it brings (IV, i, 128–35).

The play's closing Chorus adds to the ambiguity of Shakespeare's handling of Henry V's career in a different fashion. Having celebrated Henry throughout the play, it sounds a sombre note at odds with the comic mood of the final scene, which shows Henry wooing the French Princess. Victorious in love as well as war, the closing chorus praises Henry as 'This star of England', but draws attention to the short-lived nature of his success and to the fact that his son, Henry VI's weak rule would see England descend into civil war (V, Epilogue, 9–12), an event dramatised previously in Shakespeare's *Henry VI* plays.

ROMANCE AND TRAGICOMEDY

Early Elizabethan dramas were 'neither tragic nor comic in the classical sense'.[68] Many were romances, episodic plays based on classical or continental tales of chivalry and adventure. The turn of the seventeenth century brought with it fresh interest in plays which blurred the boundary between tragedy and comedy (such as romance), and led to tragicomedy becoming 'the single most important dramatic genre of the period 1610–50'.[69]

Shakespeare's late plays (*Pericles*, *Cymbeline*, *The Winter's Tale*, *The Tempest*) played an important part in re-popularising romance on the professional stage, although the plays were not described as such by contemporaries (see Glossary). Like classical and native romances (in verse and prose), those of Shakespeare and his fellow dramatists present miraculous tales of suffering, heroism and adventure and feature a number of recurrent motifs. These include the journeying of the hero (or heroes) towards home, a series of hardships and trials (often including a shipwreck and the separation of lovers or parents and children), and the culmination of the tale with the happy reunion of the hero and his/her loved ones through a series of marvellous events or divine intervention.[70]

Other playwrights interested in tragicomedy were influenced by the work of contemporary Italian playwright, Giovanni Battista Guarini. In his *Compendio della poesia tragicomica* (1603) Guarini outlined his theory of tragicomedy, as exemplified in his pastoral play, *Il Pastor Fido* (1590). According to Guarini, tragicomedy shares tragedy's focus on 'noble characters' but presents 'a story which is credible but not historically true, heightened yet tempered effects, delight not sorrow' and 'the danger not the death' of tragedy. From comedy it borrows 'laughter . . . a feigned crisis, an unexpected happy ending and – above all – the comic plotting'.[71]

One of the first English playwrights to experiment with Italianate tragicomedy was John Marston. At the start of the seventeenth century he wrote a series of plays which combined tragic and comic elements, including *Antonio and Mellida* (1602), *Antonio's Revenge* (1602) and *The Malcontent* (1604). The influence of Guarini's model of tragicomedy is even more obvious in the work of Samuel Daniel and John Fletcher, both of whom wrote plays inspired by *Il Pastor Fido*: Daniel's *The Queen's Arcadia* (performed 1605) and Fletcher's *The Faithful Shepherdess* (performed 1608). As well as identifying his play as a tragicomedy, Fletcher prefaced the printed version of *The Faithful Shepherdess* (1610) with an explanation of the genre. In this he explains that the play is a tragicomedy not because it combines 'mirth and killing, but in respect it wants deaths, which is enough to make it no tragedie, yet brings some neere it which is inough to make it no comedie'.[72] Fletcher and his collaborator, Francis Beaumont, went on to write a series of influential courtly tragicomedies, including *Philaster* (in 1608–10) and *A King and No King* (in 1611). Like *The*

Malcontent, Fletcher's and Beaumont's tragicomedies eschew the pastoral setting and characters of *Il Pastor Fido* in favour of a focus on court life and noble characters, and their comic endings generally turn on startling but rational revelations, rather than supernatural miracles of the kind found in Shakespearean romance. Other Stuart writers, including Thomas Middleton, Philip Massinger and James Shirley, were to follow their example, favouring artfully plotted, courtly tragicomedy over Guarini's pastoral version of the genre.

Romance and tragicomedy proved popular with audiences but their mixing of genres was not welcomed by all contemporaries. In his *Defence of Poesy* (1595) Sir Philip Sidney famously complained that early Elizabethan plays were 'neither right tragedies nor right comedies', but rather 'mongrel tragic-comedy'.[73] As his phrasing suggests, Sidney regarded tragicomedy as impure and inferior to tragedy and comedy. In similar fashion Ben Jonson attacked Shakespearean-style romances as unnatural and improbable in his Induction to *Bartholomew Fair* (performed 1614).

Modern responses to Renaissance romances and tragicomedies have been similarly divided. Some critics have shared Sidney's and Jonson's distaste for their artificial plots and their mixing of the tragic and comic. Others have dismissed the plays as escapist. For much of the twentieth century it was, likewise, common to regard the plays as politically conservative. As Martin Wiggins notes, the fact that the plays' conclusions often 'encourage audiences to welcome the intervention of a benevolent figure of authority, whether it be the skilful dramatist outside the play or a manipulative disguised duke within it', has led some critics to equate the genre with a 'complacently acquiescent royalism'.[74] But fresh interest in Renaissance tragicomedy in recent years has drawn attention to the ways in which such plays use their treatment of subjects like love and rule to engage with politically topical issues such as 'the limits of absolutism and the royal prerogative'.[75] Similarly, although critics continue to disagree about the politics of Shakespeare's romances, most accept that their preoccupation with abuses of royal power renders the tragicomedies of other leading playwrights, such as Beaumont and Fletcher, 'anti-court' (rather than pro-court) dramas.[76]

The Winter's Tale (performed c. 1609–11)

Shakespeare's *The Winter's Tale* was first published (1623) as a comedy but it comes close to tragedy, especially during its first three acts which focus on the terrible consequences of King Leontes's mistaken conviction that his wife Hermione is pregnant with the child of his friend, King Polixenes of Bohemia. Enraged by their imagined infidelity, Leontes plots against Polixenes's life and puts his wife on trial. Despite being declared innocent by the oracle of Apollo, Leontes sentences Hermione to death and orders Antigonus to abandon their new-born child (Perdita). His judgement is quickly followed by the news of his son's death and Hermione's apparent expiration. At this point there seems little prospect of a comic conclusion.

The opening of Act Four transforms the play: Time announces that sixteen years have passed and that Perdita has survived, preserved by a family of humble Bohemian shepherds. As the play turns to the story of her preservation and her romance with Florizel (disguised son of Polixenes), Sicilian winter gives way to Bohemian spring, the court to the countryside, and tragedy to comedy. Shakespeare flirts with the prospect of further tragedy, when Polixenes threatens to disown his son for his union with Perdita, but the play ends happily. The revelation of Perdita's royal identity renders the couple's union acceptable and leads not only to their reconciliation with Polixenes but to Polixenes's reconciliation with Leontes and Leontes's reunion with his lost child. These happy events are crowned by the miraculous revelation of Hermione's preservation. Taken to see what they believe is a cunningly life-like statue of the dead Queen, Leontes and Perdita are amazed when the statue comes to life and Hermione reveals that she has lived concealed by Paulina.

Shakespeare's main source for the play was Robert Greene's prose romance *Pandosto* (1588), but the transformation of Leontes's tale from tragedy to comedy, and the marvellous preservation of Hermione are Shakespeare's invention. Shakespeare's tragicomic version of the tale is similarly original in its artistically pointed concern with hybridity and the relationship between art and nature. These concerns come to the fore during the sheep-shearing festival when Polixenes (in disguise) meets Perdita, and the pair discusses the relative merits of pure and mixed varieties of flower. The lost princess reveals that she keeps no cross-bred flowers, favouring nature's own varieties of plant over those created by man's art. This prompts Polixenes to defend hybrid flowers and the human skill which creates them, arguing that the art which 'adds to nature is an art / That nature makes' (IV, iv, 90–1) and which improves nature. Although superficially about horticulture, their conversation has wider implications. In arguing for the merits of cross-breeding, Polixenes is testing the superficially lowly-born Perdita: he wants to know if she hopes to mix herself with his royal stock. At the same time, by phrasing their discussion in terms of 'art' and 'nature', Shakespeare invites audiences to see their conversation as potentially pertinent to the play's 'mixed' breed. Like Perdita, the detractors of romance complained that its art was at odds with nature. Although he may not mean what he says, Polixenes's defence of cross-breeding and 'art' as 'natural' serves not only as a justification of cross-class marriage but of the romantic mixing of tragedy and comedy.

Early twentieth-century critics often interpreted *The Winter's Tale* as a Christian allegory about suffering and repentance. Heightened critical interest in romance in recent years has prompted a variety of other interpretations of the play. While psychoanalysts have been especially fascinated by its treatment of jealousy, historicist and feminist critics have focused on the play's handling of patriarchal power and gender. Like many of the flawed kings of Stuart tragicomedy, Leontes misuses his power as monarch to serve his jealous ends. In doing so he exposes himself to accusations of tyranny. Paulina warns him as much in Act Two scene Three, when she observes that his 'most cruel usage' of the queen 'not able to produce more accusation / Than your own weak-hinged fancy – something savours / Of tyranny' (II, iii, 117–20). Just as Leontes's courtiers worry about his abuse of power and the rights of subjects, so many contemporaries were concerned about the potentially tyrannical nature of absolute monarchy: the model of rule espoused by James I (see Introduction).

At the heart of Leontes's misplaced jealousy of Hermione lies an implicit fear of female sexuality and its perceived threat to his masculinity. Such fears are not confined to Leontes and are not unusual in Renaissance literature (see Introduction). The idyllic pastoral world which Polixenes invokes when recalling their youthful friendship is an ideal from which women and their sexuality are, likewise, absent. Leontes's anxiety about female sexuality is reflected in his misogynistic stereotyping of women as inherently false and sexually uncontrollable. In his view there is 'no barricade for a belly . . . / It will let in and out the enemy / With bag and baggage' (I, ii, 205–7). Hermione's heavily pregnant body with its visible proof of her sexuality appears to heighten these anxieties. Accusing Hermione of adultery becomes one way of distancing himself from her sexuality.[77]

The second half of the play witnesses the redemption of Leontes's character, and the symbolic recuperation of women. While 'Perdita serves as the focal point' for the 'recovery of a positive image of the feminine', Florizel embodies a new mode of masculinity which is at ease with femininity.[78] Unlike Leontes, Florizel actively 'embraces the female' and demonstrates 'an unwavering male faith in women'.[79] Some feminist critics see the play's second half as privileging female values but the 'order' which is restored at the play's conclusion is explicitly patriarchal.[80] The women are celebrated for embodying virtues 'congenial to patriarchal expectations', such as chastity, and the play's noblemen remain in command.[81] Leontes is rewarded with the restoration of Hermione and his heir; Florizel discovers that his 'queenly' shepherdess is in fact royal; and the previously outspoken Paulina is married off to Camillo. The roles of women may be 'central' to the play's world but, as Peter Erickson notes, they are ultimately 'circumscribed'.[82]

The Tempest (performed 1611)

The Tempest tells the story of Prospero, the deposed Duke of Milan, who is overthrown by his brother (Antonio) after allowing his sibling to rule in his stead while he devoted himself to scholarship. Antonio forces his brother to flee Milan by sea with his infant daughter (Miranda). The pair land on a remote Mediterranean island inhabited by a lone native (Caliban); there they remain until fortune brings an Italian ship, carrying Antonio and his collaborator in

Prospero's overthrow (Alonso, King of Naples) close to their shores. Aided by Ariel, an island spirit, Prospero conjures a tempest which wrecks the ship and brings all the passengers ashore, where he seeks to reform his foes, and contrives the peace-making marriage of his daughter to Ferdinand, son of Alonso.

The shipwreck with which the play opens seems to have been suggested to Shakespeare by William Strachey's account of the shipwreck of a group of English colonists in the Bermudas in 1609. The rest of the play is largely Shakespeare's invention, but it shares its narrative shift from tragic suffering and loss, to reunion and redemption with Shakespeare's previous romances. Unusually, much of Prospero's suffering precedes the action and the play observes the classical 'unities' (see Glossary), confining its action to one location (the Island) and one day.

In focusing his play on a powerful magus (or magician) Shakespeare was catering for popular interest in magic (see Introduction), but the play also draws analogies between magic and theatre as 'arts' of illusion. This has led many critics to read *The Tempest* as (in part at least) 'an allegory about artistic creation' in which magic stands in for theatre and is used to explore theatre's evocative power.[83] Throughout the play Prospero's magic is conceptualised as an 'art' and is associated with the creation of compelling illusions, such as the opening tempest. The theatricality of this 'art' becomes most evident when Prospero chooses to mark the betrothal of Ferdinand and Miranda with a magical masque and explains to Ferdinand that the performers of the entertainment are 'Spirits, which by mine art / I have from their confines called to enact / My present fancies' (IV, i, 120–2). As many critics have noted, Prospero's words could be those of a playwright describing his performed play.

Although modern critics continue to be interested in the play's concern with theatre and artistic creation, the rise of postcolonial criticism has encouraged scholars to reconsider the play in terms of European colonialism. Knowing that the play was partly inspired by the shipwreck of the *Sea Adventure* off the Bermudas, some critics have interpreted the play as a commentary on the European colonisation of America. Allusion is made to 'the still-vexed Bermudas' (I, ii, 230), but other references make it clear that the isle is located in the Mediterranean rather than the New World. This does not mean that original audiences could not have appreciated the play's relevance to the colonisation of America, but, as Meredith Skura points out, there is 'no *external* evidence that seventeenth-century audiences thought the play referred to the New World' and Shakespeare's depiction of Caliban is not wholly in keeping with contemporary travellers' descriptions of American Indians.[84] It is not even clear that he is dark-skinned. Prospero's initial description of him as a 'freckled whelp' could indicate that Shakespeare imagined him as pale-skinned (I, ii, 285–6). If Prospero's description of Sycorax as a 'blue-eyed hag' (I, ii, 270) alludes to her eye-colour, rather than the blue eye-lids associated with pregnant women, it could mean that Shakespeare imagined Caliban sharing the blue or grey eyes associated with northern European races, too. That Caliban may be white has encouraged some critics to read the play in terms of England's troubled colonisation of Ireland. There is internal evidence to link Caliban with the Irish, including his wearing of a 'gaberdine' cloak (II, ii, 36). As Barbara Fuchs notes, this garment, and Caliban's use of it for shelter as well as clothing, is suggestive of the mantle which native Irishmen were famous for wearing, that served as 'house, bed, and garment'.[85]

Like contemporary European colonisers, Prospero leaves his native state to journey to a 'new' country where he and Miranda initially befriend (and are befriended by) its native inhabitant, but peaceful co-existence gives way to discord and Prospero ends up enslaving Caliban and seizing control of the island. Prospero's initial justification for enslaving Caliban is his alleged attempt to rape Miranda, but he and Miranda continue to justify Caliban's subjection by demonising him as rebellious, savage and inherently wicked. Miranda even claims that he is incapable of learning virtue (I, ii, 354–5). In a similar manner, European colonisers often claimed retrospective justification for their actions in the alleged savagery of the native inhabitants of the lands they colonised.[86]

Whether the play endorses Prospero's actions and his perspective on events is more contentious. Some critics argue that it does. The demeaning of Caliban as less than human is not confined to Prospero and his daughter, and his plot against Prospero is treated in 'fully comic mode': this implicitly renders Caliban ridiculous and, at the same time, appears to confirm his 'natural' treachery as a savage.[87] On the other hand, Prospero's account of events on the island does not go uncontested. Caliban characterises Prospero as a 'tyrant' who has 'cheated' him 'of the island' (III, ii, 40–1) which he claims by inheritance from his mother (I, ii, 334–5). As Stephen Orgel notes, such a system of inheritance was commonplace in Europe so that, 'historically speaking', his 'claim to the island is a good one'.[88] Caliban insists in similar fashion on the unfairness of the cruelty and privation Prospero subjects him to, and likens himself to an overthrown king. In doing so he implies that the usurped Duke has turned usurper and recasts Prospero's subjection of him as politically (rather than morally) motivated.

Further questions are raised about Prospero's perspective as coloniser by the fact that Shakespeare does not present Caliban as stereotypically 'savage'. Although he does not deny Miranda's attempted rape and openly curses and plots against Prospero's life he is not presented as an unfeeling brute. He revels in the 'sounds and sweet airs' of the isle, showing that he apprehends the natural magic of the island as sensitively as the play's protagonist commands it. Sympathy for Caliban and his plight has led some critics and performers to reinterpret him as the play's hero and Prospero as its tyrannical villain.

COURT MASQUES

Masques were an elite, multimedia form of entertainment, combining music, dance, spectacle, and, occasionally, speech. They were sometimes performed at noble houses and the Inns of Court, but the Royal Court was the main venue for these private, visually spectacular entertainments. There, they were performed to mark special occasions. Sponsoring such lavish entertainments allowed English monarchs to display their power and wealth.

Like court 'pageants', these specially commissioned shows were typically allegorical or mythical in subject and complimentary in mode, offering idealised representations of the court for which they were written. Many trace a transformation of discord into concord made possible by the presence of the monarch who 'consistently appears as a source of order and harmony in both the physical and political domains'.[89] The idealisation of royal power in court masques is unsurprising. Overt critiques of the monarchy would not have been tolerated or wise; but masques were not always, or simply, vehicles for flattery or royal ideology. As recent research has shown, contemporary masque writers were sensitive to the political and didactic potential of the genre and sometimes used masques to offer coded advice as well as praise.

Professionals like Ben Jonson were generally hired to write and perform the speaking parts in masques, but other masque performers were members of the court and could include women and royalty. The performance typically concluded with the masquers inviting their fellow courtiers to join them in dancing. This made for a form of entertainment which blurred the boundary between performers and spectators. At the same time, the presence of the monarch, often on a raised stage opposite the performance area, highlighted the fact that masques, like all court entertainments, were part of a larger royal 'show' in which the monarch was the chief spectacle as well as the main spectator.

The earliest masques in England were staged by Henry VIII, but the genre became increasingly popular under James I and Charles I, in keeping with the 'new estimate of the usefulness of ceremonial in projecting the wealth and power of the court' in early seventeenth-century Europe.[90] In the early sixteenth century, masques were not dramas in a conventional sense. As Martin Butler notes, 'the typical Henrician revel was a neo-medieval tilt or an entry into the court by disguised dancers on a spectacular pageant wagon such as a castle or a rock'.[91] Although some of these disguisings included speeches, others did not. Under Elizabeth I the genre developed in two distinct directions, with masques tending 'to be either wholly literary and dramatic' or 'wholly choreographic and theatrical'. During James I's reign the two types of masque re-converged but the style and performance of masques was developed in a variety of new ways.[92] At the heart of many of these developments was the collaboration of Ben Jonson and designer Inigo Jones. Under Jonson the spoken part of the masque assumed a new primacy. He insisted that the text of the masque was vital to its meaning, describing it as the 'soul' and the design as 'the bodily part' of the show.[93] He made increasing use of dramatic scenarios and dialogue, and called for the masque dances to be related symbolically to his text. Thus in *Pleasure Reconciled to Virtue* (performed 1618), the eventual reconciliation of pleasure and virtue was not only described but acted out when the masquers who personified the pleasures and virtues danced together. In 1609, inspired by a suggestion made by Queen Anne, Jonson adapted the tradition of the 'ante-masque' (a prefatory show) to create what became known as the 'anti-masque', as well. This introductory scene would be performed before the masque-proper, to which it served as a foil, typically featuring grotesque, comic or ugly characters, who were subsequently banished by the entry of the idealised courtly masquers.

Jonson's textual innovations were matched by a series of technical innovations in the performance of masques, for which Inigo Jones was responsible. These included the importation of the proscenium arch and perspective staging from Europe, and the use of the '*scena ductilis* or system of sliding flats which enabled the entire setting, and not only one unit, to be changed at a stroke'.[94] These developments allowed for the creation of more varied and spectacular settings, especially in the Caroline era (when it became customary to have 'three major scene changes').[95] Jones's innovations changed the relationship between masque audiences and performances, too. The monarch was traditionally the political and 'ethical centre of court productions' but Jones's use of perspective meant that he became 'the centre' in 'a physical and emblematic way', as well.[96]

The Masque of Blackness (performed 1605)

The Masque of Blackness was written by Ben Jonson and designed by Inigo Jones for performance at court on Twelfth Night. The masquers included the Queen and a number of her court ladies, and the performance was attended not only by King James and his courtiers, but also by several international ambassadors. The masque was performed at the lower end of the banqueting hall in Whitehall Palace, against the backdrop of a seaside landscape and a sea-machine. Jonson explains how the 'artificial sea was seen to shoot forth, as if it flowed to the land' (line 22); while the twelve female maskers first appeared 'in a great concave shell like mother of pearl, curiously made to move on those waters and rise with the billow' (lines 47–8). The costuming for the performance was similarly lavish. Most of the masquers wore rich blue or sea-green gowns and were blackened with make-up.

The action proper included sophisticated props and special effects, the most notable being the spectacular 'discovery' of Aethiopia (the moon goddess). Jonson describes how she was suddenly revealed 'in the upper part of the house, triumphant in a silver throne, made in figure of a pyramid' (lines 187–8). Jones's set made innovative use of perspective staging, too. Such staging was frequently used in theatres on the European continent but had never been used before in England. Jones's set design could only be viewed perfectly from King James's centrally positioned throne, a fact which reinforced symbolically his central importance as monarch and chief spectator.

The splendour of the spectacle did not impress everyone. In a letter written shortly after the performance Sir Dudley Carleton acknowledged the mechanical sophistication of the stage machinery but mocked Jones's illusory sea, observing that 'there was all fish and no water'.[97] He was similarly critical of the female masquers' attire and the fact that they used black make-up, complaining that their 'Apparell was rich, but too light and Curtizan-like for such great ones' and that their black paint 'became them nothing so well as their red and white'.[98] As Carleton's comments suggest, such attire and make-up was at odds with the conventionally idealised representation of court women in English masques.

The Masque of Blackness dramatises the quest of the River Niger and his daughters, the Aethiopian princesses, to find the land ruled over by a Sun who has the power to transform their blackness into white. Arriving off the shores of England, Niger is met by his father, Oceanus and Aethiopia who reveals that Britain is the land Niger and his daughters have sought. She praises it as a 'world divided from the world' (line 219) and reveals that it is ruled over by 'a sun' (a metaphor for King James) who possesses the power to 'blanch an Ethiop and revive a cor's' (or corpse) (line 226). Having danced with the men of the British court, Aethiopia reveals that the Princesses will be transformed in a year's time into beautiful white princesses by the light of the British 'sun'.

Although the masque can be interpreted as a moral Christian allegory about redemption from spiritual 'blackness' or sin, it is, more obviously, an allegorical compliment to England's new king, James I. By presenting him as the source of the 'sciential light' that can 'salve the rude defects of every creature' (line 228) the masque attributes to James a God-like power to redeem people. In similar fashion, Jonson's repeated references to the country as Britannia (rather than England) and his celebration of the Island as 'a world divided from the world' (line 219) implicitly promotes James's well-publicised (but ultimately unsuccessful) desire to re-establish the ancient kingdom of Britain, through the union of his two realms (England and Scotland).

Queen Anne provided the initial inspiration for the masque, requesting that Jonson devise a performance in which she and her ladies appeared as 'blackamoors'. For the story of the Aethiopian Princesses Jonson turned to several classical sources and proverbial wisdom: 'blanching an Ethiop' was a stock phrase for achieving the impossible. Whereas Jonson would later use the characters in the 'anti-masque' as a counter-point to the idealised world of the court, in *Blackness* this 'foil' is figured through the blackness of Niger's daughters. Why Anne wished herself and her ladies to 'masque' as black is a thornier question. As the antagonistic response of Sir Dudley Carleton reveals, the usual connotations of blackness in Renaissance England were negative: it was associated with ugliness, sinfulness, sexual lustiness and depravity. Anne may have wished to surprise the English courtly audience with something exotic and novel to them, but recent research suggests that her choice of dramatic conceit may have been politically pointed, too. The character she performs in *Blackness* is a 'marginal figure, an alien princess indelibly stamped with an inferior colour and in search of a social legitimacy in the Jacobean court'. Hardin Asand argues that this symbolically parallels Anne's own position as a Danish, Catholic princess seeking to establish her identity and become integrated within the English, Protestant, male-dominated court.[99]

The mirror that *Blackness* holds up to the Jacobean court and Anne's place within it is not without ambiguity. The masque's hyperbolic praise of the British court is countered by Jonson's description of its male courtiers as 'Sirens of the land' (line 266) (an analogy which suggests that the court may be a dangerous as well as an attractive place) and by the fact that 'nothing really happens' at its climax. As Stephen Orgel notes: 'the significant action, the metamorphosis of blackness to beauty, takes place *between* the masque and its sequel, *The Masque of Beautie* (1608), in which the nymphs are already white when they appear'.[100] Part of the explanation for the deferred transformation is likely to have been pragmatic, but the absence of a physical transformation scene potentially qualifies the masque's celebration of the King's power.

SUMMARY OF KEY POINTS

- **Secularisation:** Growing restrictions on religious drama in the late sixteenth century contributed to the secularisation of English theatre.
- **Professional Stage:** The late sixteenth century saw the establishment of the first permanent theatres and the professionalisation of the English theatre world.
- **Acting Companies:** Acting was company-based and all-male. Women were not allowed to act publicly. Acting companies were generally of two types: adult and boy companies.
- **Playwriting:** There was a massive expansion in the number of plays in English in the late sixteenth century; many were written collaboratively; they drew on a variety of sources and classical and Medieval dramatic traditions.
- **Regulation:** All plays had to be licensed for performance and for printing; some were subject to censorship, generally because they dealt too directly with living individuals or contentious issues.
- **Publication:** Plays were generally written for performance not reading; only some were printed. Printed versions of plays were not necessarily the same as each other or as the versions that were originally performed in the theatre.
- **Staging:** Renaissance plays had to be adaptable for a variety of venues and therefore generally relied on a minimalist staging style; scenery and sets were not used; settings were usually evoked through textual allusions.

- **Academic Drama:** It was common to study and perform classical plays in schools and at the universities, as a way of training students in Latin, rhetoric and oratory.
- **Inns of Court Drama:** Lawyers occasionally hosted professional performances and mounted their own plays and masques. Their own entertainments were often politically topical in theme and satirical in mode.
- **Court Drama:** Dramatic entertainments were a central part of court culture. As well as hosting play and masque performances, monarchs were accustomed to being entertained with short 'shows' when they went on progress round the country. These often combined flattery with advice or requests for patronage.
- **Household/Closet Drama:** Noblemen and women sometimes patronised and played host to professional players; some also staged amateur performances and/or wrote their own plays and masques. Some of these texts are 'closet' dramas (intended for reading), others appear to have been written for performance.
- **Attitudes to Drama:** The large audiences drawn to players' performances point to a popular taste for public theatre, but the stage had its opponents. Some complained that plays were morally corrupting; others were concerned that theatres were magnets for crime, disease and disorder. Opponents of the theatre were often characterised as puritans but not all puritans were opponents of drama or vice versa.
- **Comedy:** Comedies dominated the professional stage in the late sixteenth century; they were defined by their happy endings rather than their use of humour, and borrowed from classical and European comic writing.
- **Tragedy:** The first English tragedies were written in the Renaissance and were influenced by Senecan tragedy and Medieval *de casibus* tales. Tragedy only became one of the dominant genres in the Jacobean period.
- **History:** History plays dramatised the stories of (reputedly) historical characters and events and were particularly fashionable in the 1590s; many were based on material found in the wave of historical chronicles published in the sixteenth century.
- **Romance and Tragicomedy:** Early Elizabethan plays often mixed tragedy and comedy. In the early seventeenth century

there was a renewed taste for plays which mixed the genres, including romances and tragicomedies. Some contemporaries complained about such generic hybrids, but tragicomedy became the dominant dramatic genre on the Stuart stage.

- **Masques:** The masque was a lavish, multimedia form of entertainment developed in the Renaissance and particularly popular at the Stuart court. The proscenium arch, perspective staging, and female performance were pioneered in England in court masques.

NOTES

1. Andrew Gurr, *The Shakespearian Playing Companies* (Oxford: Clarendon, 1996), p. 114.
2. Herbert Berry, 'Playhouses', in *A Companion to Renaissance Drama*, ed. Arthur F. Kinney (Oxford: Blackwell, 2004), pp. 147–62 (p. 149).
3. See Geoffrey Bullough, *Narrative and Dramatic Sources of Shakespeare*, 8 vols (New York: Columbia University Press, 1957–75).
4. See Martin Wiggins, *Shakespeare and the Drama of His Time* (Oxford: Clarendon, 2000), pp. 18–25.
5. Christopher Marlowe, *Tamburlaine Parts One and Two*, ed. Anthony B. Dawson (London: A & C Black, 1998), Prologue, l–6. All subsequent references to this edition are given in the text.
6. A. R. Braunmuller, 'The Arts of the Dramatist', in *The Cambridge Companion to English Renaissance Drama*, ed. A. R. Braunmuller and Michael Hattaway, 2nd edn (Cambridge: Cambridge University Press, 2003), pp. 53–92 (p. 72).
7. Richard Dutton, *Licensing, Censorship and Authorship in Early Modern England* (Basingstoke: Palgrave, 2000), p. 6.
8. Richard Dutton, 'Jurisdiction of Theater and Censorship', in *A Companion to Renaissance Drama*, ed. Arthur F. Kinney (Oxford: Blackwell, 2004), pp. 223–36 (p. 228).
9. Annabel Patterson, *Censorship and Interpretation: The Conditions of Writing and Reading in Early Modern England* (Madison, WI: University of Wisconsin Press, 1984), p. 18.

10. Janet Clare, *'Art made tongue-tied by authority'*: *Elizabethan and Jacobean Dramatic Censorship*, 2nd edn (Manchester: Manchester University Press, 1999), p. 217.

11. For further information, see Peter W. M. Blayney, 'The Publication of Playbooks', in *A New History of Early English Drama*, ed. John D. Cox and David Scott Kastan (New York: Columbia University Press, 1997), pp. 383–422.

12. *Documents of the Rose Playhouse*, ed. Carol Chillington Rutter, revised edn (Manchester: Manchester University Press, 1999), p. 136.

13. Cited in Andrew Gurr, *The Shakespearean Stage, 1574–1642*, 3rd edn (Cambridge: Cambridge University Press, 1992), pp. 195–6.

14. Ibid., p. 182.

15. Wiggins, p. 131.

16. Cited in T. H. Vail Motter, *The School Drama in England* (London: Longman, 1929), p. 273.

17. J. B. Leishman (ed.), *The Three Parnassus Plays (1598–1601)* (London: Ivor Nicholson & Watson, 1949), IV.iv.1835.

18. Martin Butler, 'Private and Occasional Drama', in *The Cambridge Companion to English Renaissance Drama*, ed. A. R. Braunmuller and Michael Hattaway, 2nd edn (Cambridge: Cambridge University Press, 2003), pp. 131–63 (p. 155).

19. William Shakespeare, *The History of King Henry the Fourth, as revised by Sir Edward Dering*, ed. George Walton Williams and Gwyne Blakemore Evans (Charlottesville, VA: University of Virginia Press, 1974), p. xi, p. viii.

20. *REED: Kent: Diocese of Canterbury*, ed. James M. Gibson, 2 vols (London: The British Library and University of Toronto Press, 2002), II, p. 917.

21. *REED: Lancashire*, ed. David George (Toronto: University of Toronto Press, 1991), pp. 180–1, p. 354.

22. Arbury Hall, Nuneaton, Newdigate Family Library, MS A414, fos 145–94.

23. See John Northbrooke, *A treatise wherein dicing, dauncing, vaine playes or enterluds with other idle pastimes [et]c commonly used on the Sabboth day, are reproued* (London: George Byshop, 1577).

24. Philip Stubbes, *The anatomie of abuses* (London: Richard Jones, 1583), p. 90.

25. Ibid., p. 91.

26. Cited in David Mann, *The Elizabethan Player* (London: Routledge, 1991), p. 97.

27. Stephen Gosson, *Playes confuted in fiue Actions* (London: Thomas Gosson, 1582), no page number.

28. Margot Heinemann, *Puritanism and Theatre: Thomas Middleton and Opposition Drama under the Early Stuarts* (Cambridge: Cambridge University Press, 1980), p. 35, p. 31.

29. Thomas Nashe, *Pierce Penniless his Supplication to the Devil* (London: Iohn Busbie, 1592), p. 26.

30. Thomas Heywood, *An Apology for Actors* (London: Johnson Reprint Company, [1612] 1972), sig. E3.

31. Ibid., sig. C3v.

32. Ibid., sig. F3.

33. Jill Levenson, 'Comedy', in *The Cambridge Companion to English Renaissance Drama*, ed. A. R. Braunmuller and Michael Hattaway, 2nd edn (Cambridge: Cambridge University Press, 2003), pp. 254–91 (p. 263).

34. William C. Carroll, 'Romantic Comedies', in *Shakespeare: An Oxford Guide*, ed. Stanley Wells and Lena Cowen Orlin (Oxford: Oxford University Press, 2003), pp. 175–92 (p. 175).

35. Wiggins, p. 68.

36. Brian Gibbons, *Jacobean City Comedy*, 2nd edn (London: Methuen 1980), p. 4.

37. See Lisa Jardine, 'Twins and Travesties: Gender, Dependency and Sexual Availability in *Twelfth Night*', in *Erotic Politics: Desire on the Renaissance Stage*, ed. Susan Zimmerman (London: Routledge, 1992), pp. 27–38 (p. 33).

38. See Mihoko Suzuki, 'Gender, Class, and the Ideology of Comic Form: *Much Ado About Nothing* and *Twelfth Night*', in *A Feminist Companion to Shakespeare*, ed. Dympna Callaghan (Oxford: Blackwell, 2001), pp. 121–43 (p. 138).

39. R. W. Maslen, '*Twelfth Night*, Gender, and Comedy', in *Early Modern English Drama: A Critical Companion*, ed. Patrick Cheney et al. (Oxford: Oxford University Press, 2006), pp. 130–9 (p. 137).

40. Ibid., p. 137.
41. Ben Jonson, *The Alchemist*, in *Ben Jonson's Plays and Masques*, ed. Richard Harp, 2nd edn (London: Norton, 2001), I.ii.135. All subsequent references to this play are given in the text.
42. Ian Donaldson, *Jonson's Magic Houses: Essays in Interpretation* (Oxford: Clarendon, 1997), p. 82.
43. See Cedric Watts, *Hamlet* (Harvester New Critical Introductions to Shakespeare) (Brighton: Harvester, 1988), pp. xxiii–xxxii, p. xli.
44. Sigmund Freud, *The Interpretation of Dreams* (1900), ed. Ritchie Robertson (Oxford: Oxford University Press, 1999), p. 204.
45. See Steven Mullaney, 'Mourning and Misogyny: *Hamlet, The Revenger's Tragedy*, and the Final Progress of Elizabeth I, 1600–1607', *SQ*, 45 (1994), 139–62 (139).
46. See David Leverenz, 'The Woman in *Hamlet*: An Interpersonal View', in *New Casebooks: Hamlet*, ed. Martin Coyle (London: Macmillan, 1992), pp. 132–53.
47. Lisa Jardine, *Still Harping on Daughters: Women and Drama in the Age of Shakespeare*, 2nd edn (London: Harvester, 1989), p. 71.
48. Joyce E. Peterson, *Curs'd Example: The Duchess of Malfi and Commonweal Tragedy* (Columbia, MO: University of Missouri Press, 1978), p. 78.
49. Frank Whigham, 'Sexual and Social Mobility in *The Duchess of Malfi*', in *The Duchess of Malif: A Casebook*, ed. Dympna Callaghan (Basingstoke: Macmillan, 2000), pp. 167–200 (p. 178); Dympna Callaghan, '*The Duchess of Malfi* and Early Modern Widows', in *Early Modern English Drama: A Critical Companion*, ed. Patrick Cheney et al. (Oxford: Oxford University Press, 2006), pp. 272–86 (p. 273).
50. William Empson, 'Mine Eyes Dazzle', *Essays in Criticism*, 14 (1964), 80–6 (82).
51. Mary Beth Rose, 'The Heroics of Marriage in Renaissance Tragedy', in *The Duchess of Malfi: A Casebook*, ed. Dympna Callaghan (London: Macmillan, 2000), pp. 122–43.
52. John Webster, *The Duchess of Malfi*, in *The Norton Anthology of English Literature*, ed. Stephen Greenblatt et al., 8th edn

(London: Norton, 2007), I, I.ii.95–113. All subsequent references to this play are given in the text.

53. Richard Helgerson, 'Writing Empire and Nation', in *The Cambridge Companion to English Literature, 1500–1600*, ed. Arthur F. Kinney (Cambridge: Cambridge University Press, 2000), pp. 310–29 (p. 318).

54. Paulina Kewes, 'The Elizabethan History Play: A True Genre?', in *A Companion to Shakespeare's Works, Volume II: The Histories*, ed. Richard Dutton and Jean Howard (Oxford: Blackwell, 2005), pp. 170–93 (p. 177).

55. Graham Holderness, *Shakespeare: The Histories* (London: Macmillan, 2000), p. 8.

56. Richard Helgerson, 'Shakespeare and Contemporary Dramatists of History', in *A Companion to Shakespeare's Works: Volume II: The Histories*, ed. Richard Dutton and Jean Howard (Oxford: Blackwell, 2005), pp. 26–47 (p. 31, p. 43).

57. Sean McEvoy, *Shakespeare: The Basics*, 2nd edn (London: Routledge, 2005), p. 175.

58. Cited in Emily C. Bartels, *Spectacles of Strangeness: Imperialism, Alienation and Marlowe* (Philadelphia, PA: University of Pennsylvania Press, 1993), p. 58.

59. Wiggins, p. 37.

60. Roy W. Battenhouse, *Marlowe's Tamburlaine: A Study in Renaissance Moral Philosophy* (Nashville, TN: Vanderbilt University Press, 1964), p. 258.

61. See David Daiches, *More Literary Essays* (London: Oliver & Boyd, 1968), p. 68.

62. Anne Barton, 'Eloquent Carnage', *TLS*, 11 September 1992, 19.

63. See Richard Levin, 'The Contemporary Perception of Marlowe's Tamburlaine', *MRDE*, 1 (1984), 51–70.

64. Jonathan Dollimore and Alan Sinfield, 'History and Ideology: the instance of *Henry V*', in *Alternative Shakespeares*, ed. John Drakakis (London: Methuen, [1985] 1996), pp. 206–27 (p. 225).

65. See, for example, Stephen Greenblatt, 'Invisible Bullets: Renaissance Authority and its Subversion, *Henry IV* and *Henry V*', in *Political Shakespeare: Essays in Cultural*

Materialism, ed. Jonathan Dollimore and Alan Sinfield, 2nd edn (Manchester: Manchester University Press, 1996), pp. 18–47.

66. Phyllis Rackin, 'English History Plays', in *Shakespeare: An Oxford Guide*, ed. Stanley Wells and Lena Cowen Orlin (Oxford: Oxford University Press, 2003), pp. 193–211 (p. 205).

67. Norman Rabkin, 'Rabbits, Ducks, and *Henry V*', *SQ*, 28 (1977), 279–96 (279).

68. Madeleine Doran, *Endeavours of Art: A Study of Form in Elizabethan Drama* (Madison, WI: University of Wisconsin Press, 1954), p. 186.

69. Gordon McMullan and Jonathan Hope, 'Introduction: The Politics of Tragicomedy, 1610–1650', in *The Politics of Tragicomedy: Shakespeare and After*, ed. Gordon McMullan and Jonathan Hope (London: Routledge, 1992), pp. 1–19 (p. 1).

70. Michael O'Connell, 'The experiment of romance', in *The Cambridge Companion to Shakespearean Comedy*, ed. Alexander Leggatt (Cambridge: Cambridge University Press, 2000), pp. 215–29 (p. 216).

71. Cited in David L. Hirst, *Tragicomedy: The Critical Idiom* (London: Methuen, 1984), p. 4.

72. Cited in Maurice Hunt, 'Romance and Tragicomedy', in *A Companion to Renaissance Drama*, ed. Arthur F. Kinney (Oxford: Blackwell, 2004), pp. 384–98 (p. 393).

73. Sir Philip Sidney, *The Defence of Poesy* (1595), in *The Major Works*, ed. Katherine Duncan-Jones (Oxford: Oxford University Press, 2002), p. 244.

74. Wiggins, p. 121.

75. Ibid., p. 113.

76. McMullan and Hope, p. 11.

77. Janet Adelman, *Suffocating Mothers: Fantasies of Maternal Origin in Shakespeare's Plays, 'Hamlet' to 'The Tempest'* (London: Routledge, 1992), p. 193.

78. Peter Erickson, *Patriarchal Structures in Shakespeare's Drama* (Berkeley, CA: University of California Press, 1988), p. 160.

79. Adelman, p. 229; Erickson, p. 164.

80. See Carol Thomas Neely, '*The Winter's Tale*: Women and Issue', in *Shakespeare: The Last Plays*, ed. Kiernan Ryan (London: Longman, 1999), pp. 169–86 (p. 175).

81. Erickson, p. 160.

82. Ibid., p. 168.

83. Jyotsna Singh, 'Post-colonial criticism', in *Shakespeare: An Oxford Guide*, ed. Stanley Wells and Lena Cowen Orlin (Oxford: Oxford University Press, 2003), pp. 492–507 (p. 501).

84. Meredith Anne Skura, 'Discourse and the Individual: The Case of Colonialism in *The Tempest*', *SQ*, 40 (1989), 42–69 (47, 57, 48–9).

85. Barbara Fuchs, 'Conquering Islands: Contextualising *The Tempest*', in William Shakespeare, *The Tempest, A Norton Critical Edition*, ed. Peter Hulme and William H. Sherman (London: Norton, 2004), pp. 265–85 (pp. 269–71).

86. See Francis Barker and Peter Hulme, 'Nymphs and reapers heavily vanish: the discursive con-texts of *The Tempest*', in *Alternative Shakespeares*, ed. John Drakakis (London: Methuen, [1985] 1996), pp. 191–205 (p. 200).

87. Ibid., p. 203.

88. Stephen Orgel, 'Prospero's Wife', in William Shakespeare, *The Tempest, A Norton Critical Edition*, ed. Peter Hulme and William H. Sherman (London: Norton, 2004), pp. 201–15 (p. 209).

89. Stephen Orgel (ed.), *Ben Jonson: The Complete Masques* (New Haven, CT: Yale University Press, 1975), p. 3.

90. Martin Butler, '*The Masque of Blackness* and Stuart Court Culture', in *Early Modern English Drama: A Critical Companion*, ed. Patrick Cheney et al. (Oxford: Oxford University Press, 2006), pp. 152–63 (p. 153).

91. Butler, 'Private and Occasional Drama', p. 141.

92. Stephen Orgel, *The Jonsonian Masque* (New York: Columbia University Press, 1981), p. 116, p. 117.

93. Ben Jonson, *The Masque of Blackness*, in *Ben Jonson's Plays and Masques* (A Norton Critical Edition), ed. Richard Harp, 2nd edn (London: Norton, 2001), p. 316. All subsequent references to the masque are given in the text.

94. Butler, 'Private and Occasional Drama', p. 144.
95. Butler, '*The Masque of Blackness*', p. 157.
96. Stephen Orgel and Roy Strong, *Inigo Jones: The Theatre of the Stuart Court*, 2 vols (London: Sotheby Parke Bernet, 1973), I, p. 7.
97. Ibid., p. 89.
98. Cited in Orgel, *Ben Jonson*, p. 4.
99. Hardin Asand ' "To blanch an Ethiop, and revive a corse": Queen Anne and *The Masque of Blackness*', *SEL*, 32:2 (1992), 271–85 (276).
100. Orgel, *The Jonsonian Masque*, p. 128.

CHAPTER 2

Poetry

Nature's 'world is brazen, the poets only deliver a golden'.[1]

OVERVIEW

Sir Philip Sidney's *Defence of Poesy* (1595) argues for the social and cultural value of poetry and the poet as maker. In making his case Sidney was implicitly responding to the perceived decline in the reputation of poetry in the early modern world. Whether there was any real decline in poetry's reputation is more contentious. If there was, it had little impact on authors' readiness to engage with the genre: poetry flourished in the late sixteenth and early seventeenth centuries, as writing in English became the norm and writers experimented with a range of traditional and newer poetic genres.

This flourishing of vernacular verse was accompanied by lively debates about poetry. While the argument about the vernacular's suitability for poetry had largely been won by the late sixteenth century (see Introduction), there was less agreement about the form English poetry should take. There were, for instance, those who objected to the use of rhyme. Such critics usually cited the example of classical 'quantitative' verse. Rather than using rhyme, classical poems were given form by their patterned use of long and short syllables. During the late sixteenth century a number of English poets experimented with the adaptation of classical meters to English, including Sir Philip

Sidney and Thomas Campion. Campion even produced a guide to writing quantitative verse, illustrated with examples of his own poetry: *Obseruations in the Art of English Poesie* (1602). Part of the reason for experimenting with quantitative meter was a desire to emulate the admired poetry of Greek and Roman authors, and to create a more learned form of English poetry that might merit comparison with that of the ancient world. But quantitative verse did not become popular, and other writers championed rhyme, including George Gascoigne in *Certayne Notes of Instruction Concerning the Making of Verse or Rhyme in English* (1575) and Samuel Daniel in his *Defence of Ryme* (1602). Even Sidney, who was interested in quantitative verse, did not condemn the use of rhyme, arguing that 'English, before any vulgar language I know, is fit for both sorts' of verse.[2]

Contemporary writers were similarly interested in the role and purpose of poetry and the poet. While some stressed poetry's didactic potential and others its recreational role, most accepted the view of classical writers such as Horace that poetry should both teach and delight its readers, and that poetry was a social art, which inevitably engaged with the world in which the poet lived. Some poets, such as Ben Jonson, went further and argued that it was the poet's duty to reflect society and to offer its readers political and ethical counsel.

Influences

The growth of poetry in Renaissance England was influenced in profound ways by renewed interest in classical poetry. The poets of the ancient world not only encouraged Renaissance authors to regard the poet as a God-like maker, but provided poets with a rich storehouse of poetic styles and genres. At the same time, the traditions of classical poetry influenced the way that Renaissance poets thought about the genres they inherited. It was customary, for example, to regard pastoral as the humblest poetic mode and epic as the most prestigious, as had the ancient authors. For this reason, some of the most ambitious Renaissance poets imitated the poetic career of Virgil by beginning their poetic apprenticeships as authors of pastoral poetry before gradually working their way up to epic (a poetic pathway sometimes described as the 'Virgilian wheel').

Among the most influential writers in Renaissance England were Theocritus, Homer, Virgil, Ovid, Horace and Juvenal. Theocritus's *Idylls* (written 3rd century BC) and Virgil's *Eclogues* (written c. 37 BC) and *Georgics* (written c. 29 BC) were the main inspiration for Renaissance pastoral and georgic verse, while Homer's *The Iliad* and *The Odyssey* (written c. 600 BC) and Virgil's *The Aeneid* (written c. 29–19 BC) served as models for the period's epic poetry. Ovid (43 BC–AD 17) was to have a similarly far-reaching influence on Renaissance love poetry. His *Metamorphoses* (translated in 1565) was to prove especially influential: its mythological tales not only offered poets diverse stories about desire and its power to transform individuals, but a model of stylistic elegance and variety of a kind especially prized in the Renaissance. As an ethical model Ovid's poetry was more controversial, with Renaissance critics divided between those who regarded him as 'a teacher of great wisdom and learning' and those who condemned him as a 'dissolute and dangerous misleader of youth'.[3] Horace and Juvenal offered poets similarly contrasting models for their satiric poetry (see below).

Writers borrowed from native and contemporary European poetic traditions, too. English pastoral verse was influenced by the poetry of Medieval English authors such as William Langland and contemporary continental pastoralists such as Jacopo Sannazaro, as well as Virgil; and England's most famous epic poets Edmund Spenser and John Milton were inspired not only by classical epics, but by Medieval English romances (such as *Sir Gawain and the Green Knight*, written c. 1375–1400), and Renaissance poems such as Dante's *The Divine Comedy* (written c. 1308–21), Ariosto's *Orlando Furioso* (1516, 1532) and Tasso's *Gerusalemme Liberata* (1581).

Renaissance Italy was the source of one of the other major influences on sixteenth-century English poetry: Petrarchism. This poetic mode takes its name from the Italian poet Francesco Petrarch (1304–74). Petrarch is most famous for his *Canzoniere* (written c. 1327–68), a sequence of 366 lyric poems about the poet's unfulfilled love for a beautiful woman called Laura. The majority of the lyrics are sonnets, a new type of poem thought to have been invented by fellow Italian, Giacomo da Lentino in the thirteenth century, but popularised across Europe by Petrarch. Petrarchan sonnets have a regular rhyme scheme (abbaabba cdecde) and tend to divide into two sections: the octave and the sestet. The shift between the two parts is known as the 'turn' or 'volta' and is often a turning point in the poem in mood, tone, or subject.

As well as establishing a fashion for sonnets Petrarch's poems have a number of recurrent features which gradually became conventional *topoi* (or motifs) in European love poetry, and constitute what we now describe as a 'Petrarchan' mode. These include a beautiful, chaste but unattainable mistress; the figuring of sexual love in religious terms; 'contests between eye and heart, beauty and virtue'; 'the power of poetry to immortalize the beloved'; the lover as slave of the beloved; the pining and sleeplessness of the lover during the absence of the beloved; and the use of antitheses to describe the poet's emotions.[4] Given their pervasive influence it is perhaps not surprising that some poets rejected Petrarchan conventions, but over time 'anti-Petrarchism' itself became conventional, and is often found in the sonnets of Renaissance English poets alongside poems clearly indebted to Petrarchan traditions.

Contexts

In the sixteenth century poetry was a genre closely identified with the royal court. Those who wrote poetry were generally either courtiers or educated, aspiring men (and occasionally women) in search of court preferment. For Elizabethan courtiers the ability to write artful poetry was part of being an accomplished gentleman (or woman), but it was also a way of cultivating the kind of persuasive skills essential in the world of Renaissance politics and diplomacy. For the most skilful, poetry could itself be a way of advancing one's personal or political agenda, providing a vehicle through which one could make requests or offer advice to fellow courtiers and the monarch. Similarly, for those beyond the court but desirous of royal or noble patronage, writing poetry could be a way of impressing and winning favour. Such favour was not only desired by those ambitious for professional advancement in the government, the law or the church, but by the new generation of would-be professional poets, men who sought to make a living from their pens. For them elite patronage provided not only status but a potential income. Given this, it is no surprise that so many of the period's poets write about and, implicitly, for the court.

The court continued to be the centre of political power and preferment in the seventeenth century, but was no longer the only hub of wealth and influence. The rise of the merchant classes and the thriving of the metropolitan economy saw the city become a place of growing power, and offered new opportunities for those in search of riches and status. This is perhaps partly why we see a diversification in seventeenth-century poetry. While courtly modes of poetry remain important we find a growing number of poets turning their attention to the city. At the same time, heightened anxieties about urbanisation and the perceived corruption of the Stuart court led others to turn their attention to the alternative world of the country. A similar pattern emerges in the world of Jacobean drama where courtly and pastoral dramas were staged alongside new forms of urban drama such as city comedies and domestic tragedies.

Circulation

Most Renaissance poetry was circulated in manuscript (see Introduction), but a series of landmark publications in the late sixteenth and early seventeenth centuries set a precedent for printing poetry collections and helped to make print a more common form of poetic transmission. One of the ground-breaking texts in this respect was the *Songs and Sonnets* published by Richard Tottel in 1557. *Tottel's Miscellany* (as it is better known) consisted of previously unpublished lyrics by Henry Howard, Earl of Surrey, Sir Thomas Wyatt and a number of other early Tudor poets. As Michelle O'Callaghan notes, the 'movement from manuscript into print' distanced the poems from their original context of production and 'from the relatively cohesive scribal community' that had given 'them meaning'. In some cases, this obliged Tottel to add 'titles' or explanatory prefaces.[5] As well as showing how originally private forms of poetry, such as the lyric, could be presented to a wider readership, the success of *Tottel's Miscellany* showed that there was a market for printed poetry.

The posthumous publication of Sir Philip Sidney's sonnet sequence *Astrophil and Stella* (1591) and his collected works (1598) was to have a similarly significant impact on the history of printed poetry. Together these editions helped to render printed poetry more acceptable, especially amongst elite poets. The Sidney volumes, likewise, set a precedent for the publishing of single-author collections which poets and publishers were to exploit in the early seventeenth century. In 1616 Ben Jonson was to take a particularly radical step, overseeing the publication of his own poetic and dramatic *Works* in a handsome Folio edition (a format generally reserved for learned publications). This was followed by the analogous First Folio of Shakespeare's plays (1623) and editions of the poems of John Donne and George Herbert in 1633.

Elizabethan Poetry

Early Elizabethan poetry was generally designed to teach its readers religious, ethical or civic lessons. Later Elizabethan poets continued to be concerned with instruction but believed that poetry was more likely to teach its readers if it amused and entertained them. At the same time, in a culture in which there was potentially strict control of political and religious commentary, poets continued to be conscious of the need for discretion when offering potentially contentious advice or instruction. For these reasons, poets increasingly favoured genres which were indirectly, rather than overtly, educative or topical such as the two most popular poetic genres in the late Elizabethan period: pastoral poetry (which superficially concerned itself with the lives and loves of shepherds) and the sonnet (conventionally associated with expressions of male, heterosexual love).

Critics have linked the late Elizabethan fashion for love poetry to the fostering of Petrarchism at the Elizabethan court. As Gary Waller notes, 'Elizabeth systematically encouraged her (male) courtiers to relate to her in the role of Petrarchan lovers'.[6] For Elizabeth and her courtiers the conventional subordination of the Petrarchan lover to his powerful mistress modelled the kind of loyal male submission Elizabeth expected from her courtiers but which was potentially difficult to command at a time when women were generally expected to be subordinate to men and the monarch had no standing army to enforce his or her authority. As modern historicist critics such as Arthur Marotti have made clear, writing poetry about love within such a culture becomes not simply a way of fictionalising personal erotic desires but a potential vehicle for expressing courtiers' political wishes and frustrations. Marotti goes further, in fact, and suggests that 'love', in most Elizabethan love poetry, 'is not love', but rather political ambition.[7]

Love is perhaps more often 'love' in another genre of poem that briefly flourished alongside the sonnet in 1590s England: the epyllion (or mini-epic). Although the generic name associates these narrative poems with the epic verse of Homer and Virgil, they typically have an erotic, rather than a martial theme, and the grand style in which they are written is often 'calculatedly close to self-parody'.[8] In this, and their frequent sexual frankness, they are indebted to the playful, erotic poetry of Ovid.

In its tendency towards parody the epyllion can be seen to anticipate another important trend in poetry at the turn of the century: the emergence of poetic satire (often in the form of epigrams or verse epistles). It is perhaps no coincidence that this was a time when disillusion with Elizabeth I and her court was at a height. Those involved in the development of poetic satire drew their principal inspiration from the example of classical poets, Persius and Juvenal, both of whom were famed for the biting, aggressive quality of their satires. Later English satirists (such as Ben Jonson) were to owe a similar debt to the more measured satires of Horace. One of the key texts in establishing the 1590s fashion for verse satire was Joseph Hall's *Virgidemiarum* (1597). Hall's example was quickly followed by a series of other satirical works, including Everard Guilpin's *Skialetheia, or A Shadow of Truth in Certain Epigrams and Satyres* (1598) and John Marston's *Pygmalion's Image and Certain Satyres* (1598). The subversive quality of these satires soon caught the attention of the authorities and led to the so-called Bishops' Ban on the printing of satires and epigrams (1599).

Stuart Poetry

The lyric mode first flourished in the sixteenth century but dominated English poetry in the early seventeenth century, as an understanding of the genre as verse intended for singing gave way to the modern conception of lyric as a 'short poem, often written in the first person and primarily contemplative or emotive rather than narrative in emphasis'.[9] Heather Dubrow links this development to the Reformation, observing that lyric poetry was 'clearly very congenial' to the Protestant 'emphasis on interior states and meditation'.[10] In this context it is perhaps not surprising that one of the forms of English poetry which flourished in the seventeenth century was the religious lyric.

The religious lyricists of the early seventeenth century exploited the genre's association with the spoken voice and confession to develop a poetry that was intimate and immediate. Among the most distinctive lyric voices of the period are those evoked in the religious poems of John Donne, George Herbert and Henry Vaughan. While Donne's famously impassioned 'Holy Sonnets' showed how the religious poet might appropriate traditionally secular lyric genres, Herbert and Vaughan provided a model for the compilation of compendia of religious lyrics with *The Temple, Sacred Poems and Private Ejaculations* (1633) and *Silex Scintillans, or, Sacred Poems and Private Ejaculations* (1650), respectively. For these writers, the religious lyric was not simply a vehicle for spiritual self-examination but a mode of prayer which spoke to their religious calling, while the custom of sharing such poems made the religious lyric a public as well as a personal genre in which poets offered readers models for their own religious meditations.

The fashion for sonnet-writing and Petrarchan love poetry waned with the end of the sixteenth century, but the taste for love lyrics did not. On the contrary, the love lyric continued to be an important arena of poetic display and was especially popular with the younger generation of male poets, many of whom were keen to challenge earlier poetic conventions. Modern critics have often divided the latter into two main movements: 'metaphysical' and 'cavalier' poets.

Today the most famous of the so-called 'metaphysical' poets is probably John Donne, but George Herbert, Henry Vaughan, Andrew Marvell, Thomas Carew and Richard Crashaw have each been described as 'metaphysical' writers. Among the features associated with 'metaphysical' poetry are a plain verbal style, an

argumentative structure or diction, irregular metre, a preoccupation with abstract philosophical speculation, an avoidance of conventional poetic images and a taste for elaborate 'conceits'.
Characteristically, these 'conceits' involve the discovery of surprising analogies between seemingly unlike objects or subjects, as when
Donne compares separated lovers to the parted legs of a compass in
'A Valediction: Forbidding Mourning'.

The 'cavalier' poets, who are usually said to include Robert
Herrick, Richard Lovelace, Sir John Suckling and Thomas Carew,
take their name from the term used to describe those who supported
the royalist cause in the English Civil War. As this connection suggests, they share a belief in loyalty to one's monarch and are generally royalist in sympathy. As writers mostly active in the Caroline era,
this meant that they participated in the royal idealisation of the relationship between Charles I and Henrietta Maria, composing poems
which celebrated Platonic (as well as sensual) love of the kind the
royal couple espoused, and loyal devotion to one's beloved ruler (see,
for example, Herrick's, *Hesperides*, 1648 and Lovelace's *Lucasta*,
1649). Other shared values include a prizing of friendship, hospitality and a commitment to the classical concept of the 'Good Life'.
Many of these values, and the neo-classical poetic style with which
they are associated, were inherited from Ben Jonson.

Alongside the flourishing of the religious lyric and new types of
love lyric, the early seventeenth century witnessed a fashion for
various forms of occasional poetry and encomiastic verse (poetry of
praise), such as verse epistles praising individuals, epithalamiums
(or wedding poems), epitaphs and elegies. In similar fashion, a
number of early seventeenth-century poets wrote poems which celebrated particular places or buildings. Probably, the most famous
of these are the so-called 'country-house' poems which became
popular following the publication of Aemilia Lanyer's 'The
Description of Cookham' (1611) and Ben Jonson's 'To Penshurst'
(1616) (see below).

Women's Poetry

Female literacy levels remained low in the Renaissance and women
who were literate were generally discouraged from writing or

publishing literature. Despite this women's poetry appears to have flourished in the early modern period, though comparatively few ventured into print. Most of the women's poetry that was published was religious (like that preserved in manuscript), probably because devotional writing was more acceptable. This includes one of the earliest printed collections of women's poetry in sixteenth-century England: Anne Locke's *A Meditation of a Penitent Sinner* (1560). Locke's *Meditation* was appended to her translation of four sermons by John Calvin and consisted of a sequence of sonnets which paraphrase Psalm 51. It was the first printed sonnet collection in England, and appeared shortly after Locke's return from a period of continental exile during the reign of Mary I. The religious subject matter of the collection helped to render it more acceptable but Locke's decision to publish her poems remained a radical move, implicitly in keeping with her Protestant belief in the importance of Biblical study and women's right to spiritual self-expression.

Many later women poets were, likewise, inspired by the Psalms (which were widely perceived as examples of divine poetry) including one of the period's most renowned literary women, Lady Mary Sidney. As well as being a famous patron of poets, such as Samuel Daniel, and responsible for overseeing the posthumous publication of her brother, Sir Philip Sidney's poetry and prose, she was herself a sophisticated author, writing original courtly verse, and translating Robert Garnier's French play *Marc Antoine* (1592), Philippe de Mornay's *A Discourse of Life and Death* (1592) and Petrarch's *The Triumph of Life and Death*. But she was to be most widely admired as a poet for her completion of the ambitious sequence of metrical Psalm paraphrases begun by her brother Philip. The completed sequence demonstrates both her technical skill and inventiveness as a poet, employing 'a dazzling array of some 126 different verse forms, including ottava rima, rime royal, terza rima, two sonnet forms, and some highly original stanzaic forms'.[11]

As Mary Sidney's example demonstrates, women poets did not confine themselves to devotional literature; some wrote secular verse. The first Englishwoman to publish such poetry under her own name or initials was Isabella Whitney in *The Copy of a Letter* (1566–7): a collection of 'four jaunty love complaints, two in female and two in male voice'.[12] Her second poetry collection, *A Sweet*

Nosegay (1573) was more varied and poetically complex, but (again) predominantly secular, including poems for and about her family and friends, and a mock-serious 'Wyll and Testament', addressed to London.

Despite the appearance of printed collections like Locke's and Whitney's, most Elizabethan and Stuart women continued to circulate their poetry in manuscript, if at all. Print publication was to be rendered a more acceptable forum for the woman poet by Lady Sidney, who published several of her own works, including an elegy for her brother ('A Dolefull Lay of Clorinda', 1595) and 'A dialogue between two shepherds, *Thenot* and *Piers*, in praise of *Astrea*' (1602).

One of the poets who appears to have been inspired by Sidney's example is Aemilia Lanyer. In 1611 she became the first seventeenth-century English woman to publish a solo-written poetry collection under her own name: *Salve Deus Rex Judaeorum* (Hail, God, King of the Jews). Like the poetry publications of her female forerunners, Lanyer's poetry is dominated by religion but aims to advance the cause of women. At the heart of her collection stands her title poem about the Passion of Christ, which offers a radical reinterpretation of the Bible in order to stress God's special esteem for women and their important part in Biblical history. More controversially, in 'Eve's Apology' Lanyer downplays Eve's part in mankind's 'Fall' into sin and argues that man's crucifixion of Jesus represents a far greater crime than Eve's error in the Garden of Eden. Lanyer's female-centric perspective on the Passion is matched by her decision to preface her collection with a series of poems dedicated to the praise of royal and aristocratic women, and her conclusion of the collection with a poem which celebrates her patron, Lady Margaret Clifford, Countess of Cumberland: 'The Description of Cookham' (see the Country-House Poem, below).

Lady Sidney's poetic career provided similar inspiration for another of the early seventeenth century's pioneering female poets: Lady Mary Wroth. Lady Wroth (née Sidney) was the oldest daughter of Lord Robert Sidney, and niece to Lady Mary Sidney and Sir Philip Sidney. Given that she was born into one of the period's most famously literary families it is perhaps not surprising that Wroth proved interested in writing. While clearly indebted to the example of her aunt and uncle, Mary Wroth was an innovator: she became the first English woman to write a prose romance (*The Countess of Montgomery's Urania*, 1621) (see Chapter 3), a masque (*Love's Victory*, written c. 1621), and an original secular sonnet sequence (*Pamphilia to Amphilanthus*, 1621). Wroth's sonnet sequence is concerned with the lead characters of her prose romance: Queen Pamphilia and her cousin and lover, Amphilanthus. Like Wroth's romance, the sonnets tell the story of Pamphilia's constant love for her inconstant lover and are believed to offer a fictionalised treatment of Wroth's affair with her cousin, William Herbert, third Earl of Pembroke. In their preoccupation with frustrated love many of the poems recall the conventional scenario found in earlier Petrarchan sonnets. Wroth's use of imagery of imprisonment and slavery to figure her love, and her apostrophes to personified figures such as Time and Love, likewise recall common Petrarchan motifs, but her sequence is distinctive for its focus on a female lover and a male beloved: an inversion of the conventional genders of poet and beloved which works to subvert the typical objectification of women in Petrarchan love poetry.

PASTORAL VERSE

Pastoral poetry focuses on the lives and loves of shepherds and idealises country life, often in contrast with court or city life. Traditionally, pastoral was the humblest form of verse but it became one of the most popular poetic genres in Renaissance Europe. While some poets turned to it as part of an apprenticeship intended to invoke the career of Virgil, others were attracted by pastoral's traditional association with covert political and social satire. Contemporary commentators on pastoral often defended the 'lowly' genre on these grounds. Sidney, for example, wrote of pastoral's shepherds being able to 'show the misery of people under hard lords or ravening soldiers'.[13] As Sidney hints, such commentary was potentially radical, affording a voice to those disaffected with their ruler or government. On the other hand, in its depiction of a world in which the distinction between high and low classes is generally taken for granted, pastoral potentially served to reinforce traditional social hierarchies. Louis A. Montrose believes that this explains the genre's special popularity in the late sixteenth century when there was anxiety about increased social mobility.[14]

Pastoral poetry finds its origins in the *Idylls* of Syracusan poet, Theocritus (born c. 310 BC). Theocritus's poems are set in his native Sicily and concerned with a group of shepherds, including figures such as Lycidas, Daphnis and Corydon. The poems were distinctive not only for their idealisation of the simple life of shepherds, but for their rustic language. Theocritus's first 'Idyll' about the death of Daphnis was to prove especially influential, leading to the development of pastoral elegy, the genre to which Milton's 'Lycidas' belongs.

A number of later classical poets imitated Theocritus's pastoral verse including Bion (late 2nd–1st century BC), Moschus (2nd century BC) and, most significantly, Virgil (70–19 BC) in his *Eclogues*. Eclogues are poems which involve a singing competition or verse exchange between two or more shepherds in which they describe or lament their usually unhappy love lives, mourn their dead friends, or compete to be recognised as the best poet. Virgil's collection consists of ten such poems. Like Theocritus's *Idylls*, Virgil's *Eclogues* present the pastoral world of the countryside as an idealised realm, but in Virgil the idealised landscape is Arcadia, rather than Sicily, and he presents it in terms which evoke the classical myth of the 'Golden Age' (see Glossary). The association of country life with the Golden Age and, in later Christian pastoral, with pre-lapsarian life in the Garden of Eden, was to become a common feature of Renaissance pastoral poetry.

At the heart of Virgil's sequence are two contrasting shepherds: the fortunate Tityrus (who appears to have been a figure for Virgil) and the unfortunate, exiled shepherd Meliboeus. Together, these two figures are often seen as representing the different fortunes of Virgil and his peers during the reign of the emperor Augustus Caesar: while Virgil enjoyed the patronage of Augustus, other Romans faced exile and dispossession, as Augustus seized their land in order to reward his soldiers. As Michelle O'Callaghan notes, the contrasting situations of Tityrus and Meliboeus provided subsequent poets with 'a version of pastoral that was double-coded; simultaneously available for panegyric and satire'.[15]

In the Renaissance Virgilian pastoral was adapted and Christianised by continental poets such as Petrarch, Mantuan and Sannazaro. In their poetry the shepherd becomes a figure not only for the poet and the good citizen (as in Virgil) but for Christ and his ministers, and the pastoral eclogue becomes a medium for ecclesiastical as well as social satire. In adapting pastoral for Christian ends, and equating shepherds with Christ and his ministers, the so-called Christian pastoralists were drawing on Biblical tradition and the example of medieval poets such as William Langland who had used pastoral to satirise social and ecclesiastical corruption. In the Bible the relationship between the shepherd and his flock regularly serves as a metaphor for the relationship between Christ and his followers, and ministers and their congregations (see, for example, the Gospel of St John where Christ describes himself as 'the good shepherd', 10:14). Biblical authors make similarly potent use of the image of wolves preying on sheep to suggest the general threat posed to Christians by Satan and sin, and to figure the specific danger of corrupt religious leaders, as in Matthew 7:15 where good Christians are warned: 'Beware of false prophets, which come to you in sheep's clothing, but inwardly they are ravening wolves'.

Edmund Spenser, *The Shepheardes Calender* (1579)

The anonymous publication of Edmund Spenser's *The Shepheardes Calendar* marked the start of Spenser's public life as a poet. In choosing to begin his poetic life writing pastoral poems Spenser (1552–99) was imitating the career of Virgil and making a bid to be recognised as 'the' national poet of England (as Virgil had been for the Roman Empire). At the same time, Spenser's decision to write in English and his revival of obsolete and archaic native words signalled his poetic commitment to the vernacular and his wish to create a native poetic tradition which rivalled that of the ancient world.

The Shepheardes Calender consists of twelve eclogues (one for each month of the year). Each has three parts: an opening woodcut and headnote, the eclogue proper, and one or more emblems. In theory, the woodcuts and emblems are illustrative of the themes or characters featured in the poems but, as Richard McCabe points out 'the interaction of word and picture is seldom straightfor-ward'.[16] Each eclogue is also accompanied by an explanatory note and textual glossary attributed to someone identified as 'E. K.' (pos-sibly a pseudonym for Spenser). E. K.'s elaborate glosses recall the kind of textual commentaries provided in Medieval and Renaissance editions of Virgil's *Eclogues* and invite readers to see the *Calender* as a 'classic' work. Like Virgil's eclogues, Spenser's generally consist either of dialogues, poetic contests or laments, which E. K. divides into three main modes: plaintive (poems which offer some kind of lament or complaint), recreative (poems con-cerned with love or praise) and moral, but the poems are formally diverse, employing a variety of different and complex rhyme schemes and metres.

Like the classical and Christian pastoralists who inspired him, Spenser uses his eclogues to engage with topical issues. This is perhaps most evident in the 'moral' eclogues, at least three of which are concerned with anti-Catholic ecclesiastical satire: 'May', 'July', 'September'. In each eclogue, Catholic ministers are implicitly con-demned as ambitious, selfish and corrupt. In using pastoral as a vehicle for satirising ecclesiastical abuses, Spenser was following the example of the Bible and earlier Christian pastoralists. Medieval and continental pastoral provided him with inspiration for other aspects of the *Calender*, too. As John N. King notes, Spenser's 'flat plain style', his use of alliteration and 'his transformation of the medieval persona of the blunt truth-telling plowman into various shepherd characters' all 'allude to' and borrow from 'the ancient tradition of English estates satire and complaint', while the name and persona that Spenser adopts in the poem ('Colin Clout') is indebted, as Richard McCabe notes, to 'the garrulous, aggressive Colyn Cloute of John Skelton's court satires and the pensive, elegiac Colin of Clément Marot's plaintive pastorals'.[17]

Following Virgil's example, Spenser uses pastoral to engage with the world of contemporary politics as well as religion. This engage-ment is most obvious in the eclogues which allude to Elizabeth I. At the time that Spenser was completing the *Calender* the Queen was involved in negotiations about a possible marriage to the French King's brother, the Catholic Duke of Alençon. Like many people in the English court (including Spenser's powerful patron, Robert

Dudley, the Earl of Leicester) Spenser was opposed to the French match, and used the *Calender* to advise the Queen against marriage, by warning of the dangers of misgovernment attendant on love, and by praising and celebrating the Queen for her virginity.

One of the first examples of such (implied) advice is offered through the figure of Colin when he observes, in the opening eclogue, that his preoccupation with love has led him to neglect his flock:

> Thou feeble flocke, whose fleece is rough and rent,
> Whose knees are weake through fast and euill fare:
> Mayst witnesse well by thy ill gouernment,
> Thy maysters mind is ouercome with care.[18]

As Spenser's political metaphors suggest, the shepherd is potentially a figure not just for the poet or the cleric, but for the monarch. By implication, the life of the lover is not compatible with effective government and the Queen is in danger of neglecting her 'flock' (like Colin) as a consequence of love's distractions.

In other poems such as 'April' Spenser celebrates the Queen's virginity, praising her as 'The flower of Virgins' (line 48). This was to become customary in later courtly literature but was risky when the Queen appeared to be on the brink of relinquishing her virgin state. Colin's 'November' elegy for Dido appears to offer an even more provocative and sombre warning about the consequences of a foreign marriage. As many critics have noted, the 'mayden of greate bloud' (p. 138) mourned by Colin is, implicitly, a figure for the Queen, and her name recalls that of Dido, Queen of Carthage, who was destroyed by her love for a foreign prince (Aeneas). Spenser's elegy suggests that pursuing a union with a foreign prince will lead to the metaphoric death of England's Prince and her land, in similar fashion.

Poetry's social power and place is Spenser's other dominant concern in the *Calender* and is the explicit subject of the debate between Piers and Cuddie in 'October'. Cuddie echoes the complaints of many of Spenser's peers, claiming that poetry is neglected and that the career of the Elizabethan poet is hard and the rewards few (lines 7–10). Such pessimism is echoed elsewhere in the collection by implied doubts about its efficacy. In the 'February' eclogue, for example, Thenot's tale about the briar and the oak fails to teach Cuddie the lesson Thenot intends about the importance of respecting age; and Piers's attempt to teach Palinode about the dangers of deceivers using the fable of the foolish kid proves similarly ineffective in Spenser's 'May' eclogue.

Piers challenges such pessimism by insisting on the praise and glory poetry can bring, and by emphasising its power to move and teach its readers ('October', lines 19–24), but his optimism about poetry is tempered by an implicit acknowledgement that it could be better supported. He calls on the court to fulfil this role; a call which suggests that such princely support was felt to be lacking: 'O pierlesse Poesye, where is then thy place? / If nor in Princes palace thou doe sitt: / (And yet is Princes palace the most fitt)' ('October', lines 79–81).

Spenser's doubts about poetry's power to influence others may have been assuaged for a time by the success of *The Shepheardes Calender*. Although fellow poets such as Sidney and Jonson expressed reservations about his archaic diction the *Calender* was widely admired and much imitated. The collection was not to enjoy the same popularity during the next three hundred years, as literary tastes changed and Spenser's *Faerie Queene* generally eclipsed the *Calender* in reputation. The *Calender* continued to be neglected even in the early twentieth century (probably because it did not lend itself to the kind of ahistorical close-reading popular until the 1960s). Since then, changing critical fashions have led to a radical reappraisal of *The Shepheardes Calender* and a resurgence in its reputation. While the rise of genre studies in the 1960s and 1970s encouraged new work on Spenser's engagement with pastoral and allegory, the emergence of New Historicism and Cultural Materialism in the 1980s drew attention to the politicising of the pastoral mode in Elizabethan culture. Unlike earlier scholars such as C. S. Lewis, recent critics have been keenly interested in the historicity of the poem and what it reveals about Spenser's relationship to Elizabethan courtly culture. Louis A. Montrose's work, for example, has emphasised Spenser's political engagement with Elizabethan ideology, while Richard Helgerson has explored what Spenser's poetry reveals about the significant but circumscribed role of the poet in sixteenth-century society.[19]

John Milton, 'Lycidas' (1638)

Milton's 'Lycidas' is a pastoral elegy, written to commemorate Edward King, a fellow graduate of Christ's College, Cambridge who drowned at sea on 10 August 1637. King was planning to take Holy Orders and is reputed to have written poetry. Milton (1609–74) does not appear to have been a close friend but evidently knew King by reputation. His elegy was written for inclusion in a collection of poems to be published in King's memory (*Justa Eduardo King Naufrago*, 1638).

Milton's figuring of King as the shepherd 'Lycidas' signals his debt to pastoral tradition. Lycidas was a well-known pastoral name occurring in Theocritus's 'Seventh Idyll' and Virgil's 'Ninth Eclogue'. Like the pastoralists he imitates, Milton adopts the persona of a 'shepherd mourning the death of a beloved companion whose departure has afflicted the entire natural world with grief'.[20] The poem is similarly indebted to Biblical and vernacular pastoral traditions. Perhaps most obviously, Milton, like Spenser, draws on the Biblical identification of the shepherd with Jesus and the religious pastor, as well as the classical conception of the shepherd as poet. He also exploits the Biblical and native association of the pastoral mode with ecclesiastical satire. By the 1630s when Milton wrote 'Lycidas' pastoral was largely out of fashion. Like Spenser before him, Milton's early engagement with pastoral and his later composition of an epic (*Paradise Lost*, between 1667–74) was implicitly a way of courting comparison with the famous Roman poet, Virgil, and of asserting his desire to be considered the major poet of his generation.

Milton's imitation of earlier pastoral poetry is creative, as is illustrated by his use of his chief model, Virgil's 'Tenth Eclogue'. Virgil's eclogue commemorates 'the death of the famous soldier, statesman, and poet, Cornelius Gallus' after becoming a victim of unrequited love.[21] Some contemporaries interpreted the elegy as a warning about erotic love; others saw it as an allegory about the dangers of political ambition. By contrast, Milton's poem mourns 'a studious virgin' who eschewed political and erotic 'love' and '*died by accident*'. As J. Martin Evans notes, this produces a poem which raises questions not about love or politics, but 'the validity of the "fugitive and cloistered virtue" exemplified by Edward King' and Milton.[22]

Milton is similarly bold in his engagement with the formal conventions associated with pastoral. The poem lacks the 'the usual pastoral frame that introduces poem, speaker, and occasion' and gives room to the speeches of other characters such as Phoebus Apollo (the classical god of poetic inspiration), Neptune (god of the sea), and St Peter, despite claiming to be a monody.[23] Milton is unconventional in his handling of rhyme, metre and stanza form, too. Most of the poem is written in irregular verse paragraphs modelled on the *canzone* (or songs) of Italian poets such as Petrarch, but unusual in English poetry. The rhyme scheme is, likewise, irregular and ten lines are unrhymed: a device perhaps intended to reflect the discord which characterises the speaker's mood through much of the poem. The only moment where Milton abandons his irregular scheme is in the closing eight lines which are written in ottava rima, the verse form associated with sixteenth-century epic. As well as signalling an end to the discord which has dominated the poem Milton's shift to ottava rima possibly points to his intention of writing epic poetry.

As the headnote added to the poem in 1645 makes clear, 'Lycidas' is a work of ecclesiastical satire and Protestant prophecy, as well as mourning, foretelling 'the ruin of our corrupted clergy, then in their height'.[24] While Spenser and earlier vernacular pastoralists focused most of their attention on satirising the Catholic Church, Milton's poem is concerned with the perceived corruption of the Anglican clergy in the 1630s. Like Milton, many radical Protestants were anxious about the direction in which the church was being led by leading Caroline cleric, Archbishop William Laud. As Stella Revard notes, Laud was responsible for 'imposing an oppressive programme' of 'ecclesiastical reform' which many saw as taking the Church closer to Catholicism'.[25]

From the opening words, 'Yet once more', Milton invites readers to expect a poem with a topical religious agenda: the phrase comes from the Biblical Epistle of Paul the Apostle to the Hebrews 12:26–7 and evokes its apocalyptic threat of religious upheaval and violent reformation. The same apocalyptic note is struck in the closing section of the poem by the speaker's invocation to 'Weep no more, woeful shepherds, weep no more' (line 165). As Michael

Wilding observes, this line recalls the prophecy in Revelation 7:17 that after the apocalypse 'God shall wipe away all tears from their eyes'. In Wilding's view this echo suggests that 'apocalyptic change' is 'shortly to come in the society at large'.[26]

What it is that needs reforming (in Milton's view) becomes clear in St Peter's speech. Like the characters that precede him, St Peter joins Milton's narrator-shepherd in lamenting the untimely death of Lycidas, but his speech takes an aggressive turn when he contrasts Lycidas with many of the shepherds he has left behind (lines 113–31). Drawing on the Biblical equation of the shepherd and the religious pastor, and on King's identity as would-be minister, Milton uses St Peter to offer a stinging attack on the existing Anglican clergy as self-serving, ambitious and neglectful of their duties. His characterisation of them as 'blind mouths' (line 119), consuming all that they can while depriving those they care for, is an especially pointed pun, playing ironically 'on the etymologies of "bishop" (person who sees) and "pastor" (person who feeds)'.[27] Equally contentious is St Peter's suggestion that such men are corrupting and endangering those within their care, by exposing them to 'foul contagions' (line 127) and 'the grim wolf with privy paw' (line 128), both symbols it seems for sin and the perceived threat of Catholicism. Like Spenser's elegy for Dido ('November') 'Lycidas' becomes, at this moment, as much an elegy for England as for King.

Having spoken of his readiness to spare Lycidas, St Peter promises that the period's many corrupt men will be punished, enigmatically observing that 'that two-handed engine at the door / Stands ready to smite once, and smite no more' (lines 130–1). A famous crux in Milton criticism, there has been much debate about the 'two-handed engine' to which St Peter alludes, but, clearly, it is an instrument of justice which Milton imagines punishing the unworthy while the virtuous are spared. St Peter's words mark the start of the poem's transformation, as classical despair gives way to 'Christian triumph', and elegy to celebration.[28] Having listened to St Peter, the speaker's remembrance of Christ's sacrifice teaches him not to mourn for Lycidas, because in Christian terms Lycidas is not lost but saved by 'the dear might of him that walked the waves' (Jesus) (line 173). The speaker's 'pastoral elegy' is rendered an 'elegant but irrelevant fiction'.[29]

THE EPIC

Epic poems are defined by their ambitious scale, their elevated language, and their characteristic concern with the fate of a nation. Most are long narrative poems, dominated by subjects such as war and ideals such as honour, loyalty and virtue. The cast of characters is often large, but predominantly male. Epic verse was the most prestigious form of poetry in the Renaissance, inheriting its high reputation from the fame of Greek and Roman epic poetry. Foremost among these works were the poems of Homer and Virgil. Like the Renaissance movement more generally, the epic revival was initiated on the European continent by writers such as Ariosto and Tasso. Their poems enjoyed considerable popularity in England, and heroic verse was highly esteemed; but few English poets wrote epic. The notable exception in the late sixteenth century was Edmund Spenser.

Edmund Spenser, *The Faerie Queene* (1590, 1596)

Keen to model his poetic career on that of Virgil, Spenser followed up his pastoral *Shepheardes Calender* with *The Faerie Queene*. The poem is epic in scale and style, but its structure and world is that of Medieval and Renaissance romance: wandering knights go on quests; the protagonists are knights and ladies; and the culture of the Faerie Queene's court is chivalric. At the same time, Spenser invites readers to interpret his characters and his narrative symbolically, describing the poem as a 'continued Allegory or darke conceit'.[30] On one level, the poem is a political allegory in which Faery Land serves as a fictionalised version of England and the Faery Queene as a figure for Queen Elizabeth, but it is also a moral allegory (teaching readers about virtue and vice) and a religious allegory through which Spenser champions the cause of Protestantism and condemns Catholicism, as he did in *The Shepheardes Calender* (see above).

Karl Marx may have been deliberately provocative when he described Spenser as Elizabeth I's 'arse-kissing poet' but he reflected a common view of Spenser's work in the early twentieth century. Up until the 1970s it was usual to think of Spenser as a court poet, and to interpret *The Faerie Queene* as a poem which endorsed the values of Elizabeth I. Influenced by the rise of New Historicism and Cultural Materialism, more recent critics have paid closer attention to Spenser's relationship to the court and to the poem's topical allegory. Such attention has emphasised Spenser's marginalised position, and suggested that the poem's treatment of Elizabeth is more ambivalent and adversarial than its royal dedication and overt flattery of the monarch would suggest. As David Norbrook notes, there is, for example, an 'undercurrent of fear of women' and an implicit unease with female rule and Spenser champions the pursuit of an aggressive foreign policy in Ireland and Europe, whereas Elizabeth was always a reluctant military campaigner.[31]

As initially conceived, *The Faerie Queene* was to consist of twelve books (each concerned with a different Aristotelian virtue), but Spenser produced only six and fragments of a seventh. The first three books were printed in 1590. In 1596 these were reissued (with revisions) along with Books IV to VI. The two cantos of Mutability were printed for the first time when a new edition of *The Faerie Queene* was published posthumously in 1609.

In writing an epic Spenser may have been staking his claim to be England's 'Virgil', but the overt purpose of the poem was didactic, as he explained in the prefatory letter to Sir Walter Raleigh (1590): 'The generall end therefore of all the booke is to fashion a gentleman or noble person in virtuous and gentle discipline' (p. 714). Rather than moralising directly about the virtues he thought gentlemen should practice, Spenser 'conceiued' that his teaching 'shoulde be most plausible and pleasing, being coloured with an historicall fiction, the which the most part of men delight to read, rather for variety of matter, then for profite of the ensample' (pp. 714–15). The history Spenser decided to use was that of King Arthur, who he describes as 'the image of a braue knight, perfected in the twelue priuate morall virtues' (p. 715). Spenser was deliberately opting for a native hero and catering for the Elizabethan taste for romance.

Keen to distinguish his epic poetry from that of his Renaissance contemporaries, Spenser invented a new nine-line stanza form for *The Faerie Queene* (rhyming ababbcbcc). Spenser was similarly creative in his handling of character. Most of his figures have symbolic names and invite allegorical interpretation. Duessa, for example, has a name which means 'double essence'. This is symbolically appropriate as she is identified in the poem's moral allegory with duplicity. Her association with this vice also leads to her being used as a figure for the Catholic Church and Mary, Queen of Scots. Significantly, Spenser does not reveal Duessa's name or her complex allegorical role immediately; only over time do we learn her name and discover what she stands for. In this respect, Spenser's handling of Duessa is characteristic. He rarely reveals characters' names or their symbolic identity when he first introduces them, choosing to describe them instead through their appearance and/or their words and actions. Like Spenser's knights, readers are obliged to interpret the visual puzzles such characters present, and, like the knights, may make misjudgements. As well as lending the poem a degree of realism, Spenser's habit of deferring the revelation of characters' names is a way of encouraging readers to be morally alert and to share in the learning of his knights.

Spenser invites readers to be similarly attentive to the landscape through which his knights pass. Like his characters, they invite allegorical interpretation. Whether places are described as high or low, light or dark, or simple or showy, and whether they are reached by narrow or wide paths is often a symbolic indication of whether they are places of virtue or vice. The moralised landscape of Faery Land is epitomised in each book by its juxtaposition of two or more symbolically opposed 'houses' or locations. Thus in Book I the showy and corrupt House of Pride contrasts with the modest and virtuous House of Holiness. In each case Spenser's symbolic 'houses' and gardens serve as places of concentrated moral education.

Book I (Holiness)

The virtue of Holiness and the struggles Christian man faces in sustaining it are enacted through the trials faced by the Red Cross Knight as he goes on a quest to defeat the dragon which besieges Princess Una's parents. Later identified as St George (the patron saint of England), the 'red cross' he wears associates Spenser's first hero with England and with the holiness of Christ: an association reinforced by the parallels earlier and contemporary writers drew between George's famous defeat of the dragon, and Christ's vanquishing of the Devil.[32] Like Spenser's subsequent knights, Red Cross learns to perfect his virtue partly as a result of his initial errors and failures in its defence. Thus in the first half of Book I Red Cross allows himself to be separated from Una and distracted from his quest by the wiles of Archimago and the seductions of Duessa. The moral and spiritual danger of Red Cross's failure to trust Una and to pursue his quest is suggested when Red Cross ends up being imprisoned by the giant Orgoglio, and has to be saved by Arthur. The second half of the book is concerned with Red Cross's return to physical and spiritual health. This begins with his visit to the House of Holiness and culminates in his defeat of the dragon on the third-day of their contest.

In symbolic terms the book offers an encyclopedia of Christianity. As well as teaching readers how to be holy, Red Cross's difficult quest exemplifies the ongoing trials and temptations faced by the Church and Christian man (including the dangers of religious error, deceit and sin). Similarly, his reliance on the intervention of Arthur and Una symbolically illustrates man's ultimate dependence on divine mercy and grace; a lesson in keeping with the Calvinist theory of 'predestination' (see Glossary). Read more topically, Book I is also an allegory about the conflict between what Spenser regards as the 'true' Protestant Church and the 'false' Catholic Church. This opposition is figured most obviously and memorably through his juxtaposition of Una and Duessa. As well as representing truth and deception, the two women serve as figures for the rival 'true' and 'false' churches. From the beginning Una is implicitly associated with a Christ-like virtue and modesty, whereas Duessa's red and gold attire and her later riding of the many-headed beast recall the Biblical Whore of Babylon and associate her with falsehood. In personifying the rival churches as true and false women Spenser drew on the Protestant tradition of reading St John's apocalyptic story of the conflict between a woman 'clothed with the sun' (Revelation 12:1) and the Whore of Babylon as an allegory about the eventual triumph of the 'true' Protestant church over Satan and the 'false' Catholic church.

Book II (Temperance)

Temperance was understood to consist in the governing of one's passions so as to achieve a temperate, virtuous mean in one's conduct. Achieving and maintaining such moderation was acknowledged to be difficult for 'fallen' man. This is perhaps why Spenser's name for his champion of Temperance is borrowed from 'gyon', meaning 'wrestler'. During his quest to capture the sorceress Acrasia, Guyon is obliged to wrestle with various forms of intemperate behaviour, ranging from the excessive love which leads Amavia to kill herself rather than outlive her faithless lover Mordant, and the fury of the brothers Pyrrocles and Cymochles, to the intemperate lust of Acrasia and her victims at the magical garden, the Bower of Bliss. Like Red Cross, Guyon requires assistance during his quest and must be saved at a crucial moment by Arthur.

More challengingly, Guyon's quest involves learning about the limits of the virtue he champions. Although the Castle of Medina and the moderate rule of Medina over her two sisters, Elissa (defect) and Perissa (excess), presents Guyon with an early model of the temperate mean Aristotle deemed desirable, Guyon's subsequent adventures suggest that temperance is not always possible or desirable. There can be no tempering of Acrasia's wickedness, for example.[33] When Guyon finally arrives on her island it is, therefore, with the intention of overcoming her entirely: he takes her captive and destroys her Bower (the most visible manifestation of her intemperate rule).

The force with which Guyon razes Acrasia's beautifully wrought Bower has prompted much debate. As many readers have noted, it itself seems intemperate (Book II, canto xii, verse 83, lines 1–4). For some scholars Guyon's 'wrathfulnesse' undermines Spenser's championing of temperance. For others, such as Stephen Greenblatt, it points rather to the interconnection of temperance and excess, suggesting that temperance 'must be constituted paradoxically by a supreme act of destructive excess'.[34] The equation of Acrasia's Bower with beautiful but deceptive art has, likewise, led some scholars to read this controversial episode as part of Spenser's persistent critique of wilfully deceptive art.

Book III (Chastity)

Like the books which precede it, Book III is concerned with a personal virtue but, Britomart is inherently chaste, while Red Cross and Guyon must prove themselves holy and temperate. Chastity was a highly esteemed virtue in Christian culture and was considered especially important for women. This helps to explain why, for the first time in the poem, the knightly protagonist is a woman.

In praising chastity Book III might seem especially well calculated to appeal to Spenser's Virgin Queen, but the chastity which Spenser celebrates is not the chaste virginity associated with Elizabeth I, but married chastity. At the heart of Britomart's adventures is the quest to find and marry her future husband, Artegall. Spenser may have discouraged his monarch from marrying the Duke of Alençon in *The Shepheardes Calendar* but his positive portrayal of Britomart involves an implied critique of Elizabeth's long-term rejection of married love.

Unlike the quests of Spenser's previous heroes, Britomart's extends beyond Book III and is interwoven with the stories of several other lovers, including Belphoebe and Timias (figures for Queen Elizabeth and Sir Walter Raleigh), Amoret and Scudamore, and Florimell and Marinell. In its use of *entrelacement* (the interweaving of multiple related narratives) Book III borrows from Medieval and Ariostan romance, and differs from Books I and II, both of which are essentially linear narratives. Such a mode lends itself symbolically to Book III's exploration of love and the relationships that connect men and women.

As in Books I and II, the difference between virtue and its opposite is figured through the contrasting symbolism of Book III's most evocative locations: the Garden of Adonis and the House of Busyrane (where Amoret is imprisoned). Like the Castle of Medina, the Garden of Adonis is, implicitly, held up as a virtuous model, offering readers a picture of natural, chaste, creative love (Book III, canto vi, verse 30, lines 1–6). By contrast, the House of Busyrane is 'a place of delusion and art in which the natural and passionate impulses of chaste love are transformed to fears and false imaginations'.[35]

Amoret's imprisonment within Busyrane's House and Scudamore's inability to penetrate it are signs of their mutual susceptibility to Busyrane's magic and the temptations of false or lustful love. By contrast Britomart's resolute chastity and the purity of her love for Artegall render her impervious to the erotic delusions and temptations of the House. This makes it possible for her to enter it and free Amoret unharmed.

Britomart's rescue redeems Amoret and paves the way for her reunion with Scudamore. In the 1590 edition of the poem this reunion concludes the book and is figured as a blissful conjoining which leads to the miraculous transformation of the lovers into one being, who is both man and woman (Book III, canto xii, verses 45–6). In the 1596 edition Spenser revised this ending, deferring the pair's union and the resolution of their tale: Britomart and Amoret emerge from Busyrane's House to discover that Scudamore has fled in despair.

Book IV (Friendship)

Book IV extends Spenser's concern with the relationships between men and women to consider 'the various kinds of alliance, worthy and unworthy, wrought by love' and friendship.[36] Although Spenser introduces new characters, including two new heroes (Cambel and Triamond), Book IV is, in many respects, a continuation of Book III. As well as sharing a preoccupation with love, Book IV continues several of Book III's stories, including those of Belphoebe and Timias, Amoret and Scudamore, and Britomart and Artegall. While Timias continues to struggle for the good opinion of Belphoebe and with the temptations of lust, Book IV brings with it the postponed reunion of Amoret and Scudamore, and the meeting and betrothal of Britomart and Artegall.

As in Book III, Spenser's concern with human relationships again leads him to adopt the romance technique of *entrelacement*. The same thematic concern probably accounts for the close relationship he establishes between his two lead characters and for his decision to have two heroes (rather than one): Cambel and Triamond become brothers as well as friends and allies when they are betrothed to each other's siblings (Cambina and Canacee). Their joint championing of friendship serves to illustrate that true friendship is created and sustained mutually rather than individually.

The siblings Cambel and Canacee are partly based on the characters of the same name that appear in Chaucer's unfinished 'Squire's Tale', while Spenser's story of the two knights' friendship is a rewriting of Chaucer's famous 'Knight's Tale' and the tragic story of Palamon and Arcite. In Chaucer's tale the life-long friends become enemies after they fall in love with the same woman. By contrast, Spenser's poem tells the story of Cambel and Triamond's transformation from bitter enemies into exemplary friends and allies. The same pattern of discord giving way to concord and union is acted out in several of Book IV's stories and finds a fitting emblem in the book's closure with a pair of symbolic marriages, between the Medway and the Thames (canto xi), and Marinell and Florimell (canto xii).

Book V (Justice)

Like Book IV, Book V has sometimes been read as a continuation of the two books which precede it, partly because Britomart's quest spans all three, but its style and tone are very different and the virtue it examines is more overtly public. Like Books I and II, Book V adopts a linear narrative structure, focused primarily on the adventures of the titular protagonist, but its perspective on the society it depicts (and, by implication, Elizabethan England) is more sombre. Thus Book V opens with a Proem which complains of the moral degeneration and corruption of society and ends with its champion under attack from Envy, Distraction and the Blatant Beast (a figure for slander). At the heart of the book is Artegall, Britomart's lover, and the knight brought up to administer justice equitably by Astrea, classical goddess of justice. His quest is to rescue Irena from the tyrant Grantorto, and to restore justice in her land. Like previous heroes, Artegall faces various tests of his 'justice' and ends up having to be rescued. While modern critics have found the justice which Artegall metes out in various ways problematic, Spenser suggests that Artegall's key error is his showing of mercy when he fights Amazon warrior Radigund (Book IV, canto v, verse 13, lines 1–4). Having promised to serve Radigund should she defeat him,

Artegall's mercy leaves him in her control. He is only saved and able to continue his quest after Britomart defeats the Amazon Queen and frees him from his unmanly servitude.

As in previous books, the names of Spenser's chief characters are indicative of their symbolic meaning. Artegall's name suggests his association with equitable justice ('art equal'), while Irena's name, which means 'peace' in Greek and is the classical name for Ireland, points to the fact that Book V is (in part) an allegory about Elizabethan Ireland. In theory Ireland was an English colony but the Elizabethan era witnessed a series of rebellions against the ruling regime (see Introduction). These were troubles that Spenser witnessed first-hand as the secretary of Elizabeth's Lord Deputy in Ireland, Arthur Lord Grey de Wilton. Lord Grey became infamous for the severity of his treatment of the Irish. Spenser implicitly uses Artegall's quest to defend the actions of his former patron, controversially suggesting that force is necessary to achieve justice and peace. That Spenser shared Grey's commitment to the use of force in Ireland is made more explicit in the prose tract he wrote about the troubled English colony during the same period, *A View of the Present State of Ireland* (written 1596).

The troubles in Elizabethan Ireland are Spenser's most pressing, but not his only political concern in this, the most topical book of the *Faerie Queene*. Spenser also alludes to the defeat of the Spanish Armada (1588) (Book V, canto viii, verses 28–42), the trial of Mary, Queen of Scots for her part in the Babington plot against Queen Elizabeth's life (Book V, canto ix, verses 38–50), and England's part in the religious wars against the Spanish in the Netherlands (1585–7) (Book V, cantos x–xi) (see Introduction). In each case Spenser's handling of history serves to emphasise what he perceived to be the necessity of acting forcefully against one's religious opponents and on behalf of one's religious allies.

Book VI (Courtesy)

Book V ends with Artegall intent on pursuing the Blatant Beast. In Book VI he gives over this quest to Calidore, the knight of Courtesy. Like justice, courtesy is conceived as a public virtue and is specifically associated with the court, although there is a significant ambiguity in Spenser's comment on this connection: 'Of Court it seemes, men Courtesie doe call, / For that it there most vseth to abound' (Book VI, canto i, verse 1, lines 1–2). It is not clear if Spenser is saying that courtesy is named after the court because that is where it is most often found or because that is where it used to be found. As Calidore's adventures reveal, courtliness and courtesy do not necessarily coincide in the world of Faery Land (or, by implication, in England): Calidore encounters a series of courtly figures that are discourteous (such as Turpine) and uncourtly figures (such as Tristram and the shepherds) who are naturally gracious. Equally troubling, is the book's suggestion that courtesy faces countless threats in Faery Land and therefore 'needs to be supplemented by violence', like Artegall's justice.[37]

As in previous books, Calidore's adventures involve him undergoing trials which test his own virtue. These include a period when he is temporarily diverted from his quest, but in circumstances more benign than those which waylay Spenser's other heroes. Rather than becoming a captive or being rendered vulnerable to his foes, Calidore is distracted from his mission by his encounter with a community of peaceable shepherds and his meeting with a beautiful and virtuous shepherdess, Pastorella. Although the narrator of the poem notes that Calidore's pastoral retreat leads him to neglect his quest he later suggests that Calidore's time has not been misspent because he has used it 'To shew the courtesie by him profest, / Euen vnto the lowest and the least' (Book VI, canto xii, verse 2, lines 4–5).

For some critics Calidore's eventual capture of the Blatant Beast closes the poem on a triumphant note. Others find the ending more troubling. As they note, Spenser is careful to point out that Calidore's victory is temporary and that the Beast later escapes and becomes an even greater problem than before (Book VI, canto xii, verse 40, lines 4–9). Some scholars detect a similar sombreness in Spenser's closing couplet which seems to question poetry's power to educate the court: 'Therfore do you my rimes keep better measure, / And seeke to please, that now is counted wisemens threasure' (Book VI, canto xii, verse 41, lines 8–9). According to Spenser's narrator, the wise poet is now obliged to confine himself (or herself) to pleasing rather than teaching readers.

The Mutability Cantos

The Mutability Cantos appear to be a fragment of a seventh book on constancy. They consist of two complete cantos (numbered vi and vii) and two stanzas of a third (viii). At the heart of the cantos is Mutability's claim to be the dominant force on earth and in the heavens. Mutability's claim takes the form of a court case, judged by Nature, during which Mutability presents evidence in support of her claim to rule life. Nature accepts the argument that all life changes but argues that this does not make it subject to change. On the contrary, she argues that mutability is purposeful (or divinely planned) and one of the ways in which 'all things' improve themselves (Book VII, canto vii, verse 58, lines 2–9). Mutability is a common theme in Renaissance literature and Spenser's interpretation of change as providential is a convention of Protestant thinking. The significance of the cantos and their relationship to Spenser's preceding books is more contentious: some critics see them as a complementary coda to the rest of the poem, while others argue that they undermine or challenge Spenser's prizing of constancy elsewhere in the poem.[38]

THE EPYLLION

The epyllion (or mini-epic) flourished briefly in England in the 1590s. Like the epic poems from which their modern name derives, epyllia are narrative poems. There is no set stanza form or length but epyllia are usually written in an elevated or consciously poetic style that sometimes comes close to parody (as noted above). Rather than dealing with war and martial bravery (the key subjects of classical epic) they are usually concerned with erotic love and are often classical in their subject matter. In their focus on desire and their sexual frankness they offered contemporary readers what Robin Sowerby describes as 'a holiday from morality'.[39]

Whereas Homer and Virgil were the chief inspiration for Renaissance epic poetry, the erotic verse of Ovid was the key model for Renaissance epyllia. There was a tradition of reading Ovid's works to 'exemplify Christian doctrine', as Coppélia Kahn notes, but the Roman poet was more often admired in the Renaissance for 'the elegance and flexibility of his verse forms, the copious and playful use of rhetorical devices' and 'the easy scepticism of his attitude' to love and desire.[40] Contemporary readers and authors were especially fascinated by his *Metamorphoses*. As well as affording a rich storehouse of erotic tales it provided writers with a suggestive way of thinking about the transformative effects of love and desire.

Thomas Lodge's *Scilla's Metamorphosis* (1589) is usually credited as the earliest published epyllia, telling the story of Scilla's transformation into a monster after she rejects the sea-god Glaucus. Many more epyllia were published in the next decade, including Thomas Heywood's *Oenone and Paris* (1594), Michael Drayton's *Endymion and Phoebe: Idea's Latmus* (1595), Thomas Edwards's *Cephalus and Procris* (1595), John Weever's *Faunus and Melliflora* (1600) and Francis Beaumont's *Salmacis and Hermaphroditis* (1602), but the two most influential examples of the genre were to be Christopher Marlowe's *Hero and Leander* (written late 1580s) and Shakespeare's *Venus and Adonis* (1593). Most of these witty, sexually risqué poems catered for the sophisticated tastes of the classically educated aristocrats and gentlemen associated with the London law schools and the universities.

Christopher Marlowe, *Hero and Leander* (1598)

Marlowe's *Hero and Leander* tells the tragic story of Leander, the mythical lover from Greek legend who dies while swimming the Hellespont to see his beloved, Hero. Marlowe (1564–93) probably knew the story of Leander from Ovid's *Heroides* but his main source for the poem is the version of the tale told by fifth-century Greek poet Musaeus. Marlowe's version of the story is incomplete, ending after Hero and Leander have become lovers but before Leander's death. It largely follows Musaeus's account although Marlowe makes Hero Venus's nun rather than her priestess, an adaptation which intensifies the frisson of her seduction and the implicit irony of a story which sees one of the goddess of Love's attendants become a victim of love. Marlowe's account of the lovers' tragedy was completed by fellow poet George Chapman and published in 1598.

Unlike Chapman's closing sequence which finds 'a clear-cut moral lesson' in the lovers' tale, Marlowe's opening rejects any simple moralising of their story.[41] Instead, following the example of Ovid's erotic verse, Marlowe develops 'an ironic treatment of the two young lovers, finding in their naive vulnerability both comedy and pathos'.[42] This is perhaps most evident in the contrast between Marlowe's humorous handling of the couple's first sexual encounter and Leander's ill-fated meeting with Neptune. In the former episode, Leander's naivety and inexperience as a lover is demonstrated in amusing fashion, when it becomes apparent that he does not know how to have sex. As Marlowe's narrator explains Leander enjoys his embraces with Hero but initially supposes 'nothing else was to be done'.[43] The same innocence has more tragic consequences when Leander meets Neptune while swimming to see Hero. Although he does not understand the sea-god's homo-erotic desires the pity he shows leads Neptune to believe that Leander loves him, a misapprehension that Marlowe implies will later lead the sea-god to drown the young lover. Although there is light comedy in Leander's rebuffing of the lusty god, the narrator's pessimistic comments about love's power to delude and the reader's awareness of Neptune's subsequent part in Leander's tragedy invest the episode with an underlying pathos (lines 703–6).

Just as Marlowe rejects overt moralising in favour of a blend of light humour and pathos so he eschews romantic tenderness for a focus on sensuality and alternates between a humorous and a cynical perspective on love. Thus the narrator is willing to accept the concept of love at first sight, famously observing 'Who ever loved, that loved not at first sight?' (line 176) but this concession to romantic convention is counter-pointed by his insistence elsewhere that love is essentially heartless: 'Love is not full of pity as men say, / But deaf and cruel, where he means to prey' (lines 771–2). At the same time, like other epyllia poets, Marlowe makes a point of combining learned allusions and elegant rhetorical set-pieces with 'titillating erotic episodes', which tease the reader with the expectation of sex without ever fulfilling this expectation.[44] Georgia Brown likens Marlowe's teasing treatment of sex to the flirtatious strategies his narrator attributes to Hero and women more generally. Just as Hero heightens Leander's desire by resisting his advances in the temple, and by refusing to have sex with him when he visits her at her tower, so Marlowe's technique of teasing the reader with the possibility of sexual scenes is implicitly a way of keeping them reading in the 'hope for mo[re]' (line 312).[45]

The poem's homoerotic dimension is similarly provocative. As critics have long noted, Marlowe pays more attention to the physical beauty of Leander than Hero. The narrator's opening accounts of the lovers are characteristic. Marlowe's extended description of Hero is mostly devoted to her beautiful dress (lines 5–50), while his portrait of Leander dwells on the young man's physical charms and looks, which he claims embody 'all that men desire' (line 84). Hero's love for Leander is representative of his attractiveness to the opposite sex, while the homoerotic desire his beauty provokes is figured through the character of Neptune and his attempted seduction of the boy (lines 665–73). Marlowe's 'casual' treatment of same-sex desire is unconventional but equally provocative is the narrator's implicit attempt to provoke homosexual as well as heterosexual desire in his predominantly male readers.[46]

Like his sensual account of Neptune's desires, the narrator's lingering descriptions of Leander's beauty invite the (male) reader to regard him as a sexual object, as we see when the narrator begins to describe Leander's body at the start of the poem, but stops his account suggestively short:

> I could tell ye
> How smooth his breast was, and how white his belly,
> And whose immortal fingers did imprint
> That heavenly path, with many a curious dint,
> That runs along his back; but my rude pen
> Can hardly blazon forth the loves of men,
> Much less of powerful gods. (lines 65–71)

As Bruce Smith has pointed out, such moments invite the lustful male reader to fantasise about Leander, rather than Hero; a reversal of Renaissance poetic as well as sexual conventions.[47] This, combined with the largely comic handling of the bedroom scenes between Hero and Leander, could lead one to conclude that the poem is more concerned with homoeroticism than it is with the heterosexual desire overtly at the heart of the story; a possibility which some scholars have linked to Marlowe's alleged homosexuality and which anticipates his interest in homoerotic desire in *Edward II* (1594).

William Shakespeare, *Venus and Adonis* (1593)

Venus and Adonis was the first work which Shakespeare (1564–1616) published under his own name. He dedicated the poem to Henry Wriothesley, the young and dashing Earl of Southampton. As well as a bid for noble patronage, Shakespeare's composition of a rhetorically sophisticated Ovidian epyllion suggests a wish to be recognised as a narrative poet, and a desire to 'outdo' his most famous contemporary, Christopher Marlowe.[48] The poem became a bestseller, going through sixteen editions by 1640.

Venus and Adonis tells the mythical story of the goddess of love's unrequited passion for a beautiful young man, Adonis, and her subsequent grief when Adonis is tragically killed by a boar. Shakespeare's version of the tale is based on Ovid's account of the lovers in his *Metamorphoses*, and is consciously Ovidian in its combination of witty rhetoric and learned allusions, and its blending of light humour and pathos, but Shakespeare adapts the story in significant ways. The classical setting of Ovid's tale is exchanged, for example, for a rural backdrop that is conspicuously English, and Adonis is transformed from a 'passively compliant' lover to a 'resistant' one.[49] Even more significantly, Shakespeare reinterprets the mythical tale so that Venus's tragedy becomes the explanation of all subsequent lovers' unhappiness. In Shakespeare's reading Venus's grief over Adonis's death leads her to curse the love she presides over.[50]

At the heart of many of the modern debates about the poem is the question of how serious or comic it is. As A. Robin Bowers notes, some critics 'have emphasized the witticism and farce of the work' and some 'the tragic, lapsarian qualities', while others have argued that the poem is deliberately ambiguous, or that its tone shifts from light humour to pathos.[51] That there are variations between the comic and the serious in the poem is clear. Much of the humour of the poem is to be found in its handling of Venus's wooing

of the reluctant Adonis in the first half, and derives from the irony
that 'She's Love; she loves; and yet she is not loved' (line 610).

Most of the poem's opening sequence is devoted to Venus's
largely unsuccessful quest to seduce Adonis. In the contrast it
sets up between the assertive, physically powerful goddess and the
resistant, femininely beautiful Adonis, the poem recalls *Hero
and Leander* and Marlowe's handling of the encounter between
Neptune and Leander. In both cases the feminised hero finds
himself subject to the unwanted attentions of an older more aggressively lusty character, and is presented as the poem's chief sex
object. But, whereas Neptune's wooing of Leander is unconventional because it is homoerotic, Venus's wooing is unconventional
because she assumes the traditionally masculine role of suitor.

Shakespeare's essentially comic handling of this inversion of
conventional gender roles is epitomised by his account of the
couple's first encounter, during which Venus plucks Adonis off his
horse and tucks him under her arm (see lines 29–32), actions which
emphasise Venus's superior size and strength as well as her domi-
nance. A similar humour derives from Venus's inability to arouse
Adonis sexually despite thrusting herself upon him literally more
than once.

On the other hand, there are moments of sombreness even within
the first half of the poem (see lines 613–60) and some comedy in the
second half, including Venus's rapid oscillation between despair
and optimism as she waits for news about the boar hunt (lines 877–
1026). Such blending of humour and pathos is typical of Ovidian
erotic verse, and, in the case of *Venus and Adonis*, can be seen as part
of what Robin Sowerby describes as its 'sophisticated exploration
of sexual passion in all its comic and serious aspects'.[52]

Critics have been similarly fascinated by Shakespeare's handling of his lovers. Many scholars have interpreted the pair alle-
gorically, and assumed that Venus is a figure for the flesh and lust,
while Adonis represents youthful innocence and spirituality.[53]
Adonis characterises himself and Venus in similar terms, and
specifically argues that her passion is not love but an indiscrimi-
nate physical desire (lines 789–94). He goes on to distinguish
between love and lust, making it clear which he believes Venus's
passion to be (lines 799–804). Whether readers are meant to share

Adonis's perspective is more debateable. As Catherine Belsey notes, the authority of Adonis's definition is implicitly undermined by his open acknowledgement that he 'knows nothing of love', and by the fact that the distinction he draws between love and lust had yet to be firmly established in the sixteenth century.[54] The modern tendency to follow Adonis in equating Venus with fleshly lust rather than love is, likewise, complicated by the way in which Shakespeare's representation of the goddess varies across the poem. Although he sometimes depicts her as earthy and sensual, at other times he emphasises her godly powers, her spirituality and her mythical persona. Similar variations characterise Venus's representation in contemporary mythography, suggesting that she was often understood to represent both sexual desire and spiritual love.[55]

Alongside the poem's preoccupation with Venus's passion runs a concern with the maturation of the male hero. Coppélia Kahn argues that the poem presents Adonis with a choice between two ways of being initiated into manhood: through love (and sex) or through hunting (and violence).[56] Venus counsels Adonis to choose love as the safer rite of passage, but the poem suggests that the rites are related and potentially equally dangerous. Perhaps most obviously, the poem invites us to see the boar not simply as 'Venus's opposite but rather as a surrogate for her that mirrors and carries out the destructive aspects of her desire'.[57] The animalistic aspect of Venus's passion for Adonis is acknowledged several times in the poem, and the analogy between the goddess and the boar is highlighted by Venus herself, when she speculates that the boar killed Adonis while trying to kiss him: 'Had I been toothed like him, I must confess / With kissing him I should have killed him first' (lines 1117–18).

What lesson we are to draw from Adonis's death (if any) is more contentious. Like his inability to master Venus, Adonis's failure to overcome the boar can be attributed to his youthful inexperience, or seen as a failure of masculinity. Other scholars believe that it offers a moral lesson about the dangers of lust, as does the Ovidian version of their story. However, Shakespeare resists drawing any simple or overt moral, leaving readers free to judge the significance of his death as they choose.

THE SONNET SEQUENCE

Invented in the thirteenth century and popularised across Europe by Petrarch, the fashion for sonnet writing came to England comparatively late (see above for a discussion of the origins of the sonnet and Petrarchan conventions). Its pioneers were two well-travelled noblemen: Sir Thomas Wyatt (1503?–42) and Henry Howard, Earl of Surrey (1517?–47). Wyatt was the first English poet to write sonnets.[58] Most are translations or variations of Petrarchan poems, but Wyatt's sonnets are distinctive for their 'emphasis on the moral dilemmas of erotic experience, and in the relative neglect of the spiritual allegory of Petrarch's love for Laura'.[59] Wyatt was innovative formally, too, modifying the Italian rhyme scheme to introduce a final rhyming couplet: abbaabba cddcee. This was to become standard in English sonnets. Characteristically epigrammatic, these closing couplets could be used in a variety of ways, including to summarise, to reflect on, or to contrast with the preceding lines.

The Earl of Surrey's small body of sonnets is, likewise, indebted to Petrarch consisting mainly of translations or adaptations of the Italian poet, but, like Wyatt, Surrey focuses on the poet's earthbound love and adapts the sonnet form that he inherited. The rhyme scheme which Surrey devised (abab cdcd efef gg) was much looser, and changed the internal shape of the sonnet from an octave and sestet, into three quatrains and a couplet. The transition between each part of the Surrey sonnet could be used to mark changes in mood, imagery and idea, just as the 'turn' between the octave and sestet was often used as a symbolic as well as a literal turning point in conventional Petrarchan sonnets. The flexibility of the Surrey sonnet perhaps explains why it became the most common form used by English Renaissance sonneteers.

Like most early sixteenth-century poets, Wyatt and Surrey circulated their poetry in manuscript. In their own lifetimes this meant that their sonnets were confined to an elite circle of courtly friends and allies. Their poems were to reach a larger audience following their posthumous publication in *Tottel's Miscellany* (1557). Separated from their original contexts, Wyatt's and Surrey's sonnets provided late sixteenth-century English poets with an artfully compressed model for writing lyric love poetry, and demonstrated 'the potential of the Petrarchan sonnet as an expression of frustrated desire – in romantic, erotic, and political terms'.[60] As has been well-documented, the Petrarchan lover's conventional desire for the favour of a powerful but distant mistress was understood to provide a model for the relationship between courtier and monarch, a model that became especially potent following the accession of a female ruler (Elizabeth I).

Wyatt and Surrey confined themselves to the composition of individual sonnets. Later English sonneteers were to become equally interested in the model Petrarch's *Canzoniere* provided for writing sequences of sonnets. As Petrarch's *Canzoniere* showed, such a sequence could be used to offer an extended anatomy of love. The earliest English writer to exploit this potential was Thomas Watson in his *Hekatompathia* (1582), but the late Elizabethan fashion for sonnet collections was started by the publication of Sir Philip Sidney's *Astrophil and Stella* (1591). A series of other poets published similar collections within the next few years, including Samuel Daniel (*Delia*, 1592), Barnabe Barnes (*Parthenophil and Parthenophe*, 1593), Thomas Lodge (*Phillis*, 1593) and Giles Fletcher (*Licia*, 1593).

The late Elizabethan vogue for love sonnets was short-lived. By the start of the seventeenth century they had (largely) fallen out of fashion, like the courtly cult of Petrarchan love (following the death of Elizabeth I). In the Stuart period sonnets became increasingly associated with devotional rather than erotic verse, although Lady Mary Wroth's Jacobean sequence, *Pamphilia to Amphilanthus* (1621) offers late proof that erotic sonnet writing was not entirely neglected. In part an homage to, and an imitation of, the Petrarchan sonnet sequences of her father and uncle (Sir Robert Sidney and Sir Philip Sidney), Wroth's ground-breaking sequence adapted Petrarchan conventions in significant ways, not least in its focus on the emotions of a female (rather than a male) lover.

Sir Philip Sidney, *Astrophil and Stella* (1591)

Sir Philip Sidney's (1554–86) pioneering Petrarchan sonnet sequence, *Astrophil and Stella*, was printed posthumously. Although it was not the first English sonnet sequence it became the most famous Elizabethan example and earned Sidney a reputation as the English Petrarch. Like the *Canzoniere* upon which it is modelled, the 108 sonnets and eleven songs which make up *Astrophil and Stella* dramatise an extended love story, between the poet-narrator, Astrophil (or 'star lover') and Stella ('star'), and appear to be based on Sidney's unfulfilled passion for a real woman: Lady Penelope Devereux, daughter of the third Earl of Essex. Whether there was ever any relationship between Sidney and Lady Devereux is unclear. Perhaps more significant is the fact that Sidney goes to great lengths to make the sequence seem biographical. This includes suggesting that Lady Devereux is to be equated with Stella, through a series of puns on her married name (as in 'Sonnet 37'), and inviting readers to see Astrophil as a figure for himself. Not only does he give his narrator-lover a name which alludes to his own but he incorporates references to his own family (in 'Sonnet 30'), and styles Astrophil as a young aspiring courtier, like himself.

Written at a time when Sidney was in disgrace at court, following his objections to the Queen's proposed marriage to the French Duke of Alençon, Astrophil's frustrated love for his mistress's favour serves as a potential figure for Sidney's struggle for courtly status, too. Indeed, critics such as Arthur Marotti have argued that *Astrophil and Stella* is primarily about Sidney's desire for political advancement. According to such readings, *Astrophil and Stella* is a prime example of 'the metaphorizing of ambition as love' in Elizabethan courtly poetry.[61] This probably overstates the case, but the analogy between romantic and political favour is one that Sidney draws within the sonnets. In several, such as 'Sonnet 107', Stella is described as a Prince, while her 'cruelty' in rejecting Astrophil's love and service is likened to the tyranny of a ruthless monarch.

Like the sonnets of Wyatt and Surrey, those included in *Astrophil and Stella* are deeply indebted to Petrarchan tradition, but Sidney's wish to distinguish himself as a love poet is made clear in his opening sonnet which serves as a mini poetic manifesto for the rest of the sequence. Not only does he adopt a different form (writing in alexandrines, or twelve syllable lines, rather than iambic pentameter, and modifying the Italian rhyme scheme to abbaabba cdcdee), but he claims to write a poetry which is more heartfelt. Having studied other writers and struggled to express his love, Astrophil claims to have turned inwards for inspiration: ' "Fool", said my muse to me, "look in thy heart, and write" '.[62]

In similar fashion, several later sonnets explicitly reject Petrarchan conventions. In 'Sonnet 6', for example, Astrophil alludes to the Petrarchan custom of expressing one's desire in terms of oxymorons and through classical myth only to reject these traditions in favour of a less artful declaration of his love: 'I can speak what I feel, and feel as much as they, / But think that all the map of my state I display, / When trembling voice brings forth that I do Stella love' (lines 12–14). Again, the implication is that Astrophil's feelings and his verses are more authentic, but Sidney's rejection of artifice and his anti-Petrarchism is a pose: expressed as a sonnet, Astrophil's love poetry is just as artificial and contrived as those of the poets he dismisses, and Sidney still makes use of Petrarchan *topoi* even if it is to reject them. As noted above, such 'anti-Petrarchism' was a conventional part of the Renaissance sonnet tradition and rarely involved an outright rejection of Petrarchan conventions

Sidney's sequence is more innovative in the kind of love story that it tells. Although some scholars have argued for reading the sequence as 'a single long poem' which tells the story of Astrophil's courtship and eventual loss of Stella, most critics agree that *Astrophil and Stella* does not document an unfolding relationship in quite the same way as Petrarch's *Canzoniere*.[63] Instead, Sidney focuses more on the effects of desire and Astrophil's changing states of mind and emotion.

Sidney's focus on physical desire is similarly unusual. Although Astrophil accepts the superiority of spiritual love and frequently presents his love of Stella in those terms, several sonnets acknowledge that his feelings are partly based on lust and that his physical desire for Stella is in tension with his virtuous love for her. 'Sonnet 71' is characteristic in this respect. It begins by celebrating Stella's ability to inspire virtuous love, but the closing line reveals that her beauty also provokes Astrophil's lust and that his longing for her is not assuaged by love alone: ' "But, ah," Desire still cries, "give me some food" ' (line 14). In this poem 'Desire' literally gets the last word.

Astrophil and Stella is similarly noteworthy for the fact that it occasionally allows Stella to speak (see Songs four, eight and eleven). In conventional Petrarchan sonnets the beloved mistress is the silent object of her male lover's desire. Stella's speeches are generally brief but in 'Song 8' Sidney allows her to respond to Astrophil more fully and thus to become more human. She reveals that she sympathises with Astrophil's suffering, but makes clear why she cannot accede to his requests to return his love: 'Tyrant honour thus doth use thee; / Stella's self might not refuse thee' (lines 95–6). As a court woman she cannot take Astrophil as her lover without forfeiting her sexual honour.

In keeping with Sidney's concern with the earthly dimensions of desire the sequence does not finish with Astrophil renouncing his passion for Stella in favour of divine love (as did Petrarch's narrator) but with Astrophil facing a life of endless division between joy and suffering ('Sonnet 108', lines 13–14). What readers are to make of this inconclusive ending and the sequence as a whole has long been a matter of debate. While some scholars have emphasised the tragicomic quality of the sequence, others see *Astrophil and Stella* as an essentially serious work, exploring the tension between courtly and pious values, and offering a specific moral lesson about the dangers of yielding to 'ungoverned sexual passion'.[64] Others argue that Sidney and the sequence are 'caught between compassion and condemnation' of his protagonist and that the poems both 'warn against yielding to desire' and 'show the need to satisfy desire'.[65] The implicit ambiguity of the sequence may stem from Sidney's own well-documented difficulties in reconciling the demands of love, virtue and public duty.

William Shakespeare, *Sonnets* (1609)

Most of Shakespeare's 154 sonnets are thought to date from the 1590s when the fashion for sonnet writing in England was at its height but they were not published as a collection until 1609. Unlike earlier sonnet sequences which were generally named after the woman they celebrated, Shakespeare's appeared without a title and included poems for more than one (unnamed) lover. The sequence, likewise, lacks the kind of clear storyline associated with earlier sonnet collections, although it has become customary to divide the sequence into two main parts: Sonnets 1–126 (which are conventionally thought to be addressed to, or about, a beautiful young man) and Sonnets 127–54 (most of which appear to be about a 'dark' lady). In actuality, most of Shakespeare's sonnets do not specify the gender of the beloved and could therefore be equally applicable to a male or female lover.[66]

Like Sidney's sonnets, Shakespeare's seem to court autobiographical interpretation. As well as incorporating a series of puns on his name ('Will'), Shakespeare's close attention to the intensity and complexity of his speaker's feelings, and his consistent use of the first-person, encourages the reader to regard the speaker as a figure for the author. As a consequence, many critics have, likewise, assumed that the young man and the dark lady are figures for real people. The dedication of the Sonnets to 'Mr W. H.' has been taken as a clue to the identity of the male addressee. Both initials are found in the names of the two men most commonly cited as possible models for Shakespeare's youth: Henry Wriothesley, third Earl of Southampton and William Herbert, third Earl of Pembroke. Both men were famously handsome and have other connections with Shakespeare's work: Southampton was the dedicatee of Shakespeare's *The Rape of Lucrece* (1594) and *Venus and Adonis* (1593), and Pembroke was to be joint dedicatee with his brother Philip of the First Folio of Shakespeare's complete works in 1623. There is, however, no firm evidence that either of them was the intended dedicatee and it would have been unusual to address a nobleman by the humble title of 'Mr'.

Attempts to identify the so-called dark lady have proved similarly inconclusive. Mary Fitton, royal lady-in-waiting and mistress of William Herbert was suggested as a possible candidate for identification with the dark lady in the late nineteenth century, but the publication of a family portrait (in 1897) revealed that she was fair, rather than dark-haired. More recently, A. L. Rowse created controversy when he argued that the poet, Aemilia Lanyer was Shakespeare's dark lady.[67] As the one-time mistress of Shakespeare's theatrical patron, Henry Carey, and the wife of a court musician, Lanyer certainly moved in circles to which Shakespeare had occasional access, and her family's Jewish-Italian

origins probably mean that she had dark hair, but there is no concrete evidence to suggest that she had a liaison with Shakespeare.
Most modern scholars are therefore sceptical about Rowse's theory.

Most of Shakespeare's sonnets are traditional in form, consisting of fourteen decasyllabic lines and adopting the English rhyme
scheme pioneered by Surrey. Like the sonnets of Sidney and his
contemporaries, Shakespeare's are indebted to the conventions
of Petrarchan love poetry; but there are notable differences in
his treatment of love and the erotic relationships he explores.
Traditional sonnet sequences celebrated the male poet's love for a
beautiful, chaste, unobtainable woman. By contrast, Shakespeare's
sonnets record the poet's (possibly homosexual) love for a beautiful
young man, and his consummated relationship with an unconven-
tionally attractive, promiscuous woman. Shakespeare's sequence is
similarly distinctive in its focus on desire. Building on the example
of Sidney, Shakespeare's sonnets offer a frank anatomy of lust as
well as love. Some of the sonnets indulge in bawdy humour about
sex like 'Sonnet 135'; others are bitter, like 'Sonnet 129' which characterises lust as the 'expense of spirit in a waste of shame / . . . Past
reason hunted; and no sooner had, / Past reason hated, as a swal-
low'd bait'.[68] At the same time, Shakespeare's sonnets ignore some
of the common motifs of Petrarchan love poetry: there is little interest in courtship or the spirit of *carpe diem* so popular in other love
poems of the period, and Shakespeare's speaker does not dwell on
himself and his sufferings, as was usual in earlier sonnets.[69] Instead,
Shakespeare's pressing concern throughout the sequence is with
'devouring' Time and how to defy it as a lover and a poet ('Sonnet
19', line 1). Collectively, the sonnets offer two answers: love's power
to transcend time and change, and poetry's power to immortalise
love and the beloved (see, for example, Sonnets 19, 55 and 116).

The unconventionality of Shakespeare's sonnets (along with the
decline of the genre) may help to explain why the sequence was comparatively unsuccessful in the seventeenth century and why it fell
out of print. There is not much evidence of critical interest in the
poems either until the nineteenth century when it became increasingly common to interpret the sonnets biographically. Whether or
not they thought the poems were autobiographical, most Victorian
critics were uncomfortable with Shakespeare's handling of the

speaker's love for the young man. Typically, they either condemned the poems or insisted that the love depicted was entirely platonic. The potentially homosexual dimension of the sequence was foregrounded when Oscar Wilde alluded to the sonnets during his 1895 trial (for alleged homosexual crimes), describing the 'love that dare not speak its name' as that 'great affection of an elder for a younger man as there was between David and Jonathan, such as Plato made the very basis of his philosophy, and such as you find in the sonnets of Michelangelo and Shakespeare'.[70]

The past century has seen considerable critical interest in, and debate, about the sonnets, especially following the rise of queer theory and feminist criticism. Central to these debates has been a continuing interest in the biographical status of the sonnets and their treatment of the speaker's love for the young man and the dark lady, which have been seen respectively as homosexual and misogynistic. For many Victorian and early twentieth-century critics, denying that the sonnets were autobiographical was a way of avoiding the suggestion that England's most famous poet may have loved a man. Other more recent scholars have argued against biographical interpretations of the sonnets on the grounds that they cannot be substantiated and that it is simplistic to assume a straightforward connection between writers' lives and their works. Thus in 1977 Stephen Booth famously dismissed those who would read the sonnets for information about Shakespeare's own sexuality, playfully observing that 'William Shakespeare was almost certainly homosexual, bisexual, or heterosexual. The sonnets provide no evidence on the matter'.[71] As such comments suggest, modern debates about the autobiographical status of the sonnets have been bound up with debates about the nature of the poet's love for the young man. While some critics argue that the love is homosexual, others contend that the 'Fair Youth' poems celebrate platonic male love in a way that was conventional in an era which prized male friendship and 'love' above men's relationships with women.

Part of the explanation for these differences of opinion lies in the variations between the sonnets apparently addressed to the young man (1–126). In some (such as Sonnets 1–17) the poet adopts the role of a friendly counsellor, whereas other poems more closely resemble conventional heterosexual love sonnets, and thus carry an erotic charge. Perhaps most contentious of all is 'Sonnet 20' in which the poet-speaker writes of his frustrated love for his 'master-mistress', a man whose beauty resembles that of a woman.

Since the late twentieth century, feminist critics have been similarly interested in Shakespeare's representation of the dark lady. Critics have long recognised that the woman in Shakespeare's sonnets does not conform to Petrarchan tradition, but some have gone further and argued that Shakespeare's characterisation of the poet's mistress is misogynistic and that the sonnets stereotype and stigmatise women. A good example of the latter tendency is found in 'Sonnet 144', in which the dark lady is demonised as an evil, sexually diseased, angel who corrupts the beautiful young man. But the same misogyny does not characterise all of the dark lady poems. Some are conventionally flattering and playful, like 'Sonnet 128' in which the poet desires a kiss from his piano-playing mistress, while in other sonnets (such as 'Sonnet 138') the poet's characterisation of his mistress as false is tempered by his acknowledgement of his own readiness to lie and deceive.

The unconventionality of the dark lady poems and their specific preoccupation with female promiscuity has led some modern scholars to argue that they, and the poet's love for an adulterous woman, would have been more controversial and transgressive in Shakespeare's time than his homoerotic poems about male love. As Margreta De Grazia explains, English Renaissance society was generally more concerned with promiscuous women and the threat illegitimate births posed to the status quo than they were with the possibility of sex between men.[72]

THE LYRIC: JOHN DONNE, 'SONGS AND SONETS' (1633)

John Donne (1572–1631) is one of the early seventeenth century's most influential and original poets. He experimented with a number of poetic genres but most of his poetry (like that of his contemporaries) was lyrical. Like many gentlemen-poets of the period, Donne preferred to circulate his poetry in manuscript rather than print, but a collection of his poetry was published posthumously (1633). This included Donne's 'Songs and Sonets', although they were not given this title until the second edition of his poetry appeared (1635). The 1633 edition of Donne's poetry helped to set a precedent for the publication of single-authored poetry collections (as noted above) and demonstrated the flexibility and richness of the lyric mode. The poems which make up the 'Songs and Sonets' cannot be precisely dated but are thought to have been written in the 1590s or 1600s.[73]

Although formally and metrically varied, the poems collected in the 'Songs and Sonets' share a distinctive style and some common themes. Like a growing number of English poets in the seventeenth century, Donne rejected the high-flown rhetoric that had come to be associated with courtly Petrarchan verse in favour of a plain style and a colloquial, conversational voice. As Achsah Guibbory notes, the poems often 'presume an occasion which has prompted the speaker's address, and some open with a dramatic outburst', spoken to an imagined hearer.[74] This lends Donne's lyrics a sense of immediacy and drama. At the same time, Donne invests his sequence of poems with variety by adopting different personae. It is probably no coincidence that he was writing at a time when the popular stage was flourishing. Like the plays he would have watched, Donne's 'Songs and Sonets' offer us a procession of different lovers and perspectives on love, sex and women.

Often the poems are argumentative as well as dramatic. Many involve Donne's speaker either debating with himself or attempting to persuade an assumed addressee to accept his petition or his point of view. C. S. Lewis thought his poems addressed his readers in the same fashion, observing that 'no poet . . . "goes for us" like Donne'.[75] The strong, often forceful voice that Donne's speakers characteristically employ is usually matched by a self-assertiveness and a reluctance to adopt humble or passive postures. For some critics this is part of Donne's consciously 'masculine' poetics and signals his rejection of the traditionally submissive position assigned to the male suitor in Petrarchan love poetry. In similar fashion, the 'Songs and Sonets' favour a realistic rather than an idealistic handling of love and eschew the Petrarchan preoccupation with chaste, beautiful and unobtainable women. In Donne's love lyrics the women may be beautiful, but they are not necessarily chaste, and are rarely unobtainable. On the contrary, many of his poems are concerned with the celebration of an achieved relationship. In this respect his poems look forward to the sensual love lyrics associated with some of the 'cavalier' poets.

Donne's poetry is similarly distinctive for its use of complex metaphysical conceits (or extended metaphors), a feature that has led many modern critics to describe Donne and his imitators as 'metaphysical poets' (see above). As Samuel Johnson observed in the eighteenth century, Donne's conceits typically involve the 'discovery of occult resemblances in things apparently unlike'.[76] In many cases the analogies that Donne draws are especially surprising or memorable because he draws on 'new sources' of imagery, such as the worlds of 'law, science, philosophy' and New World exploration.[77]

Like his life, Donne's poetry was shaped by two main concerns: love and religious salvation. While his obsession with the fate of his soul finds its most vivid expression in his 'Holy Sonnets' and hymns, the lyrics which make up the 'Songs and Sonets' represent his fullest and 'most complicated exploration of love'.[78] The sequence is especially distinctive for its voicing of multiple, sometimes contradictory, views of love and for the critical debates it has prompted. In some poems (such as 'Love's Alchemy') Donne's speaker is sceptical and bitter: he rejects the possibility of spiritual love and intellectual companionship between men and women as an 'imposture', and insists that 'love' is nothing more than physical desire.[79] By contrast, other poems (such as 'The Undertaking') idealise spiritual unions and insist upon love's emotional and intellectual dimension. Others again (such as 'The Ecstasy') stress the equal importance of physical and spiritual love, and suggest that true love involves the marrying of bodies and souls and that: 'Love's mysteries in souls do grow', while 'the body is his book' (lines 71, 72).

Many of Donne's lyrics prize mutual love in a way that was similarly innovative for the time and atypical of Petrarchan love poetry. In several cases, Donne celebrates mutual love by defining it as akin, or superior, to the public world of the court and the state. This includes favouring the world of love before that of the court and using royal and political analogies to describe his lovers, as in 'The Sun Rising' where the poet-lover claims that he and his lover are the true centre of the world and that he is its true monarch (lines 21–30). Such metaphors claim for the lovers' relationship the kind of power and significance associated with the public sphere and its rulers. It is perhaps no coincidence that most of the poems celebrating mutual love were written at a time when Donne was largely excluded from the political sphere by his controversial elopement with Ann More (1601). Like his poet-lovers Donne had a vested interest in showing love to be as significant and as rewarding as public or political power and service.

In other poems Donne attempts to lend a similar importance to love by describing it in sacred terms or by arguing for its power to sanctify lovers. Thus, in 'The Canonization' Donne's speaker provocatively imagines himself and his beloved being 'canonized' for their embodiment of true love (line 36). In similar fashion, the poet-lover of 'The Relic' appropriates the language of religious 'miracles' to describe the love he shares with his mistress, and, looking forward to the future, imagines their bodies being dug up and revered like holy relics (lines 12–23). Such images come close to sacred parody but are, implicitly, a way of suggesting the profundity of the love they describe. In a similar fashion, many of Donne's religious lyrics use provocative metaphors of erotic and married love to express and to humanise the speaker's love for God and the Church.

Variations between the poems make generalising about Donne's portrayal of love in the 'Songs and Sonets' difficult. Tilottama Rajan suggests that this is deliberate and a way of resisting a definitive perspective on passion. In her view the juxtaposition of contrasting poems makes the sequence 'continually self-reversing' so that 'the reader can no more find a resting place in the worldly cynicism of the profane poems than in the neo-platonic romanticism of the poems of mutual love'.[80]

Donne's lyrics offer similarly contradictory perspectives on women. In some poems, such as 'The Undertaking' and 'The Relic', the beloved woman is idealised. Others downplay gender differences or imply a degree of emotional and spiritual equality atypical of the period and its poetry (see, for example, 'The Good Morrow'). Other lyrics are overtly sexist or misogynist. Several poems (including 'Community') present women as only good for men's sexual 'use', while others stereotype women as fickle and false. Such negative stereotyping of women was not unusual in the period, but John Carey argues that Donne's preoccupation with female falsehood veils a deeper anxiety about his own capacity to break 'faith' (exemplified by his conversion from Catholicism to Protestantism): 'What seems to happen is that Donne, in the fantasy world of the poems, rids himself of his disloyalty by transferring it to women, and directing against them the execrations which he could be seen as meriting.'[81]

Donne's emphasis on masculine rule in love and his typical refusal to adopt the traditional Petrarchan role of the suppliant lover have led other critics to interpret his love lyrics politically. For some scholars they are evidence that he shared the disaffection with the Elizabethan regime and female rule common amongst many aspiring young men and courtiers associated with the Earl of Essex at the turn of the seventeenth century. Others see it as a more specific reaction against Donne's political marginalisation and disempowerment following his impetuous marriage. Within the world of love, Donne's lovers get to reign and exercise a power denied to their author in the public sphere for much of his career by his romantic but rash marriage to a woman his social superior.

THE COUNTRY-HOUSE POEM

The English 'country-house' poem is an invention of the early seventeenth century and is defined by its praise of a country-house estate and its (typically male) owner. Conventionally, such poems praise the house and master as embodying an ideal way of life or model social values. Sometimes this involves contrasting the estate and its master with other houses and lords; more often they are contrasted with the corruption associated with the city and the court. The country-house poet's conventional idealisation of country-house living often includes likening life on the estate to that in the classical Golden Age or the Garden of Eden, and suggesting that nature provides freely of her riches. In similar fashion, the country house and its master are usually praised for their up-holding of traditional customs of hospitality and for the sense of community that this fosters between tenants, neighbours, servants and the noble family.

The main influences on the genre are classical, including the pastoral and georgic poetry of Virgil, and the satirical verse of Horace, Martial and Pliny. Like the poets they imitated, the authors of the early English country-house poems are generally semi-professional writers. The perspective offered is thus usually that of an outsider, although the poems are often based on the poet's experience of visiting the estate described, and the host is usually an actual or desired patron.

The pioneers of English country-house poetry appear to have been Aemilia Lanyer and Ben Jonson. Lanyer's 'Description of Cookham' was the first country-house poem to be published (1611), but Ben Jonson's 'To Penshurst' (1616) may have been written around the same time or earlier. The other best known country-house poems from the period are Ben Jonson's 'To Sir Robert Wroth' (1616), Thomas Carew's 'To Saxham' and 'To My Friend G. N. from Wrest' (1640), Robert Herrick's 'A Panegyric to Sir Lewis Pemberton' (1648), and Andrew Marvell's 'Upon Appleton House' (written 1651). Lanyer's country-house poem is the most famous by a woman in the period but she is not the only seventeenth-century poetess to have written in the genre. Katherine Austen's unpublished manuscript commonplace book, likewise, includes a country-house poem about her family's estate, 'On the Situation of Highbury' (written 1665).[82]

How and why country-house poetry emerged in the early seventeenth century is a thornier question and one which has prompted much debate. The revived taste for authors such as Horace and Martial and the turn of the century fashion for satirical verse forms such as epigrams and verse epistles appear to have been one factor in its emergence. Another appears to have been the growing anxiety about urbanisation and the decline of traditional hospitality in the Stuart era. Although the early seventeenth century saw many nobles and gentlemen build or improve their country houses, the rural aristocracy and the gentle classes as a whole were spending more time in the City. In a political culture in which the monarch and the central government relied on nobles and gentlemen to oversee regional communities this was a matter of concern: their non-residence threatened to undermine effective regional government and risked making those outside the metropolis feel politically marginalised. James I and Charles I were both troubled by the migration of nobles and gentlemen to London and issued proclamations calling on them to return to the country. In their praise of country living and their prizing of hospitality, the period's country-house poems can be seen as reflecting the same desire to encourage a return to country-living and traditional customs amongst the ruling classes.

Ben Jonson, 'To Penshurst' (1616)

Ben Jonson's 'To Penshurst' celebrates the Kentish country house of Sir Robert Sidney, later Lord Lisle, brother of Sir Philip Sidney and father of Lady Mary Wroth. The house was originally built in the fourteenth century by Sir John de Pulteney but was granted to the Sidney family in 1552 by Edward VI. Like the country-house poems of his successors, Jonson's 'To Penshurst' is indebted to the georgic poetry of Virgil, the satiric verse of Horace and Martial, and the neo-classical tradition of epideictic verse (that is, poetry in praise or blame of someone or something). Like Martial's 'Epigram III' (58), which contrasts the model Baian villa of Faustinus with the villa of Bassus, Jonson's 102-line poem idealises Penshurst and its owner and characterises them as exceptional through implicit comparisons with other estates and lords.

That the poem is to be both a celebration of Penshurst and Sidney, and a veiled critique of other houses and nobles is hinted at in the opening lines when Jonson (1572–1637) begins by defining the estate in terms of what it is not: 'Thou art not, Penshurst, built to envious show'.[83] Implicitly, Jonson contrasts Penshurst with the era's fashionable 'prodigy houses', country houses built (or remodelled) at great expense in the early modern period and designed to be visually impressive rather than homely or utilitarian. Unlike these 'showy' houses (of which Jonson is critical), Penshurst is praised as 'an ancient pile' (line 4) whose beauties lie in its attractive natural location (lines 7–9) and its fertility. Drawing on the myth of the Golden Age Jonson suggests that the estate is so benign and rich in natural resources that the creatures of the estate offer

themselves up willingly for consumption. Thus the 'painted' par-
tridges are described as 'willing to be killed' (lines 29, 30), and the
'fat aged carps' are said to 'run into' the 'net' (line 33). The estate's
orchards are described as similarly bountiful, supplying the family
with an array of soft, and exotic fruits, including cherries, plums,
figs, grapes, quinces, apricots and peaches (lines 41–3).

Jonson is equally keen to stress the generosity of the Sidney
household and thus builds on his praise for the natural riches of the
estate with an account of the warm hospitality extended to those
received within its walls. At the same time, he is careful to note that
those walls were 'reared with no man's ruin, no man's groan' (line
46). By implication, the same could not be said of all country houses
in the period. Part of the explanation for the benign relationship
between Penshurst and its tenants appears to be found in the
Sidneys' moderate way of life and their even-handed generosity.
According to Jonson, not only do 'all come in' (line 48), but they
enjoy the same welcome and the 'lord's own meat' (line 62).
Jonson's well-documented taste for good food and wine and his sensitivity about his relatively humble social origins perhaps explain
his special appreciation of this seemingly egalitarian generosity and
the detailed attention he pays the experience of dining at the hall,
observing: 'Here no man tells my cups; nor standing by, / A waiter
doth my gluttony envy, / But gives me what I call, and lets me eat'
(lines 67–9). It was an example of aristocratic hospitality that contrasted with Jonson's experience of Theobalds, the neighbouring
estate of Lord Salisbury, and one of the 'showy' houses that Jonson
may have been criticising in the opening lines of the poem. During
a visit to the latter in 1607 Jonson became disgruntled when he was
served a different meal from his host.

As a final proof of Penshurst's unpretentious hospitality, Jonson
alludes to the warm and 'sudden cheer' (line 82) which reputedly
greeted King James and his son Prince Henry when they paid an
unexpected visit to the house, despite the absence of its mistress,
Lady Sidney. Jonson's commendation of Lady Sidney's house-
wifery leads on to the poem's most direct praise for Sidney and his
family, and to some of Jonson's most overt social satire. Lady
Sidney is celebrated for being 'noble, fruitful and chaste' and for
providing Sidney with children he 'may call his own, / A fortune in

this age but rarely known' (lines 91–2). While Lady Sidney is held up as a model wife, Jonson's bitter after-comment suggests that she is exceptional and that contemporary women are more often promiscuous and unchaste. Similarly, Jonson makes a point of praising Sidney and his wife for teaching their children and their household to value piety (lines 93–7), a commendation that suggests that few parents set their children or their servants a similar example. The poem closes much as it begins with an address to Penshurst, but this time, as well as distinguishing Penshurst from other houses, it distinguishes Sidney from other Lords, suggesting that he has created a home not simply a grand house (lines 99–102).

'To Penshurst' is probably the best known of the early seventeenth-century country-house poems and has been much discussed. Often the poem has been taken at face value and interpreted as a work of artful flattery, designed to earn the patronage of Sir Robert Sidney. Others suggest that the poem is as much a work of topical satire as a work of self-interested flattery, in which Penshurst and its Lord serve primarily as social and ethical models against which Jonson's contemporaries can be measured and criticised. Similarly, while some critics have found Jonson's hyperbolic commendation of Penshurst playful, others have condemned his praise as sycophantic. Following the example of Marxist critic, Raymond Williams, some later twentieth-century scholars have also criticised Jonson for his suggestion that the work of Penshurst's labourers 'is all done for them by a natural order'.[84]

More recent researchers have suggested that Jonson's praise of Penshurst and its Lord is both more realistic and more complicated than earlier critics recognised. Among the first scholars to reassess the poem was J. C. A. Rathmell (1971). He used his research amongst the Sidney family papers to demonstrate that Jonson's praise of Penshurst and the Sidney household was (implicitly) based on first-hand knowledge of the estate and the family. At the same time, his discovery that Lord Lisle was in a 'desperate financial position' during this period suggested that Jonson's praise for the estate's natural beauties and the family's 'homely virtues' may have been didactically pointed (rather than sycophantic), serving as 'a tactful means of reconciling Lord Lisle to living within his means and of persuading him that his inability to emulate the magnificence of wealthier courtiers, so far from being a cause for shame, is in fact a matter for congratulation'.[85]

Aemilia Lanyer, 'The Description of Cookham' (1611)

Aemilia Lanyer's (1569–1645) 'Description of Cookham' was the first country-house poem to be published in English but has only received sustained scholarly attention in the last thirty years following the rise of feminist criticism. Like 'To Penshurst', Lanyer's 210-line 'Description' combines praise of a place with praise of a noble patron: Lady Margaret Clifford, Countess of Cumberland. Lady Margaret stayed at Cookham in Berkshire between 1603 and 1605 during her protracted legal dispute with her estranged husband about her daughter's right to inherit the Clifford estates. Lanyer's 'Description' suggests that she, too, stayed at Cookham.

In its focus on a Lady, rather than a Lord, and a female community seemingly devoid of men, Lanyer's 'Description' is in keeping with Lanyer's sustained interest in praising her sex in her collection *Salve Deus Rex Judaeorum* (see above) but atypical of later country-house poems which tend to concentrate on the celebration of a Lord. The poem is similarly distinctive in its tone. Unlike 'To Penshurst' which is celebratory in its evocation of the Sidney estate, Lanyer's poem is elegiac and nostalgic, offering a lament for a lost female community. The elegiac quality of the poem is signalled from the beginning when Lanyer chooses to open her verse with the word 'Farewell'.[86] In presenting her poem as a 'farewell' to a place Lanyer signals her debt to Virgil's 'First Eclogue', while her subsequent emphasis upon the exemplary country-life of the Countess and her household at Cookham is indebted to Martial's Epigram on the Baian villa of Faustinus and Horace's 'Epode II'.

Unlike many other country-house poems which move from a description of the grounds and house to an account of the patron, Lanyer 'constructs her poem largely in terms of the person addressed' and frames her celebration of the Countess's virtue and piety with an account of the effect her arrival and departure has on the poet and the estate at Cookham.[87] The first part of

Lanyer's elegy describes the joy the coming of the Countess appears to provoke (lines 17–75). Not only does she claim that 'the house received all ornaments to grace it' (line 19), but she describes the natural world on the estate as being glad of her presence (see lines 19–26). In attributing human emotions to inanimate objects, Lanyer adopts the technique of pathetic fallacy, and emphasises the Countess's goodness by suggesting it is recognised even by the natural world. The same device is repeated in the closing sequence of the poem to describe the Countess's departure from Cookham. Just as nature hurried to welcome her so the grounds mimic the poet's sadness and are described as mourning Lady Clifford's departure ('Methought each thing did unto sorrow frame', line 132).

The poem is similarly distinctive in the way that it praises its patron. Other country-house poems tend to celebrate their dedicatees as socially and ethically exemplary, whereas Lanyer praises Lady Clifford more specifically as a model of religious piety, describing how she studies the natural world for proof of God's power, meditates on the Bible, and communes with 'Christ and his apostles' (line 82). In this respect the portrait at the heart of the poem is akin to those offered in saints' lives and to Lanyer's celebration of Biblical heroines and Christ in her religious title-poem. Lanyer's focus on religion and her Christian idealisation of the Countess and her life in the 'Description' have led some critics to describe the idyllic female community at Cookham as a 'redeemed' female Eden, while the poem itself has been described as having more in common with the genre of the devotional lyric than the country-house poem.[88]

On the other hand, Lanyer's praise for the Countess's piety and her professions of love sit uneasily alongside the speaker's discontent about her subsequent separation from the Countess. It is perhaps especially interesting that Lanyer's most overt praise for the Countess (and her daughter) is followed by a digression in which she laments the fact that her social circumstances prevent her from enjoying a sustained friendship with the women, 'so great a difference is there in degree' (line 106). Lanyer's speaker blames Fortune for the separation of herself and the Clifford women but at least some critics (such as Lisa Schnell) think that such comments betray an anger with, and ambivalence about, her great friends which complicates the praise she elsewhere accords them.[89]

A similar ambiguity has been detected in Lanyer's final image for the relationship between the poet-speaker and her patron. Lanyer promises that her poetry will preserve Lady Clifford's name, while the poet's heart will preserve her virtues 'so long as life remains, / Tying my life to her by those rich chains' (lines 209–10). While Lanyer's desire to preserve the Countess's memory and her praise for her virtue suggests her admiration for Lady Clifford, the figuring of their relationship in terms of 'rich chains' is ambiguous. It implies a connection which is precious but also restrictive, and suggests that Lanyer's position as lower-class poet is akin to that of a slave, rather than a loyal servant or friend. Like Jonson she (implicitly) wrestles with the role of artist-servant to the aristocratic classes and is as troubled by class as gender inequalities. For this reason, critics such as Ann Baynes Coiro have suggested that it is more useful to think about Lanyer's work in relation to that of socially aspiring writers such as Jonson, than that of the period's aristocratic women.[90]

SUMMARY OF KEY POINTS

- **General**: Poetry was traditionally the most prestigious literary genre. Some contemporaries felt its status had declined but poetry writing thrived in the Renaissance. Poetry was predominantly a social art, which actively engaged with the world in which the poet lived.
- **Influences**: Classical poetry was a major influence on English Renaissance poetry, but writers also borrowed from native and contemporary European poetic traditions.
- **Contexts**: In the sixteenth century poetry was a genre closely identified with the court and ideas of courtliness. In the seventeenth century poets paid more attention to the city and the country.
- **Circulation**: The sixteenth century witnessed the development of printed poetry collections but manuscript circulation continued to be important especially amongst gentlemen and women poets.

- **Fashions:** The two most fashionable poetic genres in late sixteenth-century England were pastoral and the sonnet. Turn of the century poetry was dominated by satire; early seventeenth-century poetry was mostly lyrical.
- **Women's Writing:** Women were generally discouraged from writing or publishing but women's poetry appears to have flourished in the early modern period. Religious poetry is especially common but some women wrote secular verse (such as love poetry), too.
- **Pastoral:** Pastoral poetry focuses on shepherds and idealises country life. Traditionally, it was the humblest poetic genre, but there was a classical tradition of using pastoral to comment covertly on political issues, and a Christian tradition of equating shepherds with Christ and his ministers. The latter led some Medieval and Renaissance poets to use pastoral as a vehicle for ecclesiastical satire.
- **Epic:** Epic poems are defined by their ambitious scale, their elevated language and their focus on a legendary hero or the fate of a nation. According to classical tradition, epic was the most prestigious literary genre. Spenser was one of the few English poets to write epic.
- **Epyllion:** The epyllion (or mini-epic) flourished briefly in England in the 1590s. They are narrative poems, usually concerned with erotic love, and often inspired by Ovid.
- **Sonnets:** The sonnet was invented in thirteenth-century Italy and popularised across Europe by Petrarch. The genre was pioneered in England in the early sixteenth century by Wyatt and Surrey but enjoyed its greatest vogue in the 1590s.
- **Lyric:** Lyric poetry flourished in the sixteenth century but dominated English poetry in the early seventeenth century, as an understanding of the genre as verse intended for singing gave way to the modern conception of the lyric as a short contemplative poem about the speaker's emotions or state of mind.
- **Country-House poems:** The English 'country-house' poem borrows from the poetry of Horace and Martial but is an invention of the early seventeenth century, and defined by its praise of a country house estate and its (typically male) owner.

NOTES

1. Sir Philip Sidney, *The Defence of Poesy*, in *The Major Works*, ed. Katherine Duncan-Jones (Oxford: Oxford University Press, 2002), p. 216.
2. Ibid., p. 248.
3. Peter Hyland, *An Introduction to Shakespeare's Poems* (Basingstoke: Palgrave Macmillan, 2003), p. 60.
4. Gary Waller, *English Poetry of the Sixteenth Century* (London: Longman, 1986), pp. 221–2.
5. Michelle O'Callaghan, 'Publication: Print and Manuscript', in *A Companion to English Renaissance Literature and Culture*, ed. Michael Hattaway (Oxford: Blackwell, 2003), pp. 81–94 (pp. 85–6).
6. Waller, p. 79.
7. See Arthur F. Marotti, ' "Love is not love": Elizabethan Sonnet Sequences and the Social Order', *ELH*, 49 (1982), 396–428.
8. Lisa Hopkins and Matthew Steggle, *Renaissance Literature and Culture* (London: Continuum, 2006), p. 67.
9. Diana E. Henderson, 'Love Poetry', in *A Companion to English Renaissance Literature and Culture*, ed. Michael Hattaway (Oxford: Blackwell, 2003), pp. 378–91 (p. 381).
10. Heather Dubrow, 'Lyric Forms', in *The Cambridge Companion to English Literature 1500–1600*, ed. Arthur F. Kinney (Cambridge: Cambridge University Press, 2004), pp. 178–99 (p. 189).
11. Margaret Patterson Hannay, 'Herbert [Sidney], Mary, countess of Pembroke (1561–1621)', *Oxford Dictionary of National Biography* (2004), http://www.oxforddnb.com/view/article/1340, accessed 18 October 2007.
12. Betty S. Travitsky, 'Whitney, Isabella (fl. 1566–1573)', *Oxford Dictionary of National Biography* (2004), http//www.oxforddnb.com/view/article/45498, accessed 18 October 2007.
13. Sidney, *Defence*, p. 229.
14. Louis Adrian Montrose, ' "Of gentlemen and shepherds": The Politics of Elizabethan Pastoral Form', *ELH*, 50 (1983), 415–59.
15. Michelle O'Callaghan, 'Pastoral', in *A Companion to English Renaissance Literature and Culture*, ed. Michael Hattaway (Oxford: Blackwell, 2003), pp. 307–16 (p. 308).

16. Edmund Spenser, *The Shorter Poems*, ed. Richard A. McCabe (London: Penguin, 1999), p. 516.

17. John N. King, 'Spenser's *Shepheardes Calender* and Protestant Pastoral Satire', in *Renaissance Genres: Essays on Theory, History, and Interpretation*, ed. Barbara Kiefer Lewalski (Cambridge, MA: Harvard University Press, 1986), pp. 369–98 (p. 375); McCabe, p. xiv.

18. Edmund Spenser, *The Shepheardes Calender*, in *The Shorter Poems*, ed. Richard A. McCabe (London: Penguin, 1999), 'January', lines 43–6. Subsequent references to the poem are given in the text.

19. See L. A. Montrose, '"Eliza, Queen of Shepheardes", and the Pastoral of Power', *ELR*, 10 (1980), 153–82; Richard Helgerson, *Self-Crowned Laureates: Spenser, Jonson, Milton, and the Literary System* (Berkeley, CA: University of California Press, 1983).

20. J. Martin Evans, 'Lycidas', in *The Cambridge Companion to Milton*, ed. Dennis Danielson (Cambridge: Cambridge University Press, 1997), pp. 35–50 (p. 35).

21. Ibid., p. 37.

22. Ibid., p. 39.

23. Stella P. Revard, 'Lycidas', in *A Companion to Milton*, ed. Thomas N. Corns (Oxford: Blackwell, 2001), pp. 246–60 (p. 247).

24. John Milton, 'Lycidas', in *The Norton Anthology of English Literature*, ed. Stephen Greenblatt et al., 8th edn (London: Norton, 2006), I, p. 1806. Subsequent references to the poem are given in the text.

25. Revard, p. 255.

26. Michael Wilding, 'John Milton: the early works', in *The Cambridge Companion to English Poetry. Donne to Marvell*, ed. Thomas N. Corns (Cambridge: Cambridge University Press, 1998), pp. 221–41 (p. 230).

27. David Norbrook, *Poetry and Politics in the English Renaissance*, revised edn (Oxford: Oxford University Press, 2002), p. 57.

28. Wilding, p. 238.

29. Ibid., p. 237.

30. Edmund Spenser, *The Faerie Queene*, ed. A. C. Hamilton et al., 2nd edn (London: Longman, 2007), p. 716. Subsequent references to this edition are given in the text.
31. Norbrook, p. 107.
32. Elizabeth Heale, *The Faerie Queene: A Reader's Guide*, 2nd edn (Cambridge: Cambridge University Press, 1999), p. 23.
33. Ibid., p. 50.
34. Stephen Greenblatt, *Renaissance Self-Fashioning: From More to Shakespeare* (Chicago, IL: Chicago University Press, 1980), p. 172.
35. Heale, p. 92.
36. Ibid., p. 97.
37. Norbrook, p. 128.
38. See Hamilton, *The Faerie Queene*, p. 17.
39. Robin Sowerby, *The Classical Legacy in Renaissance Poetry* (London: Longman, 1994), p. 293.
40. Coppélia Kahn, '*Venus and Adonis*', in *The Cambridge Companion to Shakespeare's Poetry*, ed. Patrick Cheney (Cambridge: Cambridge University Press, 2007), pp. 72–89 (p. 74); Hyland, p. 62.
41. Sowerby, p. 291.
42. Hyland, p. 57.
43. Christopher Marlowe, *Hero and Leander*, in *The Norton Anthology of English Literature*, ed. Stephen Greenblatt et al., 8th edn (London: Norton, 2006), I, line 537. Subsequent references to the poem are given in the text.
44. Kahn, p. 75.
45. Georgia E. Brown, 'Marlowe's poems and classicism', in *The Cambridge Companion to Christopher Marlowe*, ed. Patrick Cheney (Cambridge: Cambridge University Press, 2004), pp. 106–26 (pp. 116–17).
46. Alan Sinfield, 'Marlowe's Erotic Verse', in *Early Modern English Poetry: A Critical Companion*, ed. Patrick Cheney et al. (Oxford: Oxford University Press, 2007), pp. 125–35 (p. 132).
47. Bruce R. Smith, *Homosexual Desire in Shakespeare's England: A Cultural Poetics* (Chicago, IL: University of Chicago Press, 1994), p. 132.
48. Hyland, p. 57.

49. Kahn, p. 77.
50. William Shakespeare, *Venus and Adonis*, in *The Norton Shakespeare*, ed. Stephen Greenblatt et al. (London: Norton, 1997), lines 1135–40. Subsequent references to the poem are given in the text.
51. A. Robin Bowers, ' "Hard Armours" and "Delicate Amours" in Shakespeare's *Venus and Adonis*', *ShSt*, 12:1 (1979), 1–23 (1, 2).
52. Sowerby, p. 297.
53. John Doebler, 'The Many Faces of Love: Shakespeare's *Venus and Adonis*', *ShSt*, 16 (1983), 33–43 (33).
54. Catherine Belsey, 'Love as Trompe-l'oeil: Taxonomies of Desire in *Venus and Adonis*', *SQ*, 46 (1995), 257–76 (265, 266).
55. See Doebler, p. 38.
56. Kahn, p. 83.
57. Ibid., p. 84.
58. Michael Spiller, *Early Modern Sonneteers: From Wyatt to Milton* (Tavistock: Northcote House, 2001), p. 18.
59. Waller, p. 89.
60. Sasha Roberts, 'Shakespeare's Sonnets and English Sonnet Sequences', in *Early Modern English Poetry: A Critical Companion*, ed. Patrick Cheney et al. (Oxford: Oxford University Press, 2007), pp. 172–83 (p. 173).
61. Marotti, p. 400.
62. Sir Philip Sidney, *Astrophil and Stella*, in *The Major Works*, ed. Katherine Duncan-Jones (Oxford: Oxford University Press, 2002), 'Sonnet 1', line 14. Subsequent references to the sonnets are given in the text.
63. A. C. Hamilton, *Sir Philip Sidney: A Study of his Life and Works* (Cambridge: Cambridge University Press, 1977), p. 87.
64. Alan Sinfield, *Literature in Protestant England, 1560–1660* (London: Croom Helm, 1983), p. 56.
65. Waller, p. 141; Hamilton, *Sir Philip Sidney*, p. 105.
66. Margreta De Grazia, 'The Scandal of Shakespeare's Sonnets', *ShS*, 46 (1993), 35–49 (40–1).
67. A. L. Rowse, *Shakespeare's Sonnets, The Problems Solved*, 2nd edn (London: Macmillan, 1973), pp. xxxiv–xlii.

68. *The Norton Shakespeare*, ed. Stephen Greenblatt et al. (London: Norton, 1997), 'Sonnet 129', lines 1, 6–7. Subsequent references to the sonnets are given in the text.

69. J. B. Leishman, *Themes and Variations in Shakespeare's Sonnets*, 2nd edn (London: Hutchinson, 1963), pp. 99–100.

70. Cited in Paul Edmundson and Stanley Wells, *Shakespeare's Sonnets* (Oxford: Oxford University Press, 2004), p. 140.

71. *Shakespeare's Sonnets*, ed. Stephen Booth (New Haven, CT: Yale University Press, 1977), p. 548.

72. De Grazia, p. 48.

73. John Donne, *The Major Works*, ed. John Carey (Oxford: Oxford University Press, 2000), p. xxiii.

74. Achsah Guibbory, 'John Donne', in *The Cambridge Companion to English Poetry. Donne to Marvell*, ed. Thomas N. Corns (Cambridge: Cambridge University Press, 1998), pp. 123–47 (p. 126).

75. C. S. Lewis, 'Donne and Love Poetry in the Seventeenth Century (1938)', in *Donne, Songs and Sonets: A Casebook*, ed. Julian Lovelock (Basingstoke: Macmillan, 1990), pp. 113–33 (p. 117).

76. Cited in Guibbory, p. 127.

77. Lewis, p. 116.

78. Guibbory, p. 134.

79. John Donne, 'Love's Alchemy', in *The Major Works*, ed. John Carey (Oxford: Oxford University Press, 2000), line 6. Subsequent references to this edition are given in the text.

80. Tilottama Rajan, ' "Nothing sooner broke": Donne's *Songs and Sonets* as Self-Consuming Artefact', in *John Donne: New Casebooks*, ed. Andy Mousley (London: Macmillan, 1999), pp. 45–62 (p. 57).

81. John Carey, *John Donne: Life, Mind and Art*, new edn (London: Faber & Faber, 1990), p. 24.

82. See *Early Modern Women Poets: An Anthology*, ed. Jane Stevenson and Peter Davidson (Oxford: Oxford University Press, 2001), pp. 315–16.

83. Ben Jonson, 'To Penshurst', in *The Norton Anthology of English Literature*, ed. Stephen Greenblatt et al., 8th edn (London:

Norton, 2006), I, line 1. Subsequent references to the poem are given in the text.

84. Raymond Williams, *The Country and The City* (London: Chatto & Windus, 1973), p. 32.

85. J. C. A. Rathmell, 'Jonson, Lord Lisle, and Penshurst', *ELR*, 1 (1971), 250–60 (256).

86. Aemilia Lanyer, 'The Description of Cookham', in *The Norton Anthology of English Literature*, ed. Stephen Greenblatt et al., 8th edn (London: Norton, 2006), I, line 1. Subsequent references to the poem are given in the text.

87. George Parfitt, *English Poetry of the Seventeenth Century*, 2nd edn (London: Longman, 1992), p. 242.

88. Elaine Beilin, *Redeeming Eve: Women Writers of the English Renaissance* (Princeton, NJ: Princeton University Press, 1987), p. 202; Patrick Cook, 'Aemilia Lanyer's "Description of Cooke-ham" as Devotional Lyric', in *Discovering and (Re)covering the Seventeenth-Century Religious Lyric*, ed. E. R. Cunnar and J. Johnson (Pittsburgh, PA: Duquesne University Press, 2001), pp. 104–18.

89. Lisa Schnell, ' "So Great a Difference Is There in Degree": Aemilia Lanyer and the Aims of Feminist Criticism', *MLQ*, 57:1 (1996), 23–35.

90. Ann Baynes Coiro, 'Writing in Service: Sexual Politics and Class Position in the Poetry of Aemilia Lanyer and Ben Jonson', *Criticism*, 35 (1993), 357–76.

CHAPTER 3

Prose

English prose writing thrived in the Renaissance. By the end of the sixteenth century English was the usual language for literature and prose was the dominant, most diverse printed genre. English Renaissance prose has only recently attracted sustained scholarly attention. But, as such research has shown, the period's prose works are rich and varied. Authors used prose to address a wide range of subjects, from politics, religion and history, to crime, travel and domestic life, and they developed a variety of sub-genres, including familiar non-fictional forms, such as treatises and sermons and comparatively new forms such as the essay, the pamphlet and biography. The common modern distinction between non-fiction and fiction had yet to be firmly established, and several prose genres mixed fact and fiction.

Whether they were writing fiction or non-fiction, style was a common concern for Renaissance authors. The rhetorical training young men received at grammar schools and universities emphasised the importance of verbal style and introduced students to traditionally accepted models of stylistic excellence. Most of the models were Greek or Roman but the authors and styles favoured varied across the period, and there was a general shift during the seventeenth century from an emphasis upon linguistic copiousness and variety towards plainer styles of writing.

The most important models for English prose writers were the styles associated with classical authors Cicero and Seneca. The

Ciceronian style is often described as 'round' and rhythmical, because its (usually) long sentences make use of carefully balanced clauses and antitheses. In the early seventeenth century some writers reacted against this prose model, preferring styles which aimed at 'expressiveness rather than formal beauty'.[1] Anti-Ciceronian writers generally favoured or mixed what Morris Croll describes as the 'curt' style and the 'loose' style. The 'curt' style (associated with Seneca) is characterised by its terseness and the 'studied brevity' of its clauses. In this style the first part of a sentence is often 'a self-contained and complete statement of the whole idea of the period'; the other parts may be asymmetrical, rather than balanced, and ordinary linking words are often omitted, giving the whole period an air of compression and succinctness. The 'loose' style or period is characterised by the use of extended sequences of loosely linked clauses.[2]

NON-FICTION

Most English Renaissance prose is non-fictional. The most popular printed prose genres were religious, including sermons, meditations and devotional manuals. The English appetite for religious prose was fostered by the Protestant emphasis on individual worship (see Introduction) and matched by a similar taste for utilitarian literature in the period. The latter underpins the Renaissance fashion for classical and native histories (which were regarded as offering potentially valuable lessons for the present), and the early modern vogue for various forms of advice literature (which ranged from tracts on household government to political and courtly conduct books).

A number of new prose genres became fashionable, too, including the essay, character writing, biography and the pamphlet. Today, the essay is a familiar prose form, but in sixteenth-century England it was a novelty. Some of the earliest essays in English were written by Sir Francis Bacon (see below). He was inspired by the example of classical authors such as Seneca, Cicero and Plutarch, and contemporary French writer, Michel de Montaigne, while the term itself derives from 'the French *essai*, a trial or attempt, and the older French-English "assay", an examination or tasting'.[3]

Like essay writing, character writing became popular in the early seventeenth century. 'Characters' were short prose compositions which described the defining features of different social, moral and/or personality types. The genre was classically inspired, developing from the sketches of Greek author Theophrastus. The first collection of English 'characters' was Bishop Joseph Hall's *Characters of Virtues and Vices* (1608) but the two best known compilations were those of Thomas Overbury (1614) and John Earle (*Microcosmographie*, 1628). These included characters such as 'A good Woman', 'A Dissembler', 'A Courtier', 'A Country Gentleman', 'An idle Gallant' and 'A Player'.

While the popularity of 'character writing' points to a tendency to think of character in stereotypical ways, the increasing interest in biography and auto-biography in the seventeenth century suggests a growing awareness of the individuality of the self. Not only is there more evidence of people keeping diaries and journals, but the period sees the publication of the first 'lives' about, and by, English people. Like contemporary historians, early biographers were often interested in the example afforded by the lives of famous contemporaries. Probably the two best-known early biographers are Sir Fulke Greville and Izaak Walton. Greville famously wrote a biography-cum-Elizabethan-political-history based on the life of his close friend and author, Sir Philip Sidney. His celebratory account of Sidney as a model Christian courtier and soldier (written 1610–14) appeared posthumously as *The Life of the Renowned Sir Philip Sidney* (1652). Izaak Walton's first 'life' (the 'Life of John Donne') appeared around the same period having been written to accompany the edition of Donne's sermons which Walton edited with Henry Wooton (1640). Encouraged by its success, Walton prepared short biographies of four other clerics, including poet George Herbert (1670). Like Greville's, Walton's 'lives' are eulogistic, each holding up its subject as exemplary in his devotion.

Alongside such exemplary 'lives' appeared short accounts which purported to tell the story of infamous criminals, forerunners of the criminal biographies which became popular in the Restoration era. Robert Greene's *The blacke bookes messenger laying open the life and death of Ned Browne one of the most notable cutpurses, crosbiters, and conny-catchers, that euer liued in England* (1592) is a vivid example of the genre. Like Greene's pamphlet, later criminal 'lives' were usually sensational, moralistic and often only pseudo-factual, but they enjoyed a large readership, as did other accounts of rogue life such as 'cony-catching' pamphlets. As Joad Raymond notes, the usual 'premise' of the latter is 'the penetration of the criminal underworld by an honest man, who subsequently exposes their deceitful practices, explaining their confidence tricks, social struc-ture, mores and language'.[4] Popular examples such as Robert Greene's *The Art of Cony-Catching* (1591) combined instruction and entertainment in ways that middle and low-brow readers appear to have found especially appealing.

The 'pamphlet' format (see Glossary) was used for various short prose works, and came to be especially associated with topical issues. In the 1610s, for example, there was a notorious exchange of pamphlets about the nature and status of women, initiated by the publication of Joseph Swetnam's *The Arraignment of Lewde, Idle, Froward, and Vnconstant Women* (1615). The popularity of Swetnam's pamphlet, which castigated women, led to the publica-tion of three pamphlet 'answers', purportedly written by, and defending, women: Rachel Speght's, *A Mouzell for Melastomus* (1617); Ester Sowernam's, *Ester Hath Hang'd Haman* (1617); and Constantia Munda's, *The Worming of a Mad Dogge* (1617).

FICTION

English prose fiction is essentially a creation of the Renaissance: prior to the sixteenth century narratives in English were generally written in verse, not prose. The rising prestige of prose and the gradual shift towards the use of prose for narrative fiction paved the way for the development of the novel in the eighteenth century. Critics have long debated the origins of this important new genre. Some scholars trace it specifically to the prose fictions of the Renaissance and describe them as early novels; others, such as Michael McKeon, suggest that early modern prose romances and novellas are distinct in several ways from the conventionally realistic novels that came later.[5]

In choosing to write prose narratives English Renaissance writers were following the example of classical and contemporary authors of romance such as Heliodorus, Jacopo Sannazaro and Jorge de Montemayor; contemporary European writers of novellas such as François de Belleforest and Matteo Bandello; and Sir Thomas More, who used (Latin) prose for his semi-fictional, political narrative *Utopia* (written 1515–16). The sixteenth-century taste for prose fiction led to the publication of several compilations of translated prose novellas. Among the most popular were William Painter's *The Palace of Pleasure* (1566) and Geoffrey Fenton's *Certaine Tragical Discourses of Bandello* (1567). These collections brought together a variety of classical and contemporary continental stories, some based on recent factual events and ordinary people. They are typically sensational tales of lust and violence but are often moralistic in tone. While English playwrights ransacked such collections for plots and characters, Elizabethan prose writers developed their different modes of narration (with some writers focusing on plot and action, and others on rhetoric and character, as did the novella authors).[6]

The first examples of English prose fiction precede the publication of the popular novella collections but anticipate their experiments with narration. The earliest original prose fiction in English, and, according to some 'the first English novel', is thought to be William Baldwin's anti-Catholic allegory *Beware the Cat* (written 1553, printed 1570).[7] Although it was not printed for some years *Beware the Cat* showed that prose fiction could be used to engage with topical issues and provided a narrative model that was innovative in its use of first-person narration and language as a medium of characterisation.

The 1570s saw the emergence of more original prose fictions. Many shared the preoccupation with intrigue, love and violence found in continental novellas. One of the earliest and most fascinating examples is George Gascoigne's *The Adventures of Master F. J.* (1573). Often read as a satire of courtly love and romance, Gascoigne's fiction tells the story of F. J. and his relationship with two women (Elinor, the woman he desires, and Frances, his friend and confidante). Like *Beware the Cat*, *The Adventures of Master F. J.* mediates its tale of seductions and betrayals through an unreliable narrator (G. T.) and his commentary on a series of letters and poems supposedly written by the lovers.

A similar concern with courtly love characterises the most influential prose fictions of the 1570s and 1580s: John Lyly's *Euphues. The Anatomy of Wit* (1578) and its sequel, *Euphues and his England* (1580). Lyly's first fiction tells the story of Euphues, a clever but arrogant Athenian who travels to Naples and betrays his best friend, Philautus, after they fall in love with the same woman. Later, rueing his conduct, Euphues is reconciled with his friend and returns to Athens to study moral philosophy. In the sequel, Lyly's focus shifts to Philautus and his relationship with the virtuous and beautiful Camilla; Euphues features as 'one of a number of moral guides who the couple encounter on their travels'. At the end Euphues returns to Athens and writes a superficially complimentary description of England intended for the instruction of Italian women.[8] While contemporary readers appear to have enjoyed Lyly's combination of moral instruction and courtly romance, fellow authors especially admired his complex plotting and his artful prose, with its carefully patterned use of antitheses, balanced clauses and elaborate figures of speech.

In the 1590s the fashion for euphuistic fiction gave way to a vogue for prose romances, inspired by the publication of Sir Philip Sidney's *Arcadia* (1590, 1593). Sidney's romance survives in several versions. The first, known as *The Old Arcadia* (written c. 1577–81), consists of five books and is a pastoral romance about the adventures of two princes (Pyrocles and Musidorus). At a later date, Sidney began revising his romance to give more attention to the princes' heroic exploits, but the *New Arcadia* (1590) is incomplete. A composite text was published by Sidney's sister in 1593.

The *Arcadia* established romance as the dominant form of prose fiction and became one of Renaissance England's most widely read and imitated fictions. Some of the most fascinating imitations are those written by women, for whom Sidney's romance appears to have held a special appeal, perhaps because of the central role it assigns its heroines (Pamela and Philoclea). Among the most famous of these works is that produced by Sidney's niece, Lady Mary Wroth. She makes Sidney's shepherdess Urania a central character in her Jacobean romance: *The Countess of Montgomerie's Urania* (1621) (see below).

In *Jack of Newbury (or The Pleasant History of John Winchcombe)* (1597) Thomas Deloney pioneered a new type of prose romance, appropriating the genre's conventions to celebrate the rise to glory and success of a working man, rather than the usually noble protagonists of courtly romance. Other contemporaries parodied romance conventions, producing fictions today described as 'anti-romances'. One of the liveliest examples of the latter is Thomas Nashe's *The Unfortunate Traveller* (1594) (see below).

THE ESSAY: SIR FRANCIS BACON

Sir Francis Bacon (1561–1626) is the best known English Renaissance essayist but he was not the first, nor was essay-writing a wholly new phenomenon. As Floyd Gray notes, 'the essay began to take form in the epistolary writings of Cicero and Seneca' and was popularised, and given its name, by French author Michel de Montaigne, whose first collection of *Essais* appeared in 1580.[9] In England, several authors produced essay-like works in the sixteenth century, but Bacon was the first to publish a sequence of such works and to adopt the term 'essay' to describe them. Like Montaigne, Bacon appears to have been especially attracted to the genre by the implicitly provisional quality of its statements: as an 'attempt' (*essai*) an essay was open to subsequent reconsideration, as Bacon thought meditative works should be. Both authors exploited this possibility, revising their essays throughout their careers. The 1597 edition of Bacon's *Essays* contained only ten essays; in 1612 this was expanded to thirty-eight essays, and in 1625 to fifty-eight essays. As Bacon reveals, he 'enlarged' his *Essays* in 'weight' as well as number not only writing new essays but expanding and rearranging his early compositions.[10]

Bacon's essays sought to offer the reader moral and civil counsel. In this respect they are akin to the various forms of advice literature popular in the period. The topics which Bacon's 1625 *Essays* address are wide-ranging and collectively afford a 'concise user's guide to conduct and survival in the public world of the court'.[11] Although some of the advice Bacon offers is potentially relevant to a wider readership his main (implied) audience is men of a similar social background to himself: individuals who are privileged by birth but who need, or wish, to make their own way in the world. As the younger son of a gentleman in an era in which family property was traditionally inherited by the oldest male heir, Bacon was obliged to pursue a career and enjoyed considerable success, eventually serving as Lord Chancellor before being stripped of public office in 1621 on charges of corruption.

Many of Bacon's *Essays* are concerned with public and political life. This includes essays which explore national issues such as sedition, and essays which concern themselves with the appropriate conduct of individuals involved in the public sphere, such as 'Of Simulation and Dissimulation', 'Of Counsel', and 'Of Suitors'. Other essays are concerned with more abstract ethical and moral topics such as truth, death, envy and love. In the 1612 and 1625 editions Bacon offers his readers advice about private life, too, presenting his recommendations on issues of lifestyle (such as houses and gardens) and on marriage and children. As might be expected of a man who devoted his life to the public sphere, Bacon consistently privileges the public and political over the private and domestic.

In their focus on public life Bacon's essays are very different to those of his famous French contemporary, Montaigne. Montaigne's essays look inwards and are conspicuously personal, whereas Bacon's have been criticised as impersonal: he rarely talks about himself directly and only occasionally uses the first-person pronoun. On the other hand, as critics such as Stanley Fish have pointed out, the advice Bacon offers, especially in the later versions of the *Essays*, is personally inflected, being based not only on his reading of classical, Biblical and contemporary authorities, but on his own experiences.[12]

Bacon's 1597 essays are concise and aphoristic. Most consist of a series of tersely expressed statements. In choosing to write in a 'curt' Senecan manner, Bacon helped to popularise the 'plain' style amongst his contemporaries. Bacon's rejection of Ciceronian style was not simply aesthetic, but philosophical. He objected to its implicit privileging of style over content, arguing that the linguistic elegance of Ciceronian writing gave people the (often false) impression that the knowledge it expressed was definitive. This was particularly problematic in the sciences where Bacon was convinced that there were fresh discoveries to be made, as he discussed in works such as *The Advancement of Learning* (1605).

Bacon's later *Essays* still incorporate aphorisms but are longer and fuller. Not only does Bacon devote more words to each subject, but his sentences are often more complex and he makes greater use of colloquial language and vivid images. Some of Bacon's most effective metaphors and similes are those which discover unexpected correspondences between his chosen subjects and other aspects of the human or natural world. A similar concern with surprising correspondences characterises the metaphysical poetry of contemporaries such as John Donne (see Chapter 2). A good example of Bacon's imaginative use of analogy is found in his essay 'Of Adversity', where he turns to the world of embroidery for an image to help explain his argument that adversity has its merits, including its ability to reveal virtue:

> Prosperity is not without many fears and distastes; and Adversity is not without comforts and hopes. We see in needle-works and embroideries, it is more pleasing to have a lively work upon a sad and solemn ground, than to have a dark and melancholy work upon a lightsome ground: judge therefore of the pleasure of the heart by the pleasure of the eye . . . for Prosperity doth best discover vice, but Adversity doth best discover virtue. (p. 349)

Part of the explanation for this shift towards a fuller style lies in Bacon's conclusion that aphoristic writing was less effective in moral essays; but pithy statements continue to be an important feature of his writing. Many of his essays begin with a dramatic first sentence or pair of sentences, like 'Of Parents and Children' which opens with the poignant observation that: 'The joys of parents are secret; and so are their griefs and fears. They cannot utter the one; nor they will not utter the other' (p. 351). Likewise, although more concerned with establishing a line of argument than many of the 1597 essays, those of 1625 still call upon readers to make some of the connections between observations themselves, as is illustrated by the enigmatic opening of his essay 'Of Truth': ' "What is Truth?" said jesting Pilate; and would not stay for an answer.

Certainly there be [those] that delight in giddiness, and count it a bondage to fix a belief; affecting free-will in thinking, as well as in acting' (p. 341). The connection between Bacon's opening question and the following sentence is not immediately obvious so that readers are invited to engage actively with Pilate's question and Bacon's provisional answer to it.

Questions are a consistent feature of Bacon's essays. He poses many questions during the course of each essay, and teaches readers to be wary of complacently accepting received wisdom. One of the characteristic ways in which he fosters such scepticism is by introducing a 'commonly received notion' and then challenging it through 'the introduction of data that calls' its 'validity into question', as in his essay on 'Usury'.[13] The essay begins by summarising popular criticisms of the practice, which might lead readers to assume that he shares a similarly negative view, but, at the end of his summary, he insists that it is necessary and spends the remainder of the essay considering how usury should be used.

SERMONS AND DEVOTIONS: JOHN DONNE

Religious literature was hugely popular in Renaissance England. Two of the most important types were the sermon and the devotion. Sermons were religious lectures written by clerics for delivery in church, usually based on the interpretation of a selected Biblical quotation. Their primary purpose was to instruct people in Biblical precepts, but preachers were well aware that such teaching was likely to be more effective if delivered in an accessible, memorable manner. Consequently, they often made extensive, sometimes highly sophisticated, use of persuasive rhetorical techniques. Religious devotions were a more private form of religious literature, based on the personal spiritual meditations of their authors. Rather than offering explicit instruction of the kind associated with sermons, printed collections of devotions are usually presented to readers as a model for their own spiritual meditations. Such works had long been a part of Catholic religious culture but enjoyed an even greater vogue in post-Reformation England, as a result of the Protestant emphasis on spiritual self-examination.

Sermons

John Donne (1572–1631) started his literary career as a love poet but became one of the English Renaissance's most famous Anglican preachers, after he was ordained as a minister of the Church of England (1615). Like other preachers, Donne tailored his sermons for individual occasions and audiences. This is perhaps most evident in the sermons he gave at court, many of which are concerned both to display his loyalty to the crown, and to offer the monarch spiritual counsel. The potential tension between these two aims helps to explain why modern critics have not been able to agree about Donne's politics, with some arguing that he was a royalist and others that he belonged to the oppositional court faction.[14]

Donne's preaching was much admired: contemporary accounts testify both to the intellectual brilliance of his texts and to his extraordinary power to move his audiences. Izaak Walton located the force of Donne's preaching in his passionate engagement with his audience and his ability to vary his persuasive mode, describing him as a 'Preacher in earnest weeping sometimes for his Auditory, sometimes with them . . . carrying some, as St *Paul* was, to Heaven in holy raptures, and inticing others by a sacred Art and Courtship to amend their lives'.[15]

Early twentieth-century critics tended to neglect Donne's religious prose in favour of his poetry, but recent scholars have drawn attention to the parallels between them. As in his poetry, Donne is fascinated with paradoxes and surprising correspondences between man and his world, correspondences that he expresses through vivid metaphysical conceits. Some analogies recur several times, such as the paradoxical image of the womb as a grave, the conceptualisation of life as a circle, and the likening of man and the world to books authored by God.[16]

Stylistically, the sermons are varied, mixing elements associated with Ciceronian writing, such as a 'delight in antithesis and rounding off' with features more commonly associated with Senecan writing, such as ellipsis and terseness.[17] A similar diversity characterises Donne's self-representation. In some places he emphasises the difference between himself and his audience, by addressing his listeners as 'you'; in others he emphasises their affinity – for instance, as Christians fighting against sin – by identifying himself with his audience, and speaking as 'us' and 'we'.[18] On other occasions, he presents himself as a representative sinner who mirrors the frailties of his auditors, as in his sermon for Sir William Cockayne's funeral (written 1626). In this he offers a seemingly personal confession of his tendency to 'neglect God and his Angels, for the noise of a Flie, for the ratling of a Coach, for the whining of a doore', but prefaces his admission with an invitation that he and his auditors consider together 'the manifold weaknesses of the strongest devotions in time of Prayer'.[19]

Many of Donne's sermons share a preoccupation with man's personal sinfulness and the importance of spiritual self-examination, and Donne returns time and again to man's mortality and the paradox that life is a kind of death, and death the way to achieve resurrection. The latter preoccupation finds its fullest expression in Donne's final sermon, delivered only weeks before his death on 31 March 1631: 'Deaths Duell, or, A Consolation to the Soule, against the dying Life, and living Death of the Body' (25 February 1631). The sermon is an extended meditation on mortality, taking as its starting point the text: 'And unto God belong the issues of Death' (Psalms 68:20). The sermon interprets the quotation from Psalm 68 in three ways, each of which assumes that death is a form of divine deliverance to be understood through faith.[20]

Devotions

Donne's *Devotions Upon Emergent Occasions* (1624) were written while he recovered from a life-threatening fever (1623). This lends their meditations on mortality a special immediacy. The collection consists of twenty-three 'stations', each of three parts: a meditation, an expostulation and a prayer. Collectively, they chart the passage of Donne's illness, from 'the First Grudging, of the Sickness', to his recovery.[21]

Each 'station' shares a similar dynamic. Thus in the opening 'meditations' Donne's illness generally prompts him to spiritual contemplation on themes suggested by his suffering, such as mortality, personal sinfulness and salvation. His reflections (like his poems and sermons) are characterised by their preoccupation with paradoxes, and the identification of correspondences within and between man's worldly and spiritual lives, some of which will be familiar to readers of his poetry and prose. His conceptualisation of his body as a book, and his likening of his physical and mental self-examination to dissection in Meditation 9 (p. 52), recall analogies found in some of his sermons and in poems such as 'Hymn to God My God, in My Sickness', while Donne's persistent fascination with death and 'types' of grave leads him to liken the sickbed to man's mortal resting place in his third meditation (pp. 13–14). Perhaps most memorable of all is the meditation on mortality prompted by his hearing of a bell tolling. He begins by observing that the bell might toll for someone 'so ill, as that he knows not it tolls for him', possibly even himself. Further reflection leads him to conclude that the bell could be, and is, a sign for him and for all men as: 'any man's death diminishes me, because I am involved in mankind, and therefore never send to know for whom the bell tolls; it tolls for thee' (p. 103).

Donne's 'voice' in the meditations is personal, philosophic and measured. In the 'expostulations' calm reflection gives way to anxious questions and petitions, as Donne fears he may not be saved. Each opens with the same divine invocation and addresses God directly. Although the speaker is generally reverential, he occasionally adopts a more assertive stance, as in his first expostulation, where he boldly insists on his right to ask questions of God (p. 5). Like the 'expostulations', Donne's closing prayers often petition God for forgiveness, but the speaker is generally more submissive and hopeful that divine mercy will be granted. Donne's speakers alternate between assertiveness and humility, despair and hope, in similar fashion, in many of his 'Holy Sonnets' and soul-searching hymns.

ROMANCES

English prose romances flourished in the late Elizabethan period, inspired by the popularity of classical and continental romances such as Heliodorus's *Aethiopian History* (written c. 4th or 5th century AD), Sannazaro's *Arcadia* (1504), and Montemayor's *Diana* (1559). Along with the verse romances of Medieval England, the latter afforded English writers a variety of models for their prose romances and a familiar, but emotionally powerful, set of characteristic 'romance' *topoi* (see Glossary). Although superficially removed from everyday life, many Elizabethan and Stuart prose romances followed classical and contemporary European precedent and used their stories to comment indirectly on topical political and social issues. The potential topicality of prose romances appears to have contributed to the genre's 'low' reputation. While humanist scholars tended to dismiss romance as inferior to epic, others complained that their stories encouraged illicit sex and violence, and were thus a potentially dangerous influence, especially on the young men and women, who were reputed to be among the genre's most avid readers. Others defended romances as educative. As Goran V. Stanivukovic notes, prose romances were potentially a type of conduct book, especially for the young men who made up the bulk of their readership, not only offering recreation but models of 'good speaking' and behaviour.[22]

Renaissance romances were generally neglected by early twentieth-century critics. Growing interest in the genre in the second half of the century changed this and led to more prose romances being made available in modern editions. Some critics have been especially interested in prose romances as forerunners of the novel; others, such as Northrop Frye, have been concerned with their relationship to the broader genre of romance. More recently, there has been considerable interest in their relationship to the context in which they were produced. Whereas it was once usual to regard prose romances as escapist, historicist scholars have drawn attention to the ways in which Elizabethan and Stuart romances engage with topical issues such as gender, sexuality and rule. Similar concerns have underpinned the recent surge of interest in their original readership and women's pioneering role as translators and authors of the genre (see the Guide to Further Reading).

Sir Philip Sidney, *Arcadia* (1590, 1593)

The Old Arcadia (written c. 1577–81)

Sidney (1554–86) appears to have begun writing his first version of the *Arcadia* (or *Old Arcadia*) while temporarily retired from court life following his controversial criticism of Elizabeth I's proposed marriage to the French Duke of Alençon. Discovered for the first time in 1907, the *Old Arcadia* consists of five books, divided by a series of 'eclogues' performed by Arcadian shepherds (see Glossary). The structure of the romance is implicitly modelled on the five acts associated with classical drama, while its story borrows from classical and continental romances.

Sidney's yoking of pastoral and chivalric romance proved influential, as did his periphrastic prose style. Like Lyly before him, Sidney was especially admired for his ability to express ideas in a variety of different but elegantly patterned ways. His sentences are characteristically long, but carefully balanced, making frequent use of verbal parallelism and repetition. Sidney's taste for repetition and inversion was noted by contemporary John Hoskins (c. 1600), who identified antimetabole ('a sentence inverted or turned back' on itself) and synoeciosis (the 'composition of contraries'), as two of the most common rhetorical devices in the *Arcadia*.[23] As Roger Pooley notes, such figures of speech complement Sidney's thematic preoccupation with 'inner conflict and defeated intention'.[24]

Sidney's story takes its name from its traditional pastoral setting. Like Virgil's Arcadia, Sidney's is a seemingly idyllic, harmonious land, ruled over by a benign monarch, King Basilius. The peace of the kingdom is upset, however, when Basilius retreats to the countryside with his wife (Gynecia) and two daughters (Pamela and Philoclea), leaving a trusted deputy (Philanax) to rule in his stead. By retiring from public life Basilius hopes to prevent the fulfilment of an oracle which appears to predict his overthrow. At the same time, two young princes arrive in Arcadia (Musidorus and Pyrocles). The pair (who are cousins) have been travelling the world in seek of heroic adventure but decide to stay in Arcadia after they fall in love with Basilius's daughters. The Princes join the royal family in their pastoral retreat, disguised as a shepherd (Dorcas) and an Amazonian warrior (Cleophila). Complications ensue when the Princesses fall in love with the Princes, and Basilius and Gynecia both become infatuated with the disguised Pyrocles.

Although superficially concerned with a remote land, it is clear that various aspects of Sidney's Arcadia resemble Elizabethan England, and that Sidney uses his tale to comment covertly on topical political issues. Several critics have noted, for example, that there are parallels between the advice Philanax gives Basilius about maintaining his personal rule and the counsel Sidney gave Elizabeth I about not marrying the Duke of Alençon.[25] There is less critical agreement about the work's overall tone and purpose. For some critics, such as Robert Parker, the *Old Arcadia* is a comic work which engages with its genre and its courtly subject matter satirically. For others, such as Franco Marenco it is a 'gloomy, almost desperate book'.[26]

Scholars have been similarly divided in their views of the *Old Arcadia*'s morality. At the heart of these debates has been the princes' conduct. Sidney initially presents Musidorus and Pyrocles as model heroes but their pursuit of the Arcadian princesses leads them to behave in ways which are politically and morally problematic. Not only do they assume disguises which are potentially degrading, but they knowingly deceive Arcadia's monarch and encourage his daughters to defy moral and social conventions: Pyrocles ends up seducing Philoclea outside of marriage, while Musidorus persuades Pamela to elope with him and is only prevented from raping her while she sleeps by the intrusion of a group of bandits. Sidney's resolution of the romance involves a similar moral compromise. Although the princes suffer temporary imprisonment, they ultimately evade any punishment for their misconduct and are, instead, forgiven and rewarded with marriages to the Arcadian princesses.

The New Arcadia (1590)

Prior to his untimely death (1586) Sidney had started a revised version of the *Arcadia*, known as the *New Arcadia*. In its surviving form it is incomplete, consisting of only three books, the final of which ends in mid-sentence. Some scholars believe Sidney abandoned the book; others think the incompletion is accidental, a result either of his death or a problem with the transmission of his manuscript. Whatever the explanation, the *New Arcadia* is a significantly changed work. As well as revising the first two Books of the *Old Arcadia* Sidney makes substantial alterations and additions, creating an entirely new Book III and re-casting his story as a heroic romance which is both more serious and overtly political than the *Old Arcadia*. As Annabel Patterson observes, this transformation could signal a 'loss of confidence in indirect . . . discourse' of the kind associated with pastoral literature, and perhaps reflects the fact that it was written at a time when Sidney was more politically active.[27]

The new mode of Sidney's writing is apparent from the start. Rather than opening with a leisurely account of Arcadia as did his first version, the *New Arcadia* begins in *medias res*, like Heliodorus's *Aethiopian History*: a conversation between shepherds Klaius and Strephon about their beloved shepherdess Urania is interrupted by their discovery of Musidorus's seemingly dead body.[28] In similar fashion, military conflict is given greater prominence. As well as having the princes describe some of their most widely famed deeds retrospectively, Sidney's new book (Book III) introduces an epic siege and a series of one-to-one tournaments, reminiscent of Elizabethan courtly jousts and the battle for Troy in Homer's *Iliad*. Basilius and his army lay siege to the castle of two new characters – Amphialus, nephew to the king, and Cecropia, his wicked mother – after Cecropia abducts the Arcadian princesses and the disguised Pyrocles.

Sidney modifies his handling of his lead characters in similarly significant ways. Perhaps most strikingly, the *New Arcadia* omits the two actions most at odds with the heroic status of the princes in the *Old Arcadia*: Pyrocles's seduction of Philoclea and Musidorus's near rape of Pamela. Some critics argue that this change does not diminish the difference between the princes' past conduct and their largely anti-heroic actions in Arcadia, but the majority of modern scholars have seen Sidney's omissions as part of an attempt to recuperate the princes as morally exemplary heroes.

A similar preoccupation with instruction appears to shape Sidney's revision of his heroines' roles. Whereas they prove fallible in the *Old Arcadia*, in the *New Arcadia* Sidney emphasises their exemplary virtue, especially in Book III which concentrates on the siege at Amphialus's castle. Pamela in particular assumes heroic status, becoming what Helen Hackett calls 'the moral centre of the text', as she eloquently (if anachronistically) espouses her faith in a Calvinistic divine providence and proudly refuses to be cowed by Cecropia.[29]

Sidney's concern to provide readers with potentially instructive characters appears to underpin his expansion of the romance with a series of new sub-plots. Many of his new figures can be seen to typify different vices and virtues; others are more complex. Amphialus is arguably the most fascinating: he functions not only as the romance's anti-hero, but he embodies in his name (which means 'on both sides') and his frustrated life Sidney's heightened preoccupation with self-division, thwarted intentions and divine providence in the *New Arcadia*. Amphialus repeatedly fails in his attempts to command his destiny, with almost all of his actions rebounding upon him, or those he cares for, in tragic ways. As a once noble knight led to behave dishonourably by his passion for Philoclea, Amphialus is akin to the fallible princes of the *Old Arcadia* but suffers for his transgressions (as they do not), a fact which has led some critics to see him as a symbolic 'scapegoat' for the erring princes.

Thomas Nashe, *The Unfortunate Traveller* (1594)

Thomas Nashe (1567–c. 1601) was one of Elizabethan England's first professional writers, producing a variety of works during his decade-long career, including *The Unfortunate Traveller or The Life of Jack Wilton*. Up until the 1970s critics tended to regard it as 'an artistic failure' flawed by 'inconsistencies in theme, character, and authorial attitude'. Since then, a number of scholars have championed *The Unfortunate Traveller* and defended its narrative and tonal variety. Some have seen Nashe as 'a proto-postmodernist' and a 'precursor of modern journalists'; others have argued that he 'knowingly dissents from the humanist norms of his age'.[30]

According to its subtitle, *The Unfortunate Traveller* presents the 'life' of Jack Wilton, a mischievous but quick-witted page at the court of Henry VIII. The relationship Jack cultivates with his audience is familiar but Nashe makes it clear that his narrator is a skilful fabricator of tales (like himself), and therefore not wholly to be trusted. The problems with the reliability of Jack's 'life' are reinforced by the fact that his chronicle is a selective one, focused on only a handful of his youthful adventures in France, Northern Europe and Italy, culminating with his reformation and marriage. Each of the three parts of his 'life' is episodic, consisting of a sequence of tales about Jack's experiences in the different places that he visits, connected only by his part in them. Thus, the first part of *The Unfortunate Traveller* is about a series of tricks that Jack plays on companions at Henry VIII's camp in France; the second features his visits to Munster, Rotterdam, and Wittenberg; and the final section catalogues his increasingly unfortunate adventures in Italy, where he comes close to being executed. As several critics have noted, there is a gradual transformation in Jack's part in the tales he tells. Having initially been the one who mastered others (sometimes cruelly), he increasingly finds himself either a passive spectator or victim.

In its episodic structure, its focus on the wanderings and sufferings of its protagonist, and its culmination with a marriage, *The Unfortunate Traveller* owes an obvious debt to romance, but, as Madelon S. Gohlke notes, Nashe 'inverts the quest motif of romance, turning a fortunate journey into' a largely 'unfortunate one'.[31] In similar fashion he eschews the idealising mode of romance in favour of a more realistic, socially inclusive representation of life, in which lords rub shoulders with con artists, and the lovers who end up marrying are a reformed rogue (Jack) and a wily Italian widow (Diamante). This is why *The Unfortunate Traveller* is often described today as an anti-romance.

It is, likewise, common to describe Nashe's fiction as 'picaresque' (see Glossary), a prose genre developed in sixteenth-century Spain which traces the adventures of a rogue. Like *The Unfortunate Traveller*, picaresque fictions are usually episodic and cynical in perspective, but Nashe's work is more varied stylistically and tonally than such works usually are, partly because it borrows from other types of Renaissance literature, including Elizabethan jest books, travelogues, sermons and histories. In similar fashion, Nashe's fiction mixes high and low styles, juxtaposing Jack's typically witty but colloquial language with an occasionally more learned, consciously literary style.

Nashe uses Jack's irreverent tales to mock various aspects of Renaissance culture including religious fanaticism, humanism and the contemporary fashion for romantic and moralistic fiction. However, his most sustained parody concerns the contemporary cult of courtly love, and the literature associated with it.

Nashe's chief representative of both is the Earl of Surrey (the early sixteenth-century author famous for helping to popularise Petrarchan sonnets in England) (see Chapter 2). Although initially presented in flattering terms, Jack and Nashe's fiction increasingly mock the courtly love he prizes and the Petrarchan love poetry with which he seeks to immortalise it. Not only are the Surrey poems that Nashe invents conspicuously bad but Jack draws attention to their emotional insincerity and ineffectuality, observing that Surrey appears to be 'more in love with his own curious-forming fancy' than with the women he writes about and that his poems fail to seduce real women such as Diamante.[32]

In *The Unfortunate Traveller* the 'real' world is often cruel, as is reflected in Nashe's preoccupation with violence, domination and images of grotesque or broken bodies. These range from Jack's account of an old woman disfigured by the sweating sickness (p. 274) to the flaying and burning alive of Zadoch (p. 359) and the execution and disembowelment of Cutwolfe (p. 369). In many cases the horror of the violence is reinforced by the excruciatingly detailed, but understated way in which it is described. Jack's account of the torturing of Zadoch is characteristic: 'To his privy members they tied streaming fireworks. The skin from the crest of his shoulder, as also from his elbows, his huckle bones, his knees, his ankles, they plucked and gnawed off with sparkling pincers' (p. 359). He reports what was done but offers no emotional or moral comment on the episode. In other cases, the awfulness of the violence is foregrounded by Nashe's use of mundane analogies, as when Jack likens Cutwolfe's executioner to a fisherman, who uses his 'wood-knife' to 'fish for a man's heart', fetching 'it out as easily as a plum from the bottom of a porridge pot' (p. 369). There is a potentially comic dimension to such analogies, and critics have often been unsure whether Nashe's accounts of violence are to be interpreted seriously or comically. Similar difficulties have been posed by his handling of episodes such as the rape and suicide of Heraclide. Jack presents it to us as an unequivocally 'tragical tale', but his account veers towards melodrama as he describes Heraclide's decision to kill herself, and comes close to comedy when describing how her husband is woken from his seeming death when she collapses against him (p. 336). Part of the difficulty of establishing the tone at such moments lies in Nashe's chameleon-like combination of genres and styles in *The Unfortunate Traveller* and his general eschewal of overt moralising: without any consistent cues, Nashe's tone is almost inevitably ambiguous.

Lady Mary Wroth, *The Countess of Montgomery's Urania* (1621)

Lady Mary Wroth (1586–c. 1640) was the daughter of Lord Robert Sidney and wife of Sir Robert Wroth. Her marriage does not appear to have been happy and after her husband's death (1614) she became involved in an affair with her powerful cousin, William Herbert, third Earl of Pembroke. In the same period (1618–20) Wroth appears to have begun work on *The First Part of the Countess of Montgomery's Urania* (1621) which was published with an appendix of 103 sonnets and songs, supposedly written by her heroine, Pamphilia, to Amphilanthus.

Wroth was born into a famously literary family. Her father, her uncle (Sir Philip Sidney) and her aunt (Lady Mary Sidney) all wrote. She, herself, appears to have begun writing at an early age and became one of the most prolific women authors of the English Renaissance, and the first to publish an original prose romance. In writing a romance Wroth was challenging the conventional view that women authors should confine themselves to pious literature and identifying herself with Sir Philip Sidney. Like her uncle, she exploits the genre's potential for veiled social and political commentary, using her romance to critique contemporary court corruption, and specific aspects of Jacobean government such as James I's pacifist foreign policy. Some contemporaries believed that her romance was even more topical, being a *roman à clef* (that is, a story in which the fictional characters represent actual people). Although Wroth denied this, the assumption appeared to be confirmed when Lord Edward Denny complained that he and his family were satirised in the story of Sirelius, a jealous husband who saves his wife when her father attempts to kill her for her alleged adultery.

Dedicated to Wroth's sister-in-law, Susan Herbert, *Urania* consists of two parts which together chart the political and amatory 'adventures . . . of a number of closely woven, imaginary royal and noble families'.[33] At the heart of these adventures are cousins and lovers, Queen Pamphilia and Amphilanthus (later, Holy Roman Emperor). Having been divided for much of the narrative, Part I ends, in mid-sentence, with the lovers reunited.

Wroth's romance has many themes, including female rule and the potential tyranny of love and marriage, but her most persistent concern is female constancy, which she presents as a heroic virtue. This theme is given its fullest manifestation in the story of her chief lovers. While Amphilanthus's name (meaning 'lover of two') is the first of many clues to his inability to remain constant to Pamphilia, Pamphilia's exemplary fidelity is made clear when the pair visit the Throne of Love and the figure of '*Constancy*' is said to metamorphose 'herself into her breast'.[34] In making Pamphilia's chief virtue constancy, Wroth challenges the usual championing of chastity as the pre-eminent female virtue in romance.

Like conventional romances, Wroth's features a large cast of characters, multiple interlaced plots, and the separation, wandering and reunion of lovers and loved ones. In other respects, Wroth's romance is less typical. Her narrator comments satirically on romance conventions in a manner that shows the influence of Cervantes's hugely popular mock-romance, *Don Quixote* (Part I, 1605, Part II, 1615); and Wroth is distinctive in her concerns, focusing on married life rather than courtship, and the friendships, sufferings and heroism of her female characters, rather than on the adventures of her male characters. This has made her work of special interest to feminist scholars.

Part II of the *Urania* continues the story where Part I ended, but is more realistic and conspicuously concerned with war and politics. The principal characters of Part I continue to play a role, but most of Part II concerns the adventures of their children, which increasingly take place outside of Europe. It survives in a single unfinished manuscript which remained unpublished until the twentieth century. Like Part I, Wroth's continuation signals its incompletion by closing mid-sentence. In choosing to leave the endings of both Parts of the *Urania* open Wroth pays homage to Sidney's unfinished *New Arcadia*, one of the main inspirations for her romance. As well as providing her with characters and a template for interspersing poems and narrative, Sidney's revised

Arcadia provided a precedent for Wroth's focus on female heroism. Her other sources are varied, including English and continental romances, court masques and popular drama.

Wroth found further inspiration in the world and people that she knew. Several of her characters have been persuasively identified with real people and many of her female characters are implicitly self-portraits, including Pamphilia. Like Wroth, Pamphilia is a talented poet, unhappily married and secretly in love with her powerful cousin. By the same token, Amphilanthus is a figure for William Herbert, an identification which appears to be confirmed in Wroth's unpublished continuation of the romance, which attributes a poem believed to be by Herbert to Amphilanthus.[35] Other female characters, such as the Fisher Lady, Bellamira, Pelarina and Lindamira, play similar variations on Wroth's 'situation as a court lady with an unworthy husband and an unfaithful courtier-lover'.[36] The story of Lindamira, which is told by Pamphilia, is especially fascinating. The Queen pretends that it is 'a French story' (*Urania*, I, p. 499), but really it (and the seven sonnets appended to it) is her invention and reflects her own life. As such the episode offers 'a mirror image of Wroth telling the story of the *Urania*, complete with the sonnet sequence of *Pamphilia to Amphilanthus* tacked on at the end'; like her heroine, Wroth refuses 'to separate out the fiction from the fact in her stories'.[37]

SUMMARY OF KEY POINTS

- **Rise of Prose**: English prose writing thrived in the Renaissance and became the dominant, most diverse printed genre.
- **Fact/Fiction**: The modern distinction between non-fiction and fiction had yet to be firmly established, and several prose genres mixed fact and fiction.
- **Style**: The two key models for prose writers were the styles associated with Cicero and Seneca, but there was a general shift in the seventeenth century from an emphasis on linguistic copiousness and variety towards plainer writing.
- **Essays**: The 'essay' finds its roots in the work of classical authors such as Cicero and Seneca but was developed and named in the

Renaissance by Montaigne, and popularised in England by Sir Francis Bacon.

- **Sermons/Devotions:** Religious literature was hugely popular in Renaissance England. Two of the most important types of prose were the sermon and the devotion. Sermons were lectures written by clerics for delivery in church; religious devotions were a more private form of literature, based on their authors' personal meditations.
- **Prose Romance:** Early English fictions were generally written in verse. The late sixteenth-century flourishing of prose romances changed this and paved the way for the development of the modern novel. The genre was influenced by classical, medieval and contemporary continental romance, and associated with veiled political and social commentary.

NOTES

1. Morris W. Croll, 'The Baroque Style in Prose', in *Seventeenth-Century Prose: Modern Essays in Criticism*, ed. Stanley Fish (New York: Oxford University Press, 1971), pp. 26–52 (p. 27).
2. Ibid., p. 31, p. 33, p. 38.
3. John Lee, 'The English Renaissance Essay: Churchyard, Cornwallis, Florio's Montaigne and Bacon', in *A Companion to English Renaissance Literature and Culture*, ed. Michael Hattaway (Oxford: Blackwell, 2003), pp. 600–8 (p. 600).
4. Joad Raymond, *Pamphlets and Pamphleteering in Early Modern Britain* (Cambridge: Cambridge University Press, 2003), p. 17.
5. See Michael McKeon, *The Origins of the English Novel 1600–1740*, 2nd edn (Baltimore, MD: Johns Hopkins University Press, 2001).
6. See Paul Salzman, *English Prose Fiction, 1558–1700* (Oxford: Clarendon, 1985), p. 19.
7. William A. Ringler, '*Beware the Cat* and the Beginnings of English Fiction', *Novel* 12:2 (1979), 113–26 (113).
8. Andrew Hadfield, 'Prose Fiction', in *A Companion to English Renaissance Literature and Culture*, ed. Michael Hattaway (Oxford: Blackwell, 2003), pp. 576–88 (p. 581).

9. Floyd Gray, 'The essay as criticism', in *The Cambridge History of Literary Criticism*, ed. Glyn P. Norton (Cambridge: Cambridge University Press, 1999), III, pp. 271–7 (p. 271).

10. Francis Bacon, *The Major Works*, ed. Brian Vickers (Oxford: Oxford University Press, 2002), p. 712. All subsequent references to this edition are given in the text.

11. Lee, p. 603.

12. Stanley Fish, *Self-Consuming Artefacts: The Experience of Seventeenth-Century Literature* (Berkeley, CA: University of California Press, 1972), p. 80.

13. Ibid., pp. 92–3.

14. See Marla Hoffman Lunderberg, 'John Donne's Strategies for Discreet Preaching', *SEL*, 44:1 (2004), 97–119 (100).

15. Izaak Walton, *The lives of Dr John Donne, Sir Henry Wooton, Mr Richard Hooker, Mr George Herbert* (London: Richard Marriott, 1670), pp. 38–9.

16. See *The Sermons of John Donne*, ed. George R. Potter and Evelyn M. Simpson, 10 vols (Berkeley, CA: University of California Press, 1953–62), II (1955), pp. 199–200, III (1957), pp. 103–4.

17. Roger Pooley, *English Prose of the Seventeenth Century 1590–1700* (London: Longman, 1992), pp. 112–13.

18. See *The Sermons of John Donne*, ed. George R. Potter and Evelyn M. Simpson, 10 vols (Berkeley, CA: University of California Press, 1953–62), VII (1954), p. 60, p. 68.

19. Ibid., p. 264.

20. *The Sermons of John Donne*, ed. George R. Potter and Evelyn M. Simpson, 10 vols (Berkeley, CA: University of California Press, 1953–1962), X (1962), pp. 229–48.

21. John Donne, *Devotions upon Emergent Occasions and Death's Duel*, ed. Andrew Motion (New York: Random House, 1999), p. 3. All subsequent references to this edition are given in the text.

22. Goran V. Stanivukovic, 'English Renaissance romances as conduct books for young men', in *Early Modern Prose Fiction: The Cultural Politics of Reading*, ed. Naomi Conn Liebler (London: Routledge, 2007), pp. 60–78 (p. 66).

23. John Hoskins, *Directions for Speech and Style*, ed. Hoyt H. Hudson (Princeton, NJ: Princeton University Press, 1935), p. 14, p. 36.
24. Pooley, p. 23.
25. Sir Philip Sidney, *The Countess of Pembroke's Arcadia (The Old Arcadia)*, ed. Katherine Duncan-Jones (Oxford: Oxford University Press, 1990), p. 7, p. 369.
26. Robert W. Parker, 'Terentian Structure and Sidney's Original *Arcadia*', *ELR*, 2 (1972), 61–78; Franco Marenco, 'Double Plot in Sidney's *Old Arcadia*', *MLR*, 64 (1969), 248–63 (250).
27. Annabel Patterson, '"Under . . . Pretty Tales": Intention in Sidney's *Arcadia*', in *Sir Philip Sidney: An Anthology of Modern Criticism*, ed. Dennis Kay (Oxford: Oxford University Press, 1987), pp. 265–85 (p. 283).
28. See Philip Sidney, *The Countess of Pembroke's Arcadia (The New Arcadia)*, ed. Victor Skretkowicz (Oxford: Clarendon, 1987), pp. 3–5.
29. Helen Hackett, *Women and Romance Fiction in the English Renaissance* (Cambridge: Cambridge University Press, 2000), p. 122.
30. Steve Mentz, *Romance for Sale in Early Modern England* (Aldershot: Ashgate, 2006), p. 185.
31. Madelon S. Gohlke, 'Wits Wantonness: *The Unfortunate Traveller* as Picaresque', *Studies in Philology*, 73 (1976), 397–413 (399).
32. Thomas Nashe, *The Unfortunate Traveller and Other Works*, ed. J. B. Steane (London: Penguin, 1985), p. 307. All subsequent references to this edition are given in the text.
33. Gary Waller, *The Sidney Family Romance: Mary Wroth, William Herbert, and the Early Modern Construction of Gender* (Detroit, MI: Wayne State University Press, 1993), p. 249.
34. Lady Mary Wroth, *The First Part of The Countess of Montgomerie's Urania*, ed. Josephine Roberts (Binghamton, NY: Medieval and Renaissance Texts and Studies, 1995), p. 169. All subsequent references to this edition are given in the text.
35. Lady Mary Wroth, *The Second Part of The Countess of Montgomery's Urania*, ed. Josephine Roberts et al. (Tempe, AZ: Renaissance English Text Society, 1999), pp. 30–1.

36. Barbara Keifer Lewalski, *Writing Women in Jacobean England* (Cambridge, MA: Harvard University Press, 1994), p. 266.
37. Jennifer Lee Carrell, 'A Pack of Lies in a Looking Glass: Lady Mary Wroth's *Urania* and the Magic Mirror of Romance', *SEL*, 34 (1994), 79–107 (93, 85).

Conclusion

The Renaissance was a seminal era in the development of English literature. Up until the sixteenth century it was usual to regard the English language and English literature as far inferior to Latin and the literature of the ancient world. By the mid-seventeenth century this had changed. A series of transformations and a massive expansion in its vocabulary led to English being recognised as a rich and versatile tongue and contributed to the flourishing of literature in English. The rising status of vernacular literature is reflected in the fact that it became increasingly usual to celebrate native literary tradition and to liken the achievements of contemporary authors such as Spenser and Shakespeare to those of classical poets

The transformation of the vernacular and the flourishing of English literature was fostered by the rise of print publication: print allowed publishers to disseminate the works of contemporary (and past) English authors more widely and cheaply than ever before, and created a demand for new writing. This same demand made the writing and publication of literature a potentially profitable business and contributed to the professionalising of the English book trade. Although these developments did not mark an end to writing in Latin or to the manuscript circulation of literature (especially amongst gentlemen and women authors) the rising status of the vernacular and print heralded a slow revolution in English literary culture, paving the way for the thriving of printed English literature and the professional literary world.

The Elizabethan and Stuart eras witnessed more specific developments and innovations in English literary culture which were to have a similarly profound influence on its future development, including the blossoming of prose writing and the rise of secular drama. The growth of prose writing saw the emergence of a variety of new non-fiction and fiction genres, including the pamphlet, the essay, the biography and the prose romance. As well as fostering interest in prose writing many of these new genres enjoyed lasting popularity and influence. Essays and biographies remain popular genres today, while the prose romance laid the foundations for the development of the eighteenth-century novel and modern prose fiction.

The Elizabethan flourishing of secular drama was to transform English theatrical culture in similar fashion. Up until the sixteenth century most English drama was religious, but the increasing restriction of religious plays in post-Reformation England contributed to the gradual secularising of theatre and the thriving of non-religious drama: a transformation that has shaped English theatre ever since. The rise of secular drama led to the writing of the first recognisable tragedies and comedies in English, and the development of a series of new dramatic genres such as histories, romances and tragicomedies, all of which have served as models for later English playwrights. At the same time, the establishment of the first playhouses in the 1560s and 1570s, and the demand they created for new plays, led to an unprecedented growth in the number of English playwrights and plays, and the gradual professionalising of the theatre: for the first time it became possible for at least some contemporaries to make a career out of drama. Today's permanent theatres and full-time theatre practitioners find their roots in this world. The Restoration stage was to borrow in similar fashion from the theatrical innovations associated with the court masque: the late seventeenth-century use of scenery, proscenium arch stages, perspective staging and female performance all find their beginnings in court masque tradition.

The sixteenth and seventeenth centuries saw significant developments within the world of poetry, too. As well as appropriating and adapting classical poetic genres, English authors developed new forms (such as the sonnet, the epyllion and the country-house poem), and experimented with different linguistic styles and types of rhymed and unrhymed poetry (such as 'blank verse'). Such experimentation not only contributed to the creation of a much more varied corpus of English poetry but showed off the richness of the vernacular as a poetic medium. Most of the period's leading writers wrote poetry and it was through poetry that its most ambitious authors staked their claim (and the claim of English literature) to be comparable with the great authors and literature of the ancient world.

Many of the literary innovations associated with the Renaissance were stimulated by fresh interest in classical literature and authors such as Homer, Virgil, Ovid, Horace and Seneca, but Renaissance authors were not only indebted to classical writers. Medieval English literature and contemporary European authors were, likewise, important influences and sources. The plays of the Renaissance stage owe a significant debt, for example, to the dramatic models and symbolic staging traditions associated with Medieval mystery plays, moralities and saints' plays; and the period's pastoral poetry and drama is influenced not only by classical poets such as Virgil but by the pastoral literature of Medieval English authors such as William Langland and contemporary continental pastoralists such as Jacopo Sannazaro. Similarly, the period's writers of prose and stage romances borrowed from the epic and chivalric romances of Medieval England and Renaissance Europe, as well as from ancient authors such as Heliodorus. The richness of early modern England's literary heritage may help to explain the special power of its literature, reminding us that the Renaissance was not only an era of thrilling intellectual and artistic innovations but a time when writers looked to, and learned from, the past.

THE FUTURE

Scholarly criticism of Renaissance literature is largely a modern phenomenon. During the past century scholars have interpreted Renaissance texts using a range of different critical methods, from close-reading and psychoanalysis, to feminist and queer theory.

But the general trend, in recent years, has been towards readings which relate Renaissance texts to the social and historical contexts in which they were produced and/or the contexts in which they are interpreted today. This emphasis upon contextual interpretation is, in part, attributable to the far-reaching influence of the two 'historicist' schools of criticism which emerged in the 1980s (New Historicism and Cultural Materialism) but it also signals a reaction against the mid-twentieth century focus on close-reading. (See the Introduction for an overview of modern criticism of Renaissance literature.)

New Historicism and Cultural Materialism are no longer as dominant as they were in Renaissance studies in the late twentieth century, but the practice of historicising the period's literature remains central to much current Renaissance literary criticism and underpins one of the thriving schools of interpretation in the twenty-first century: 'Presentist' criticism. Rather than concerning itself with the original context in which Renaissance literature was produced, Presentist criticism is concerned with the meaning of Renaissance literature in the present. So far, most of the Presentist criticism has focused on Shakespeare, but there is obvious scope for a similar approach to the works of other Renaissance writers.

The other significant critical trend in the last thirty years has concerned the kinds of Renaissance authors and texts which scholars and students commonly study. Early twentieth-century criticism concentrated on a comparatively small number of male authors and the genres of drama and poetry. Since the 1970s, and thanks to the research of literary historians, and feminist, postcolonialist, Marxist and queer theorists, there has been an expansion in the Renaissance canon and a growing interest in politically and geographically marginal writers (such as non-male, non-white, non-elite, and non-metropolitan authors). This has led to the study of a wider range of poets and playwrights, and more work on Renaissance prose genres, popular literature, manuscript writing, regional literary and dramatic culture, and women's writing (see the Introduction for a fuller discussion of the late twentieth-century expansion of the Renaissance canon). Such work has already produced fascinating results but each aspect of the period's literary culture presents further research opportunities and is likely to feature in the Renaissance scholarship produced in coming years. Such research is likely to lead to new interpretations of more familiar Renaissance texts and authors, too, not least because scholars continue to be fascinated by traditionally canonical writers such as Spenser, Shakespeare and Jonson and their place within early modern and modern culture.

The late twentieth-century thriving of theatre history and performance criticism seems set to continue as well with theatre historians increasingly turning their attention to regional theatre, playing companies and theatre practices, and a growing number of performance critics extending their attention to non-Shakespearean drama on stage and film. New discoveries and fresh debates about the early English book trade, print and manuscript culture, and textual editing suggest that these will, likewise, be areas of ongoing critical interest in the early twenty-first century.

Further research opportunities are likely to be presented across the field of Renaissance studies by the increasing role of electronic texts and resources in the study and teaching of the period's literature. There is already a variety of meta-sites, websites and databases relevant, or dedicated, to the study of Renaissance literature (see Guide to Further Reading). Such resources seem set to multiply. At the same time, electronic editions and facsimiles of Renaissance texts and the on-line publication of academic journals and books are improving access to Renaissance literature and past and present scholarship on the period. The days of primary, archival and book-based research are far from over but such technological developments are making it increasingly possible to research and teach sixteenth and seventeenth-century literature 'virtually', and whenever and wherever suits students and tutors. Like the sixteenth-century rise of print, the on-going electronic revolution looks set to transform the way that we share literature and knowledge, including from and about this most exciting and influential of eras.

Student Resources

ESSAY WRITING ADVICE

The essay continues to be the most common form of assessment on undergraduate and graduate literature courses. Mastering the skill of writing successful, persuasive essays is therefore important. The best essays will not only offer a direct answer to the question but will be fluent, well-organised and carefully researched. Producing such essays is a matter of good preparation and practice. This section offers some general tips to help with this process. This advice is complemented (below) by a selection of example Renaissance essay topics, each accompanied by a list of suggested primary texts that could be used to illustrate an answer, suggestions for wider reading, and guidance on the points the essay could cover.

General Tips

Research

Most essays will require a combination of primary and secondary research. Primary research might include re-reading the Renaissance texts you would like to write about and reading relevant non-literary texts (for instance, if you are writing an essay about cross-dressing in Renaissance literature you might read the pamphlets written about the practice in 1620). Your secondary critical research may include research about the historical context in which your chosen texts were written but is also likely to include investigating previous scholarly interpretations of them. In order to be able to write about Renaissance literature in an informed way you need to be aware of the critical debates different texts and authors have prompted. The bibliographies or guides to further reading provided in Renaissance textbooks (such as this one) afford one starting point for your research. Most anthologies and editions of individual texts will also include suggestions for further reading. Using searchable databases, such as LION (Literature Online), provides another way of locating books and journal articles relevant to your topic. Further resources are freely accessible via the internet, but need to be used with care: not all the information found on the internet is scholarly or reliable. (See the Guide to Further Reading for information about electronic resources relevant to the study of Renaissance literature.) If you are not sure about the suitability or reliability of a website seek academic advice.

Structure

Your essay should have a clear structure. This should include an introduction (in which you address the question and offer some indication of your intended approach to it); a main body (in which you present your arguments and evidence); and a conclusion in which you return to the question and offer your final view. Within the main body of the essay there should be a rationale for the order in which you present your points; and each new point should be introduced and connected to that which precedes it.

Evidence

In order to be persuasive, the arguments that you make need to be substantiated. In some cases it may be sufficient to allude to, or to paraphrase, the evidence on which an argument is based (with a footnote or endnote providing a specific reference); in others it will be more appropriate or effective to quote from the text in question (whether that is a primary text or a historical or critical source). When you do use quotations it is important that they are integrated into your argument and that you acknowledge your source. This allows your reader to see what research your argument is built on. Different universities use slightly different referencing systems but you will usually need to provide information like the name of the author, the title of the work, the name of the publisher, the place and date of publication, and the page number (or the URL for electronic or web-based sources), so make a note of these when doing your research. Remember to make sure, too, that quotations are given in quotation marks. If you fail to acknowledge your sources properly you are potentially guilty of plagiarism, a serious assessment offence.

Style and Presentation

For your arguments to be effective they need to be fluently expressed. Computer grammar-checks and spell-checks can be useful but are not foolproof: they will try to make unnecessary corrections and will not pick up all errors (for example, the spell-check function will not pick up a spelling error if it exists as a word in its own right, such as 'thrown' for 'throne'). It is therefore important that you proofread your work carefully. Pay special attention to the spelling of the names of literary works, authors and characters. Repeated errors in the spelling of any of these can raise questions about how well you know the literature you are writing about. For similar reasons it is sensible to adopt a formal style and to make sure that your essay satisfies any required presentational standards (such as the use of double-spacing). Clear and accurate expression and presentation are the first signals to your marker that your essay has been carefully prepared.

SAMPLE ESSAY QUESTIONS AND PLANS

Question 1

'Renaissance history plays like Shakespeare's *Henry V* "can be seen to confirm the Machiavellian hypothesis of the origin of princely power in force and fraud even as they draw their audience irresistibly toward the celebration of this power"' (Stephen Greenblatt). Discuss.

This question asks you to think about the representation of power in Renaissance history plays. Any of the period's historical dramas could be used to illustrate an answer but the plays which make up Shakespeare's second tetralogy of histories (*Richard II*, *Henry IV, Parts I* and *II*, and *Henry V*) lend themselves particularly to the question, partly because they are the plays Greenblatt has in mind when he makes his assertion. As well as re-reading the plays your primary research might include reading Machiavelli's *The Prince* to give you a better understanding of Machiavelli's concept of power. Being able to allude to relevant contextual material (like *The Prince*) can be a way of offering a more impressive answer to the question.

Your secondary research would need to include a combination of general research on Renaissance history plays, and specific research on the individual plays you are writing about. A good starting point for the latter would be the essay from which Stephen Greenblatt's statement is taken: 'Invisible Bullets: Renaissance Authority and its Subversion, *Henry IV* and *Henry V*', in *Political Shakespeare: Essays in Cultural Materialism*, ed. Jonathan Dollimore and Alan Sinfield, 2nd edn (Manchester: Manchester University Press, 1996), pp. 18–47. Similar readings of Shakespeare's histories are afforded by Jonathan Dollimore's and Alan Sinfield's, 'History and Ideology: the instance of *Henry V*', in *Alternative Shakespeares*, ed. John Drakakis (London: Methuen, [1985] 1996), pp. 206–27, and Leonard Tennenhouse's *Power on Display: The Politics of Shakespeare's Genres* (London: Methuen, 1986). For a critique of such 'materialist' readings of Shakespeare's histories see Graham Bradshaw's *Misrepresentations: Shakespeare and the Materialists* (Ithaca, NY: Cornell University Press, 1993).

For more general studies of the genre and essays on the individual plays which make up the second tetralogy you could begin with the following: Michael Hattaway (ed.), *The Cambridge Companion to Shakespeare's History Plays* (Cambridge: Cambridge University Press, 2002), and Jean E. Howard and Richard Dutton (eds), *A Companion to Shakespeare's Works, Volume 2: The Histories* (Oxford: Blackwell, 2003). For more specific information about

Machiavellian thinking in the Renaissance, and its influence on Shakespeare you could look at Hugh Grady, *Shakespeare, Machiavelli and Montaigne: Power and Subjectivity from 'Richard II' to 'Hamlet'* (Oxford: Oxford University Press, 2002) and John Roe, *Shakespeare and Machiavelli* (London: D. S. Brewer, 2002).

Essay Outline

Introduction

- Discuss and contextualise Greenblatt's statement (relate it, for example, to the New Historicist focus on power and ideology); note that some scholars have questioned whether the plays celebrate the power they represent; outline which plays the essay will be exploring.

Main Body

- *Power in Medieval and Renaissance England*: Brief discussion of the fact that England was a monarchy in which the throne was passed on by succession; brief introduction to Machiavelli's concept of power and his advice to rulers, and why it was contentious in Renaissance England; discuss the influence of Machiavellian thinking on the conceptualisation of power in English Renaissance literature.
- *Richard II*: Consider the protagonist's 'traditional' view of power (he sees himself as divinely appointed); look at Richard's 'Machiavellian' mistakes as ruler (such as his seizure of Bolingbroke's inheritance); consider why Bolingbroke has been seen as Machiavellian (this includes his denial of any wish to claim the throne when he lands in England, his manipulation of Richard II into abdicating the throne, and his indirect call for Richard's murder); discuss the ambiguity of Bolingbroke's presentation.
- *Henry IV, Parts I and II*: Consider Henry IV's on-going political problems and the questions implicitly raised about his deposition of Richard II and his Machiavellian approach to power; consider the development of Prince Harry's role from seemingly

wayward youth to committed ruler, and why this transformation has been seen as Machiavellian and indicative of Henry's ability to suppress subversion.

- *Henry V*: Note the critical debates prompted by Henry's presentation in the play; consider why he might be seen as Machiavellian, including his implicit decision to follow his father's advice to 'busy giddy minds / With foreign quarrels' (IV, iii, 341–2), his apparent manipulation of the Church into offering support for his war with France, and his tricking of the traitors; consider whether or not the play celebrates Henry's power, and the opposing critical interpretations offered on this point.

Conclusion

- Note that the plays acknowledge the role of Machiavellian tactics in obtaining and retaining power but do not necessarily, or straightforwardly, celebrate or glamorise that power.

Question 2

Analyse and contextualise the handling of same-sex desire in Renaissance literature.

This question asks you to think about the representation of homosexual desire in Renaissance literature in relation to the context in which authors were writing. There was no concept of homosexuality in the Renaissance but there are examples of men being attracted to men and women to women in its literature. In some cases this desire is consciously homosexual, in others it is not. To reflect this diversity you could look at texts which include examples of both kinds of same-sex desire such as Shakespeare's *As You Like It*, Sidney's *The Arcadia*, Marlowe's *Edward II*, Shakespeare's sonnets to the Young Man, and Donne's 'Sappho to Philaenis'.

Before starting the essay you will need to have some understanding of Renaissance views of sexuality and same-sex relations. For specific information about homosexuality in the period see Alan Bray, *Homosexuality in Renaissance England* (London: Gay Men's Press, 1982) and Valerie Traub, *The Renaissance of Lesbianism in*

Early Modern England (Cambridge: Cambridge University Press, 2002). There is a growing body of research about cross-dressing, homoeroticism and homosexuality in Renaissance literature. The following provide useful starting points for your research on these topics and the individual works/authors suggested: *Queering the Renaissance*, ed. Jonathan Goldberg (Durham, NC: Duke University Press, 1994); Jean Howard, *The Stage and Social Struggle in Early Modern England* (London: Routledge, 1994), pp. 93–128; Stephen Orgel, *Impersonations: The Performance of Gender in Shakespeare's England* (Cambridge: Cambridge University Press, 1996); *Erotic Politics on the Renaissance Stage*, ed. Susan Zimmerman (New York: Routledge, 1992); (on Sidney) Robert H. F. Carver, ' "Transformed in Show": The Rhetoric of Transvestism in Sidney's Arcadia', *ELR*, 28:23 (1998), 323–52; Mark Rose, 'Sidney's Womanish Man', *RES*, 15:60 (1964), 353–63; (on Marlowe and Shakespeare) Mario DiGangi, *The Homoerotics of Early Modern Drama* (Cambridge: Cambridge University Press, 1997); Jonathan Goldberg, *Sodometries: Renaissance Texts, Modern Sexualities* (Stanford, CA: Stanford University Press, 1992); Bruce R. Smith, *Homosexual Desire in Shakespeare's England: A Cultural Poetics* (Chicago, IL: University of Chicago Press, 1991); Valerie Traub, *Desire and Anxiety: Circulations of Sexuality in Shakespearean Drama* (London: Routledge, 1992); (on Donne) Elizabeth Harvey, 'Ventriloquising Sappho: Ovid, Donne, and the Erotics of the Feminine Voice', *Criticism*, 31 (1989), 115–38; Janel Mueller, 'Lesbian Erotics: The Utopian Trope of Donne's "Sapho to Philaenis" ', in *Homosexuality in Renaissance and Enlightenment England*, ed. Claude Summers (New York: Harrington Park, 1992), pp. 103–34.

Essay Outline

Introduction

- Discuss the fact that there was no concept of, or word for, homosexuality in the Renaissance, although there is historical evidence of same-sex sexual activity; note that homosexual sex was seen as a 'sin' to which all were potentially prey; note that the strongly homosocial nature of Renaissance society may have encouraged same-sex desire especially between men; note that female same-sex desire was generally ignored; discuss the fact that there is evidence of same-sex desire in the period's literature but that it is only sometimes consciously homosexual.

- *Cross-dressing and homoeroticism (I)*: Consider the example of cross-dressing and homoeroticism on the Renaissance stage; note that cross-dressing is written into the plots of some Renaissance comedies and often leads to men temporarily desiring men and women, women (look, as an example, at Shakespeare's *As You Like It*, in which the cross-dressing of Rosalind leads to a woman falling in love with her, and the suggestion of a possible homoerotic dimension to the attraction between Rosalind and her future husband, Orlando); discuss the fact that contemporary detractors of the stage complained about the period's plays encouraging homoerotic desire, and that the incorporation of cross-dressing in such plays was possibly fostered by the fact that cross-dressing was an integral part of the all-male Renaissance stage; discuss the fact that such plays usually end with characters' seemingly unconventional desires resolved with a series of heterosexual marriages.
- *Cross-dressing and homoeroticism (II)*: Note that cross-dressing does not only result in the provocation of homoerotic desire on the Renaissance stage; look at Sidney's *Arcadia* and the consequences of Pyrocles's adoption of a female disguise as he pursues his secret passion for Philoclea (this includes the momentary provocation of desire in his friend Musidorus, Philoclea's experience of what she believes to be a homoerotic passion for the disguised Pyrocles, and the infatuation of Basilius, King of Arcadia, with the disguised young man); note that cross-dressing has more serious consequences in Sidney's *Arcadia* than in the period's dramas: it appears to compromise Pyrocles's heroic character and nearly results in tragedy.
- *Homoerotic / Homosexual love*: Note that other Renaissance texts address the possibility of consciously same-sex love and desire, particularly between men.
- *Marlowe*: Note that he writes a number of works which explore homosexual love and desire, including *Edward II*, about the

relationship between the king and his royal favourite, Piers Gaveston; discuss the way in which their relationship is represented and perceived within the play by Edward, Gaveston, and Edward's courtiers; discuss why the relationship has been seen as homosexual, and whether it is appropriate to describe it in these terms.

- *Shakespeare's Young Man Sonnets*: Briefly discuss which of the sonnets are thought to have a male addressee; note that this was unusual but not unprecedented in the period; note that some critics see the poems as expressing a consummated homosexual love, whereas others see them as platonic love poems; discuss the fact some critics (such as Bruce Smith) see the poems as among the first literary texts to articulate what could be characterised as a homosexual subjectivity.

- *Donne*: Renaissance literature exploring same-sex desire is mostly about men; link the greater preoccupation with male-male desire to the contemporary tendency to ignore lesbian desire and to the fact that most of the period's published authors were men; note that there are some texts which represent a seemingly lesbian love, such as Donne's 'Sappho and Philaenis'; discuss the poem's representation of Sappho's love; discuss the fact that Donne's use of classical poet, Sappho, as its speaker associates love between women with the ancient past rather than the present.

Conclusion

- There was no modern concept of homosexuality in the Renaissance but the historical evidence of same-sex desire and activity in the period is matched by an interest in same-sex love in Renaissance literature; most of this focuses on male-male desire and can be linked to the strongly male homosocial nature of Renaissance society; note that same-sex desire is not demonised in Renaissance literature in the same way that it was in moralistic writings and that there is some evidence of an emerging homosexual subjectivity in the writings of authors such as Marlowe and Shakespeare.

Question 3

'In English Renaissance culture racial "otherness" is typically demonised.' Discuss the treatment of blackness in Renaissance literature in the light of this statement.

This question invites you to think about the representation of race in Renaissance literature and its relationship to contemporary attitudes to racial otherness. A similar question might invite you to analyse the representation of religious or gender difference in the period's literature. A number of English Renaissance texts include black characters, representing them in varied ways. Three texts which reflect something of this variety are Shakespeare's *Titus Andronicus* and *Othello*, and Ben Jonson's *Masque of Blackness*.

In order to contextualise the representation of blackness in these texts some understanding of English Renaissance views of race and black people is needed. For background information on these subjects see Eldred D. Jones, *The Elizabethan Image of Africa* (Charlottesville, VA: University of Virginia Press, 1971) and Kim F. Hall, *Things of Darkness: Economies of Race and Gender in Early Modern England* (Ithaca, NY: Cornell University Press 1996). For more specific information about the representation of blackness and race in Renaissance literature, see Catherine M. S. Alexander and Stanley Wells (eds), *Shakespeare and Race* (Cambridge: Cambridge University Press, 2000); Hardin Asand, ' "To blanch an Ethiop, and revive a corse": Queen Anne and *The Masque of Blackness*', *SEL*, 32:2 (1992), 271–85; Emily Bartels, 'Making More of the Moor: Aaron, Othello, and Renaissance Refashionings of Race', *SQ*, 41 (1990), 433–54; Leslie A. Fiedler, *The Stranger in Shakespeare* (New York: Stein and Day, 1972); Ania Loomba, *Shakespeare, Race and Colonialism* (Oxford: Oxford University Press, 2002); Patricia Parker, 'Fantasies of "Race" and "Gender": Africa, *Othello*, and Bringing to Light', in *Women, "Race", and Writing in the Early Modern Period*, ed. Margo Hendricks and Patricia Parker (London: Routledge, 1994), pp. 84–100; Virginia Mason Vaughan, *Othello: A Contextual History* (Cambridge: Cambridge University Press, 1994); Mary Floyd-Wilson, *English Ethnicity and Race in Early Modern Drama* (Cambridge: Cambridge University Press, 2003).

Essay Outline

Introduction

• Few English people would have had direct knowledge of black people because there were few blacks in the country and few people travelled overseas; most people's views of racial otherness and blackness were based on second-hand knowledge or prejudice; note that there was a tendency to view all 'strangers' with suspicion and a tendency to demonise 'otherness'; at the same time contemporary interest in literature about race points to a curiosity about 'otherness'.

Main Body

• *Black Stereotypes*: Discuss some of the common cultural stereotypes associated with blackness (such as the negative association of blackness with sin, hot passions, intemperance, and the more positive association of blackness with strength and virility); note that negative stereotyping was predominant.

• *Stereotyping in literature/Titus Andronicus*: Note that black stereotyping is not unusual in Renaissance literature, and is often negative; look at the representation of Aaron the Moor in *Titus Andronicus*; he is presented as a stock villain, whose blackness is equated with his wickedness.

• *Othello*: Note that the representation of black characters is more complex in some Renaissance works, including Shakespeare's *Othello*; although Othello's vulnerability to sexual jealousy, his passionate reaction to Desdemona's alleged adultery and his violent murder of his wife are all potentially in keeping with the negative stereotyping of Africans as violent, intemperate and prey to hot passions, he is also shown to be a brave soldier, and a loyal and charismatic leader and lover; note that the more attractive aspects of Othello's portrayal could be linked to some of the more positive associations of blackness in the period; discuss the fact that critics have been divided about whether Shakespeare's characterisation of his hero is ultimately stereotypical and racist; discuss the negative use of imagery of 'blackness' in the play; note that such imagery is increasingly associated with Desdemona; link this to the intersection of attitudes to gender and racial 'difference' in the Renaissance and the cultural tendency to demonise women in the same way as racial others.

- *The Masque of Blackness:* Discuss the auspices of the masque (including Queen Anne's request that she and her ladies appear in black make-up); discuss the complexity of the treatment of blackness in the masque; note that blackness is accepted to be less desirable than whiteness but is not demonised; Niger defends blackness and the Aethiopian Princesses are not shown to be wicked, savage, or lustful, probably because they were to be performed by the Queen and her ladies; note that the Aethiopian princesses are more conspicuously stereotyped in terms of their gender (being presented as characteristically 'feminine' in their vanity about their beauty and their proneness to tears); relate this to the intersection of concerns about racial and gender difference.

Conclusion

- Although black stereotyping and the demonising of racial 'otherness' are not unusual in Renaissance literature they are not universal; at least some texts include more complex representations of racial difference; note that there is evidence of a mixture of anxiety and curiosity about racial 'otherness' in the period's literature (as in its culture), and a clear link between the ways in which Renaissance writers handle racial and gender difference.

GLOSSARY

Allegory

The term derives from the Greek word *allegoria*, meaning 'speaking otherwise'. In literature, it describes a story whose characters or action can be interpreted to have a hidden meaning.

Aphorism

A pithy observation or definition, often regarding society or morality.

Blank verse

Unrhymed verse written in iambic pentameter (see below).

Calvinism

The variety of Protestant theology associated with French religious reformer John Calvin (1509–64) and his followers.

Canon

A body of literary works deemed to be of the highest quality or significance.

Caroline

Of, or relating to, the reign of Charles I (1625–49).

Catholicism

The branch of Christianity presided over by the Pope in Rome. Catholicism was the dominant form of Christianity in Renaissance Europe.

Cavalier poetry

Poetry written by supporters of Charles I (1625–49). As well as a tendency to idealise the monarchy, Cavalier poetry is characterised by its prizing of friendship, hospitality, liberty and the classical concept of the 'Good Life'.

Ciceronian style

An eloquent, 'rounded' prose style, popular in the sixteenth century, based on the writing of ancient Roman author and orator, Cicero (106–43 BC).

The Civil War

The internal English war (1642–49) between the supporters of Parliament (known as Parliamentarians or Roundheads) and the supporters of the King (known as Royalists or Cavaliers). The war was won by the Parliamentarians and resulted in the overthrow and execution of Charles I (1649).

Classical

Of, or relating to, ancient Greek or Roman literature, art or culture.

Closet drama

A play written to be read rather than performed.

Comedy

In the Renaissance, comedies were defined by their happy endings and their characteristic focus on non-noble characters, rather than by their use of humour, although visual and verbal comedy is often a feature of them.

Country-house poem

The English 'country-house' poem was an invention of the early seventeenth century and is defined by its praise of a country-house estate and its (usually male) owner.

Counter-Reformation

The late sixteenth-century movement to reform the Catholic Church of Rome from within, stimulated by the Protestant Reformation (see below).

Eclogue

A short pastoral poem, often in the form of a dialogue between shepherds, derived from Virgil's *Eclogues*.

Elegy

A poem of mourning for an individual or a lament for an event.

Elizabethan

Of, or relating to, the reign of Elizabeth I (1558–1603).

Encomium

A poem or speech in praise of someone or something.

Epic

Usually a long narrative poem about the heroic deeds of a legendary figure and a nation's history.

Epigram

A short, witty poem or prose statement. In the Renaissance epigrams were often used satirically.

Epyllion

A narrative poem, resembling an epic but shorter in length, and usually erotic in theme in the Renaissance.

Essay

A short piece of writing on a particular subject or theme, popularised in England by Sir Francis Bacon's *Essays* (1597).

Euphuism

An ornate prose style, often involving parallelism, antithesis, and elaborate figures of speech, named after John Lyly's *Euphues. The Anatomy of Wit* (1578) and *Euphues and his England* (1580).

Folio

A book made up of sheets of paper folded once to create two leaves (four pages). In the Renaissance the folio format was expensive and tended to be reserved for learned or prestigious works such as the Bible.

Georgic

Poetry which represents rural life and agricultural work; its perspective on country life is usually less idealised than that associated with classical pastoral poetry (see below).

The 'Golden Age'

An idyllic time in classical mythology when there was believed to be peace, harmony, and plenty; men and women did not need to work or farm, living instead off nature's freely provided bounty.

History play

A play which dramatises a story about reputedly historical characters and events.

Homosocial

A term borrowed from social anthropology to describe social interactions between members of the same sex.

Humanism

An intellectual movement originating in Renaissance Italy that encouraged the fresh study of classical literature, and which emphasised the importance of learning as a means of improving one's self.

Iambic pentameter

Verse in which each line contains five iambic feet; an iambic 'foot' consists of an unstressed syllable followed by a stressed syllable. This is the most common metrical form in English poetry. When used for unrhymed poetry it is known as blank verse (see above).

Iconoclasm

The destruction of images used in religious worship.

Interregnum

The term used to describe the period between the end of the rule of Charles I (1649) and the restoration of the monarchy in England (1660).

Jacobean

Of, or relating to, the reign of James I (1603–25).

Lutheranism

The Protestant theology associated with sixteenth-century church reformer, Martin Luther.

Lyric

A short poem, often in the first-person, concerned with expressing the speaker's thoughts or emotions.

Masque

An elaborate form of courtly entertainment, combining music, dance, spectacle and poetry.

Metaphysical poetry

A type of seventeenth-century poetry, especially associated with John Donne, characterised by its plain, colloquial style, its metrical and rhythmic variety and its use of original, often surprising, analogies or 'conceits'.

Morality play

An allegorical moral drama dramatising the battle between good and evil in the human soul; the protagonist is usually a representative of mankind, while other characters personify abstract qualities such as virtues and vices.

Mystery plays

Short Medieval plays dramatising episodes from the Bible.

The 'New World'

The name used to describe North and South America, following Christopher Columbus's discovery of America in 1492.

Pamphlet

A short book about a single subject or theme. In the Renaissance these were usually sold unbound for a few pennies and often dealt with topical subjects.

Pastoral

Traditionally a type of poetry dealing with shepherds and country life, but extended to include pastoral drama and prose fiction in the

Renaissance. The representation of rural life is typically idealised, rather than realistic. Traditionally, pastoral was the humblest poetic genre, but there was a classical tradition of using it to comment covertly on political issues, and a Christian tradition of equating shepherds with Christ and his ministers. The latter led some Medieval and Renaissance authors to use pastoral as a vehicle for ecclesiastical satire.

Pathetic fallacy

The attribution of human feelings to inanimate objects or animals.

Petrarchan

A poetic mode that takes its name from Italian poet Francesco Petrarch (1303–74). As well as establishing a fashion for sonnets, Petrarch's poems have a number of recurrent features, which were widely imitated. These include a preoccupation with a beautiful but distant mistress and the use of antitheses to describe the extremity of the poet's love.

Picaresque

An episodic style of fiction, usually about a rogue hero, developed in sixteenth-century Spain.

Playhouse (or theatre)

The Renaissance saw the establishment of the first permanent theatres in England. There were two types initially: open-air amphitheatres and indoor hall playhouses.

Predestination

The Calvinist theory that people are predestined to be saved or damned by God even before they are born.

Protestantism

The name given to the Christian churches which broke away from the Catholic Church of Rome during the sixteenth-century Reformation (see below).

Quarto

A book in which the pages have been made by folding individual sheets of paper twice to create four leaves (or eight pages). Such books were smaller and cheaper than Folio texts (see above).

Reformation

The sixteenth-century movement to reform the Catholic Church which led to a split in the Church and the establishment of the Reformed and Protestant churches.

Rhetoric

The art of effective or persuasive speaking or writing.

Romance

A mode or type of story (usually a tale of chivalry and adventure), rather than a genre. Today, we associate 'romance' with love stories, but what characterised a work as a 'romance' in the Renaissance was its eschewal of realism, its episodic style, its focus on tales of adventure and suffering, its incorporation of miraculous or improbable events, and its conclusion with the happy reunion of the hero or heroes with their loved ones.

Saints' play

A Medieval play dramatising the life-story of a Christian saint.

Satire

Refers to literature which attacks contemporary individuals or social vices.

Senecan style

A curt prose style, characterised by the terseness and brevity of its clauses, named after Roman author, Seneca (c. 4 BC–AD 65), upon whose writing it was modelled.

Sermon

A religious talk or lecture, usually based on the interpretation of Biblical quotations, and written by clerics for delivery in church.

Sonnet

A lyric poem consisting of fourteen lines, usually written in iambic pentameter. The genre was popularised by Italian poet Francesco Petrarch. There are two main types of sonnet in the Renaissance: Italian (or Petrarchan) sonnets, which are divided into an octave and a sestet, rhyming abbaabba cdecde, and English (or Shakespearean) sonnets, divided into three quatrains and a couplet, rhyming abab cdcd efef gg.

Stuart

Of, or relating, to the reign of the Stuart royal family in Scotland (1371–1714) and Britain (1603–49, 1660–1714).

Tragedy

A serious play about the downfall of a (usually elite) protagonist, often ending with his or her death.

Tragicomedy

A play which combines elements of comedy and tragedy. Renaissance tragicomedies are often serious in tone and subject matter but generally avoid extreme suffering or death, and end 'happily'.

'Unities'

The classical dramatic theory derived from Aristotle which suggested that the action of a play should be unified and should take place in one location, over the course of one day.

GUIDE TO FURTHER READING

INTRODUCTION

The Historical Context

For a concise introduction to the history of the Elizabethan and Stuart periods see John Guy, *The Tudors: A Very Short Introduction* (Oxford: Oxford University Press, 2000) and John Morrill, *Stuart Britain: A Very Short Introduction* (Oxford: Oxford University Press, 2000). Short chapters on various aspects of Renaissance culture can be found in Julia Briggs, *This Stage-Play World, Texts and Contexts, 1580–1625*, 2nd edn (Oxford: Oxford University Press, 1997), *A Companion to English Renaissance Literature and Culture*, ed. Michael Hattaway (Oxford: Blackwell, 2003), and *The Cambridge Companion to English Literature, 1500–1600*, ed. Arthur F. Kinney (Cambridge: Cambridge University Press, 2004). Useful extracts from primary sources about English Renaissance society can be found in Kate Aughterson's two anthologies, *Renaissance Woman: A Sourcebook* (London: Routledge, 1995) and *The English Renaissance: An Anthology of Sources and Documents* (London: Routledge, 1998). More detailed information about specific aspects of Renaissance culture can be found in the following sources.

Religion

Collinson, Patrick, *The Birthpangs of Protestant England: Religious and Cultural Change in the Sixteenth and Seventeenth Centuries* (Basingstoke: Macmillan, 1988).
Duffy, Eamon, *The Stripping of the Altars: Traditional Religion in England, c. 1400–c.1580* (New Haven, CT: Yale University Press, 1992).

Politics and the Court

Haigh, Christopher (ed.), *The Reign of Elizabeth I* (Athens, GA: University of Georgia Press, 1987).

Peck, Linda Levy (ed.), *The Mental World of the Jacobean Court* (Cambridge: Cambridge University Press, 1991).

Russell, Conrad, *The Causes of the English Civil War* (Oxford: Clarendon, 1990).

Society and Home

Stone, Lawrence, *The Crisis of the Aristocracy, 1558–1641* (Oxford: Oxford University Press, 1965).

Wright, Louis B., *Middle-Class Culture in Elizabethan England* (London: Methuen, 1958).

Wrightson, Keith, *English Society, 1580–1680* (London: Hutchinson, 1982).

Gender, Marriage and Sexuality

Bray, Alan, *Homosexuality in Renaissance England* (London: Gay Men's Press, 1982).

Fletcher, Anthony, *Gender, Sex, and Subordination in England, 1500–1800* (New Haven: Yale University Press, 1995).

Stone, Lawrence, *The Family, Sex and Marriage in England 1500–1800* (London: Weidenfeld and Nicolson, 1977).

Traub, Valerie, *The Renaissance of Lesbianism in Early Modern England* (Cambridge: Cambridge University Press, 2002).

Humanism and Education

Kraye, Jill (ed.), *The Cambridge Companion to Renaissance Humanism* (Cambridge: Cambridge University Press, 1996).

O'Day, Rosemary, *Education and Society 1500–1800: The Social Foundations of Education in Early Modern Britain* (London: Longman, 1982).

Pincombe, Mike, *Elizabethan Humanism: Literature and Learning in the Late Sixteenth Century* (London: Longman, 2001).

The English Language

Barber, C. L., *Early Modern English*, 2nd edn (Edinburgh: Edinburgh University Press, 1997).

Science

Pumfrey, Stephen, Paolo L. Rossi and Maurice Slawinski (eds), *Science, Culture and Popular Belief in Renaissance Europe* (Manchester: Manchester University Press, 1991).

Exploration, New Worlds and Race

Hadfield, Andrew, *Literature, Travel, and Colonialism in the English Renaissance, 1540–1625* (Oxford: Oxford University Press, 1998).

Jones, Eldred D., *The Elizabethan Image of Africa* (Charlottesville, VA: University of Virginia Press, 1971).

Matar, Nabil, *Turks, Moors, and Englishmen in the Age of Discovery* (New York: Columbia University Press, 1999).

Shapiro, James, *Shakespeare and the Jews* (New York: Columbia University Press, 1996).

Writing

Love, Harold, *The Culture and Commerce of Texts: Scribal Publication in Seventeenth-Century England* (Amherst, MA: University of Massachusetts Press, 1993).

Lytle, Guy Finch and Stephen Orgel (eds), *Patronage in the Renaissance* (Princeton, NJ: Princeton University Press, 1981).

Patterson, Annabel, *Censorship and Interpretation: The Conditions of Writing and Reading in Early Modern England* (Madison, WI: University of Wisconsin Press, 1984).

The Critical Context

For a selection of literary criticism written in the Renaissance see *English Renaissance Literary Criticism*, ed. Brian Vickers (Oxford: Clarendon, 1999). For anthologies of modern criticism of Renaissance literature and Shakespeare see *Literary Theory/ Renaissance Texts*, ed. Patricia Parker and David Quint (Baltimore, MD: Johns Hopkins University Press, 1986) and Russ McDonald's

Shakespeare: An Anthology of Criticism and Theory 1945–2000 (Oxford: Blackwell, 2003). For overviews of modern criticism of Renaissance literature and Shakespeare see Thomas Healy, *New Latitudes: Theory and English Renaissance Literature* (London: Hodder Arnold, 1992) and *An Oxford Guide to Shakespeare*, ed. Stanley Wells and Lena Cowen Orlin (Oxford: Oxford University Press, 2002). For more specific information and examples of the different schools of criticism described in the Introduction see the sources listed in the chapter endnotes and the following suggestions.

New Historicism/Cultural Materialism

Dutton, Richard and Richard Wilson (eds), *New Historicism and Renaissance Drama* (London: Longman, 1992).

Ryan, Kiernan (ed.), *New Historicism and Cultural Materialism: A Reader* (London: Hodder Arnold, 1996).

Veeser, H. Aram (ed.), *The New Historicism* (Berkeley, CA: University of California Press, 1989).

Feminism

Callaghan, Dympna (ed.), *The Impact of Feminism on Renaissance Studies* (Basingstoke: Palgrave Macmillan, 2006).

Traub, Valerie, M. Lindsay Kaplan and Dympna Callaghan (eds), *Feminist Readings of Early Modern Culture: Emerging Subjects* (Cambridge: Cambridge University Press, 1996).

Queer Theory

Goldberg, Jonathan, *Sodometries: Renaissance Texts, Modern Sexualities* (Stanford, CA: Stanford University Press, 1992).

Goldberg, Jonathan (ed.), *Queering the Renaissance* (Durham, NC: Duke University Press, 1994).

Smith, Bruce R., *Homosexual Desire in Shakespeare's England: A Cultural Poetics* (Chicago, IL: University of Chicago Press, 1991).

Postcolonialism

Knapp, Jeffrey, *An Empire Nowhere: England, America and Literature from 'Utopia' to 'The Tempest'* (Berkeley, CA: University of California Press, 1997).

Linton, Joan Pong, *The Romance of the New World: Gender and the Literary Formation of English Colonialism* (Cambridge: Cambridge University Press, 1998).

Loomba, Ania and Martin Orkin (eds), *Post-Colonial Shakespeares* (London: Routledge, 1998).

Psychoanalysis

Armstrong, Philip, *Shakespeare in Psychoanalysis* (London: Routledge, 2001).

Holland, Norman, *Psychoanalysis and Shakespeare* (New York: McGraw-Hill, 1966).

Schwartz, Murray and Coppélia Kahn (eds), *Representing Shakespeare: New Psychoanalytic Essays* (Baltimore, MD: Johns Hopkins University Press, 1980).

Performance Criticism

Cave, Richard, Elizabeth Schafer and Brian Woolland (eds), *Ben Jonson and Theatre: Performance, Practice and Theory* (London: Routledge, 1999).

Esche, Edward J. (ed.), *Shakespeare and His Contemporaries in Performance* (Aldershot: Ashgate, 2000).

Jackson, Russell (ed.), *The Cambridge Companion to Shakespeare on Film* (Cambridge: Cambridge University Press, 2000).

Wells, Stanley and Sarah Stanton (eds), *The Cambridge Companion to Shakespeare on Stage* (Cambridge: Cambridge University Press, 2002).

Theatre History

Douglas, Audrey and Sally-Beth MacLean (eds), *REED in Review: Essays in Celebration of the First Twenty-Five Years* (Toronto: University of Toronto Press, 2006).

Gurr, Andrew, *The Shakespearian Playing Companies* (Oxford: Clarendon, 1996).

Ingram, William, *The Business of Playing* (Ithaca, NY: Cornell University Press, 1992).

Keenan, Siobhan, *Travelling Players in Shakespeare's England* (Basingstoke: Palgrave Macmillan, 2002).

McMillin, Scott and Sally-Beth MacLean, *The Queen's Men and their Plays* (Cambridge: Cambridge University Press, 1998).

Stern, Tiffany, *Rehearsal from Shakespeare to Sheridan* (Oxford: Clarendon, 2000).

Wickham, Glynne, *Early English Stages: 1300 to 1600*, 4 vols (New York: Columbia University Press, 1959–81).

Women / Women's Writing

Burke, Victoria E. and Jonathan Gibson (eds), *Early Modern Women's Manuscript Writing: Selected Papers from the Trinity / Trent Colloquium* (Aldershot: Ashgate, 2004).

Haselkorn, Anne M. and Betty S. Travitsky (eds), *The Renaissance Englishwoman in Print: Counterbalancing the Canon* (Amherst, MA: University of Massachusetts Press, 1990).

Mendelson, Sara and Patricia Crawford, *Women in Early Modern England: 1550–1720* (Oxford: Oxford University Press, 1998).

Pacheco, Anita (ed.), *A Companion to Early Modern Women's Writing* (Oxford: Blackwell, 2002).

Presentist Criticism

Hawkes, Terence, *Shakespeare in the Present* (London: Routledge, 2002).

CHAPTER 1: DRAMA

The Professional Stage

Bentley, G. E., *The Jacobean and Caroline Stage*, 7 vols (Oxford: Clarendon, 1941–68).

Braunmuller, A. R. and Michael Hattaway (eds), *The Cambridge Companion to English Renaissance Drama*, 2nd edn (Cambridge: Cambridge University Press, 2003).

Butler, Martin, *Theatre and Crisis, 1632–1642* (Cambridge: Cambridge University Press, 1984).

Cerasano, S. P. and Marion Wynne-Davies (eds), *Renaissance Drama by Women: Texts and Documents* (London: Routledge, 1996).

Chambers, E. K., *The Elizabethan Stage*, 4 vols (Oxford: Clarendon, 1923).

Cheney, Patrick, Andrew Hadfield and Garrett A. Sullivan Jr (eds), *Early Modern English Drama: A Critical Companion* (Oxford: Oxford University Press, 2006).

Clare, Janet, *'Art made tongue-tied by authority': Elizabethan and Jacobean Dramatic Censorship*, 2nd edn (Manchester: Manchester University Press, 1999).

Cox, John D. and David Scott Kastan (eds), *A New History of Early English Drama* (New York: Columbia University Press, 1997).

Doran, Madeleine, *Endeavours of Art: A Study of Form in Elizabethan Drama* (Madison, WI: University of Wisconsin Press, 1954).

Dutton, Richard, *Mastering the Revels: The Regulation and Censorship of Elizabethan Drama* (Basingstoke: Macmillan, 1991).

Gurr, Andrew, *The Shakespearean Stage, 1574–1642*, 3rd edn (Cambridge: Cambridge University Press, 1992).

Howard, Jean, *The Stage and Social Struggle in Early Modern England* (London: Routledge, 1994).

Hunter, G. K., *English Drama, 1586–1642: The Age of Shakespeare* (Oxford: Clarendon Press, 1997).

Kinney, Arthur F. (ed.), *A Companion to Renaissance Drama* (Oxford: Blackwell, 2004).

Wickham, Glynne, *Early English Stages, 1300–1600*, 4 vols (New York: Columbia University Press, 1959–81).

Wiggins, Martin, *Shakespeare and the Drama of His Time* (Oxford: Clarendon, 2000).

Private and Occasional Drama

Archer, Jayne Elisabeth, Elizabeth Goldring and Sarah Knight (eds), *The Progresses, Pageants and Entertainments of Queen Elizabeth I* (Oxford: Oxford University Press, 2007).

Astington, John, *English Court Theatre 1558–1642* (Cambridge: Cambridge University Press, 1999).

Boas, F. S., *University Drama in the Tudor Age* (Oxford: Clarendon, 1914).

Finkelpearl, P. J., *John Marston of the Middle Temple* (Cambridge, MA: Harvard University Press, 1968).

Smuts, Malcolm, *Court Culture and the Origins of a Royalist Tradition in Early Stuart England* (Philadelphia, PA: University of Pennsylvania Press, 1987).

Straznicky, Marta, 'Recent Studies in Closet Drama', *ELR*, 28 (1998), 142–60.

Straznicky, Marta, Privacy, *Play-reading, and Women's Closet Drama 1550–1700* (Cambridge: Cambridge University Press, 2004).

Westfall, Suzanne, *Patrons and Performance: Early Tudor Household Revels* (Oxford: Clarendon, 1990).

Attitudes to Drama

Gurr, Andrew, *Playgoing in Shakespeare's London* (Cambridge: Cambridge University Press, 1987).

Heinemann, Margot, *Puritanism and Theatre: Thomas Middleton and Opposition Drama under the Early Stuarts* (Cambridge: Cambridge University Press, 1980).

Wickham, Glynne, Herbert Berry and William Ingram (eds), *English Professional Theatre, 1530–1660. Theatre in Europe: A Documentary History* (Cambridge: Cambridge University Press, 2000).

Comedy

Bradbrook, Muriel, *The Growth and Structure of Elizabethan Comedy*, new edn (London: Chatto & Windus, 1973).

Gibbons, Brian, *Jacobean City Comedy*, 2nd edn (London: Methuen 1980).

Leggatt, Alexander, *Citizen Comedy in the Age of Shakespeare* (Toronto: University of Toronto Press, 1973).

Leinwand, Theodore B., *The City Staged: Jacobean Comedy, 1603–1613* (Madison, WI: University of Wisconsin Press, 1986).

Twelfth Night

Barber, C. L., *Shakespeare's Festive Comedy: A Study of Dramatic Form and its Relation to Social Custom* (Princeton, NJ: Princeton University Press, 1959).

Greenblatt, Stephen, *Shakespearean Negotiations: The Circulation of Social Energy in Renaissance England* (Berkeley, CA: University of California Press, 1988), pp. 66–93.

Jardine, Lisa, 'Twins and Travesties: Gender, Dependency and Sexual Availability in *Twelfth Night*', in *Erotic Politics: Desire on the Renaissance Stage*, ed. Susan Zimmerman (London: Routledge, 1992), pp. 27–38.

Maslen, R. W., '*Twelfth Night*, Gender, and Comedy', in *Early Modern English Drama: A Critical Companion*, ed. Patrick Cheney et al. (Oxford: Oxford University Press, 2006), pp. 130–9.

The Alchemist

Barton, Anne, *Ben Jonson, Dramatist* (Cambridge: Cambridge University Press, 1984).

Barish, Jonas A., *Ben Jonson and the Language of Prose Comedy* (Cambridge, MA: Harvard University Press, 1960).

Donaldson, Ian, *Jonson's Magic Houses: Essays in Interpretation* (Oxford: Clarendon Press, 1997).

Harp, Richard and Stanley Stewart (eds), *The Cambridge Companion to Ben Jonson* (Cambridge: Cambridge University Press, 2000).

Tragedy

Belsey, Catherine, *The Subject of Tragedy: Identity and Difference in Renaissance Drama* (London: Methuen, 1985).

Bowers, Fredson, *Elizabethan Revenge Tragedy, 1587–1642* (Princeton, NJ: Princeton University Press, 1940).

Dollimore, Jonathan, *Radical Tragedy: Religion, Ideology and Power in the Drama of Shakespeare and His Contemporaries*, 2nd edn (Hemel Hempstead: Harvester Wheatsheaf, 1989).

McAlindon, T., *English Renaissance Tragedy* (Basingstoke: Macmillan, 1986).

Neill, Michael, *Issues of Death: Mortality and Identity in English Renaissance Tragedy* (Oxford: Oxford University Press, 1997).

Hamlet

Adelman, Janet, *Suffocating Mothers: Fantasies of Maternal Origin in Shakespeare's Plays, 'Hamlet' to 'The Tempest'* (London: Routledge, 1992).

Coyle, Martin (ed.), *New Casebooks: Hamlet* (London: Macmillan, 1992).

Greenblatt, Stephen, *Hamlet in Purgatory* (Princeton, NJ: Princeton University Press, 2001).

Lee, John, *Shakespeare's Hamlet and the Controversies of Self* (Oxford: Clarendon, 2000).

McEachern, Claire (ed.), *The Cambridge Companion to Shakespearean Tragedy* (Cambridge: Cambridge University Press, 2003).

McGee, Arthur, *The Elizabethan Hamlet* (New Haven, CT: Yale University Press, 1987).

Tennenhouse, Leonard, *Power on Display: The Politics of Shakespeare's Genres* (London: Methuen, 1986).

The Duchess of Malfi

Callaghan, Dympna, *Women and Gender in Renaissance Tragedy* (Brighton: Harvester, 1989).

Callaghan, Dympna (ed.), *The Duchess of Malif: A Casebook* (Basingstoke: Macmillan, 2000).

Hunter, G. K. and S. K. Hunter (eds), *John Webster: A Critical Anthology* (Harmondsworth: Penguin, 1969).

Jardine, Lisa, *Still Harping on Daughters: Women and Drama in the Age of Shakespeare* (London: Harvester, 1983).

Peterson, Joyce E., *Curs'd Example; The Duchess of Malfi and Commonweal Tragedy* (Columbia, MO: University of Missouri Press, 1978).

History

Dutton, Richard and Jean Howard (eds), *A Companion to Shakespeare's Works, Volume II: The Histories* (Oxford: Blackwell, 2005).

Hattaway, Michael (ed.), *The Cambridge Companion to Shakespeare's Histories* (Cambridge: Cambridge University Press, 2002).

Holderness, Graham (ed.), *Shakespeare's History Plays: 'Richard II' to 'Henry V'* (Basingstoke: Macmillan, 1992).

Howard, Jean E. and Phyllis Rackin, *Engendering a Nation: A Feminist Account of Shakespeare's English Histories* (London: Routledge, 1997).

Ribner, Irving, *The English History Play in the Age of Shakespeare* (London: Methuen, 1957).

Tamburlaine the Great

Bartels, Emily C., *Spectacles of Strangeness: Imperialism, Alienation and Marlowe* (Philadelphia, PA: University of Pennsylvania Press, 1993).

Battenhouse, Roy W., *Marlowe's Tamburlaine: A Study in Renaissance Moral Philosophy* (Nashville, TN: Vanderbilt University Press, 1941).

Cheney, Patrick (ed.), *The Cambridge Companion to Christopher Marlowe* (Cambridge: Cambridge University Press, 2004).

Downie, J. A. and J. T. Parnell (eds), *Constructing Christopher Marlowe* (Cambridge: Cambridge University Press, 2000).

Leech, Clifford, *Christopher Marlowe: Poet for the Stage* (New York: AMS Press, 1986).

Levin, Harry, *The Overreacher: A Study of Christopher Marlowe* (Cambridge, MA: Harvard University Press, 1952).

Oz, Avraham (ed.), *Marlowe: New Casebooks* (Basingstoke: Palgrave Macmillan, 2003).

White, Paul Whitfield (ed.), *Marlowe, History and Sexuality: New Critical Essays on Christopher Marlowe* (New York: AMS Press, 1998).

Henry V

Bradshaw, Graham, *Misrepresentations: Shakespeare and the Materialists* (Ithaca, NY: Cornell University Press, 1993).

Dollimore, Jonathan and Alan Sinfield, 'History and Ideology: the instance of *Henry V*', in *Alternative Shakespeares*, ed. John Drakakis (London: Methuen, [1985] 1996), pp. 206–27.

Greenblatt, Stephen, 'Invisible Bullets: Renaissance Authority and its Subversion, *Henry IV* and *Henry V*', in *Political Shakespeare: Essays in Cultural Materialism*, ed. Jonathan Dollimore and Alan Sinfield, 2nd edn (Manchester: Manchester University Press, 1996), pp. 18–47.

Rabkin, Norman, 'Rabbits, Ducks, and *Henry V*', *SQ*, 28 (1977), 279–96.

Romance and Tragicomedy

Dutton, Richard and Jean Howard (eds), *A Companion to Shakespeare's Works, Volume IV: The Poems, Problem Comedies, Late Plays* (Oxford: Blackwell, 2003).

Frye, Northrop, *A Natural Perspective: The Development of Shakespearean Comedy and Romance* (New York: Columbia University Press, 1967).

Hirst, David L., *Tragicomedy: The Critical Idiom* (London: Methuen, 1984).

Knight, G. Wilson, *The Crown of Life: Essays in Interpretation of Shakespeare's Final Plays* (Oxford: Oxford University Press, 1947).

Maguire, Nancy Klein (ed.), *Renaissance Tragicomedy* (New York: AMS, 1987).

McMullan, Gordon and Jonathan Hope (eds), *The Politics of Tragicomedy: Shakespeare and After* (London: Routledge, 1992).

The Winter's Tale

Adelman, Janet, *Suffocating Mothers: Fantasies of Maternal Origin in Shakespeare's Plays, 'Hamlet' to 'The Tempest'* (London: Routledge, 1992).

Erickson, Peter, *Patriarchal Structures in Shakespeare's Drama* (Berkeley, CA: University of California Press, 1988).

Felperin, Howard, *Shakespearean Romance* (Princeton, NJ: Princeton University Press, 1972), pp. 211–45.

Paster, Gail Kern, *The Body Embarrassed. Drama and the Disciplines of Shame in Early Modern England* (New York: Columbia University Press, 1993).

The Tempest

Barker, Francis and Peter Hulme, 'Nymphs and reapers heavily vanish: the discursive con-texts of *The Tempest*', in *Alternative Shakespeares*, ed. John Drakakis (London: Methuen, [1985] 1996), pp. 191–205.

Brown, Paul, '"This thing of darkness I acknowledge mine": *The Tempest* and the discourse of colonialism', in *Political Shakespeare: Essays in Cultural Materialism*, ed. Jonathan Dollimore and Alan Sinfield, 2nd edn (Manchester: Manchester University Press, 1996), pp. 48–71.

Greenblatt, Stephen, *Shakespearean Negotiations: The Circulation of Social Energy in Renaissance England* (Oxford: Oxford University Press, 1988), pp. 129–63.

Vaughan, Alden T. and Virginia Mason Vaughan, *Shakespeare's Caliban: A Cultural History* (Cambridge: Cambridge University Press, 1991).

Court Masques

Bevington, David and Peter Holbrook (eds), *The Politics of the Stuart Court Masque* (Cambridge: Cambridge University Press, 1998).

Lindley, David (ed.), *The Court Masque* (Manchester: Manchester University Press, 1984).

Orgel, Stephen and Roy Strong, *Inigo Jones: The Theatre of the Stuart Court*, 2 vols (London: Sotheby Parke Bernet, 1973).

Ravelhofer, Barbara, *The Early Stuart Masque: Dance, Costume, and Music* (Oxford: Oxford University Press, 2006).

The Masque of Blackness

Asand, Hardin, "To blanch an Ethiop, and revive a corse": Queen Anne and *The Masque of Blackness*', *SEL*, 32:2 (1992), 271–85.

Butler, Martin, '*The Masque of Blackness* and Stuart Court Culture', in *Early Modern English Drama: A Critical Companion*, ed. Patrick Cheney et al. (Oxford: Oxford University Press, 2006), pp. 152–63.

McManus, Clare, *Women on the Renaissance Stage: Anna of Denmark and Female Masquing in the Stuart Court 1590–1619* (Manchester: Manchester University Press, 2002).

Orgel, Stephen, *The Jonsonian Masque* (New York: Columbia University Press, 1967).

CHAPTER 2: POETRY

General

Cheney, Patrick, Andrew Hadfield, Garrett A. Sullivan Jr (eds), *Early Modern English Poetry: A Critical Companion* (Oxford: Oxford University Press, 2007).

Corns, Thomas N. (ed.), *The Cambridge Companion to English Poetry. Donne to Marvell* (Cambridge: Cambridge University Press, 1998).

Parfitt, George, *English Poetry of the Seventeenth Century*, 2nd edn (London: Longman, 1992).

Waller, Gary, *English Poetry of the Sixteenth Century* (London: Longman, 1986).

Pastoral

Alpers, Paul, *What is Pastoral?* (Chicago, IL: University of Chicago Press, 1997).

Montrose, Louis A., ' "Of gentlemen and shepherds": The Politics of Elizabethan Pastoral Form', *ELH*, 50 (1983), 415–59.

The Shepheardes Calender

Es, Bart van, 'Spenserian Pastoral', in *Early Modern English Poetry: A Critical Companion*, ed. Patrick Cheney et al. (Oxford: Oxford University Press, 2007), pp. 79–89.

Herman, Peter C., '*The Shepheardes Calender* and Renaissance Antipoetic Sentiment', *SEL*, 32 (1992), 15–33.

King, John N., 'Spenser's *Shepheardes Calender* and Protestant Pastoral Satire', in *Renaissance Genres: Essays on Theory, History, and Interpretation*, ed. Barbara Kiefer Lewalski (Cambridge, MA: Harvard University Press, 1986), pp. 369–98.

Norbrook, David, *Poetry and Politics in the English Renaissance*, revised edn (Oxford: Oxford University Press, 2002).

'Lycidas'

Evans, J. Martin, 'Lycidas', in *The Cambridge Companion to Milton*, ed. Dennis Danielson (Cambridge: Cambridge University Press, 1997), pp. 35–50.

Patrides, A. C. (ed.), *Milton's Lycidas: the Tradition and the Poem* (New York: Holt, Rinehart and Winston, 1961).

Patterson, Annabel (ed.), *John Milton* (Longman Critical Readers) (London: Longman, 1992).

Epic and The Faerie Queene

Burrow, Colin, *Epic Romance: Homer to Milton* (Oxford: Clarendon, 1993).

Goldberg, Jonathan, *Endlesse Worke: Spenser and the Structures of Discourse* (Baltimore, MD: Johns Hopkins University Press, 1981).

Greenblatt, Stephen, *Renaissance Self-Fashioning: From More to Shakespeare* (Chicago, IL: Chicago University Press, 1980), pp. 157–92.

Hadfield, Andrew, *Shakespeare, Spenser and the Matter of Britain* (Basingstoke: Palgrave Macmillan, 2004).

Heale, Elizabeth, *The Faerie Queene: A Reader's Guide*, 2nd edn (Cambridge: Cambridge University Press, 1999).

Norbrook, David, *Poetry and Politics in the English Renaissance*, revised edn (Oxford: Oxford University Press, 2002).

Roche Jr, Thomas P., *The Kindly Flame: A Study of the Third and Fourth Books of Spenser's 'Faerie Queene'* (Princeton, NJ: Princeton University Press, 1964).

Epyllion

Hulse, Clark, *Metamorphic Verse: The Elizabethan Minor Epic* (Princeton, NJ: Princeton University Press, 1981).

Keach, William, *Elizabethan Erotic Narratives: Irony and Pathos in the Ovidian Poetry of Shakespeare, Marlowe, and their Contemporaries* (New Brunswick, NJ: Rutgers University Press, 1977).

Hero and Leander

Sinfield, Alan, 'Marlowe's Erotic Verse', in *Early Modern English Poetry: A Critical Companion*, ed. Patrick Cheney et al. (Oxford: Oxford University Press, 2007), pp. 125–35.

Smith, Bruce R., *Homosexual Desire in Shakespeare's England: A Cultural Poetics* (Chicago, IL: University of Chicago Press, 1991).

Venus and Adonis

Belsey, Catherine, 'Love as Trompe-l'oeil: Taxonomies of Desire in *Venus and Adonis*', *SQ*, 46 (1995), 257–76.

Hyland, Peter, *An Introduction to Shakespeare's Poems* (Basingstoke: Palgrave Macmillan, 2003).

Kahn, Coppélia, '*Venus and Adonis*', in *The Cambridge Companion to Shakespeare's Poetry*, ed. Patrick Cheney (Cambridge: Cambridge University Press, 2007), pp. 72–89.

The Sonnet Sequence

Lever, J. W., *The Elizabethan Love Sonnet* (London: Methuen, 1974).
Marotti, Arthur F., '"Love is not love": Elizabethan Sonnet Sequences and the Social Order', *ELH*, 49 (1982), 396–428.
Roche Jr, Thomas P., *Petrarch and the English Sonnet Sequences* (New York: AMS Press, 1989).
Spiller, Michael, *The Development of the Sonnet* (London: Routledge, 1992).

Astrophil and Stella

Campbell, Marion, 'Unending Desire: Sidney's Reinvention of Petrarchan Form in *Astrophil and Stella*', in *Sir Philip Sidney and the Interpretation of Renaissance Culture*, ed. Gary F. Waller and Michael D. Moore (London: Croom Helm, 1984), pp. 84–94.
Fienberg, Nona, 'The Emergence of Stella in *Astrophil and Stella*', *SEL*, 25 (1985), 5–19.
Jones, Ann Rosalind and Peter Stallybrass, 'The Politics of *Astrophil and Stella*', *SEL*, 24 (1984), 53–68.
Kennedy, William J., 'Sidney's *Astrophil and Stella* and Petrarchism', in *Early Modern English Poetry: A Critical Companion*, ed. Patrick Cheney et al. (Oxford: Oxford University Press, 2007), pp. 70–8.

Shakespeare's Sonnets

Booth, Stephen, *An Essay on Shakespeare's Sonnets* (New Haven, CT: Yale University Press, 1969).
De Grazia, Margreta, 'The Scandal of Shakespeare's Sonnets', *ShS*, 46 (1993), 35–49.
Edmundson, Paul and Stanley Wells, *Shakespeare's Sonnets* (Oxford: Oxford University Press, 2004).
Fineman, Joel, *Shakespeare's Perjured Eye: The Invention of Poetic Subjectivity in the Sonnets* (Berkeley, CA: University of California Press, 1986).
Schiffer, James (ed.), *Shakespeare's Sonnets: Critical Essays* (New York: Garland, 2000).

Smith, Bruce R., *Homosexual Desire in Shakespeare's England; A Cultural Poetics* (Chicago, IL: University of Chicago Press, 1991).

The Lyric and Donne's 'Songs and Sonets'

Carey, John, *John Donne: Life, Mind and Art*, new edn (London: Faber & Faber, 1990).

Lewalski, Barbara Kiefer, *Protestant Poetics and the Seventeenth-Century Religious Lyric* (Princeton, NJ: Princeton University Press, 1979).

Lovelock, Julian (ed.), *Donne, Songs and Sonets: A Casebook* (Basingstoke: Macmillan, 1990).

Low, Anthony, *The Reinvention of Love: Poetry, Politics and Culture from Sidney to Milton* (Cambridge: Cambridge University Press, 1993).

Marotti, Arthur F., *Manuscript, Print and the English Renaissance Lyric* (Ithaca, NY: Cornell University Press, 1995).

Mousley, Andy (ed.), *John Donne: New Casebooks* (Basingstoke: Macmillan, 1999).

Country-House Poetry

Fowler, Alastair, 'Country House Poems: The Politics of a Genre', *The Seventeenth Century*, 1 (1986), 1–14.

Hibbard, G. R., 'The Country House Poem of the Seventeenth Century', *Journal of the Warburg and Courtauld Institutes*, 19 (1956), 159–74.

Jenkins, Hugh, *Feigned Commonwealths: The Country-House Poem and the Fashioning of the Ideal Community* (Pittsburgh, PA: Duquesne University Press, 1998).

Kelsall, Malcolm, *The Great Good Place: The Country House and English Literature* (London: Harvester Wheatsheaf, 1993).

McClung, William A., *The Country House in English Renaissance Poetry* (Berkeley, CA: University of California Press, 1977).

'To Penshurst'

Cubeta, Paul M., 'A Jonsonian Ideal: "To Penshurst"', *Philological Quarterly*, 42 (1963), 14–24.

Rathmell, J. C. A., 'Jonson, Lord Lisle, and Penshurst', *ELR*, 1 (1971), 250–60.

Wayne, Don E., *Penshurst: The Semiotics of Place and the Poetics of History* (London: Methuen, 1984).

'The Description of Cookham'

Beilin, Elaine, *Redeeming Eve: Women Writers of the English Renaissance* (Princeton, NJ: Princeton University Press, 1987).

Coiro, Ann Baynes, 'Writing in Service: Sexual Politics and Class Position in the Poetry of Aemilia Lanyer and Ben Jonson', *Criticism*, 35 (1993), 357–76.

Cook, Patrick, 'Aemilia Lanyer's "Description of Cooke-ham" as Devotional Lyric', in *Discovering and (Re)covering the Seventeenth-Century Religious Lyric*, ed. E. R. Cunnar and J. Johnson (Pittsburgh, PA: Duquesne University Press, 2001), pp. 104–118.

Schnell, Lisa, '"So Great a Difference Is There in Degree": Aemilia Lanyer and the Aims of Feminist Criticism', *MLQ*, 57:1 (1996), 23–35.

Wilcox, Helen, 'Lanyer and the Poetry of Land and Devotion', in *Early Modern English Poetry: A Critical Companion*, ed. Patrick Cheney et al. (Oxford: Oxford University Press, 2007), pp. 240–52.

CHAPTER 3: PROSE

General

Fish, Stanley E. (ed.), *Seventeenth-Century Prose: Modern Essays in Criticism* (Oxford: Oxford University Press, 1971).

McKeon, Michael, *The Origins of the English Novel 1600–1740*, 2nd edn (Baltimore, MD: Johns Hopkins University Press, 2001).

Pooley, Roger, *English Prose of the Seventeenth Century 1590–1700* (London: Longman, 1992).

Raymond, Joad, *Pamphlets and Pamphleteering in Early Modern Britain* (Cambridge: Cambridge University Press, 2003).

Essays and Sir Francis Bacon

Fish, Stanley, *Self-Consuming Artefacts: The Experience of Seventeenth-Century Literature* (Berkeley, CA: University of California Press, 1972), pp. 78–155.

Gray, Floyd, 'The essay as criticism', in *The Cambridge History of Literary Criticism*, ed. Glyn P. Norton (Cambridge: Cambridge University Press, 1999), III, pp. 271–7.

Jardine, Lisa, *Francis Bacon, Discovery and the Art of Discourse* (Cambridge: Cambridge University Press, 1974).

Jardine, Lisa and Alan Stewart, *Hostage to Fortune: The Troubled Life of Francis Bacon (1561–1626)* (London: Weidenfeld and Nicholson, 1999).

Lee, John, 'The English Renaissance Essay: Churchyard, Cornwallis, Florio's Montaigne and Bacon', in *A Companion to English Renaissance Literature and Culture*, ed. Michael Hattaway (Oxford: Blackwell, 2003), pp. 600–8.

Vickers, Brian, *Francis Bacon and Renaissance Prose* (Cambridge: Cambridge University Press, 1968).

Sermons and John Donne

Ferrell, Lori Anne and Peter McCullough (eds), *The English Sermon Revised: Religion, Literature and History 1600–1750* (Manchester: Manchester University Press, 2000).

McCullough, P. E., *Sermons at Court, Politics and Religion in Elizabethan and Jacobean Preaching* (Cambridge: Cambridge University Press, 1998).

Mousley, Andy (ed.), *John Donne: New Casebooks* (Basingstoke: Macmillan, 1999).

Oliver, P. M., *Donne's Religious Writing. A Discourse of Feigned Devotion* (London: Longman, 1997).

Romances

Hutson, Lorna, *The Usurer's Daughter: Male Friendship and Fictions of Women in Sixteenth-Century England* (London: Routledge, 1994).

Liebler, Naomi Conn (ed.), *Early Modern Prose Fiction: The Cultural Politics of Reading* (London: Routledge, 2007).

Maslen, R. W., *Elizabethan Fictions. Espionage, Counter-espionage, and the Duplicity of Fiction in Early Elizabethan Prose Narratives* (Oxford: Clarendon, 1997).

Mentz, Steve, *Romance for Sale in Early Modern England* (Aldershot: Ashgate, 2006).

Newcomb, Lorie Humphrey, *Reading Popular Romance in Early Modern England* (New York: Columbia University Press, 2002).

Salzman, Paul, *English Prose Fiction, 1558–1700* (Oxford: Clarendon, 1985).

The Arcadia

Hackett, Helen, *Women and Romance Fiction in the English Renaissance* (Cambridge: Cambridge University Press, 2000).

Hamilton, A. C., *Sir Philip Sidney: A Study of his Life and Works* (Cambridge: Cambridge University Press, 1977).

Kay, Dennis (ed.), *Sir Philip Sidney: An Anthology of Modern Criticism* (Oxford: Oxford University Press, 1987).

Kinney, Clare R., 'Chivalry Unmasked: Courtly Spectacle and the Abuses of Romance in Sidney's *New Arcadia*', *SEL*, 35 (1995), 35–52.

McCoy, Richard C., *Sir Philip Sidney: Rebellion in Arcadia* (Hassocks, Sussex: Harvester, 1979).

The Unfortunate Traveller

Gohlke, Madelon S., 'Wits Wantonness: *The Unfortunate Traveller* as Picaresque', *Studies in Philology*, 73 (1976), 397–413.

Harrington, Susan Marie and Michael Nahor Bond, ' "Good Sir, Be Ruld By Me": Patterns of Domination and Manipulation in

Thomas Nashe's *The Unfortunate Traveller'*, *Studies in Short Fiction*, 24:3 (1987), 243–50.

Hutson, Lorna, *Thomas Nashe in Context* (Oxford: Clarendon, 1989).

Simons, Louise, 'Rerouting *The Unfortunate Traveller*: Strategies for Coherence and Direction', *SEL*, 28 (1988), 17–38.

Urania

Lewalski, Barbara Keifer, *Writing Women in Jacobean England* (Cambridge, MA: Harvard University Press, 1994).

Miller, Naomi J., *Changing the Subject: Mary Wroth and Figurations of Gender in Early Modern England* (Lexington, KT: University Press of Kentucky, 1996).

Miller, Naomi J. and Gary Waller (eds), *Reading Mary Wroth: Representing Alternatives in Early Modern England* (Knoxville, TN: University of Tennessee Press, 1991).

Quilligan, Maureen, 'Lady Mary Wroth: Female Authority and the Family Romance', in *Unfolded Tales: Essays on Renaissance Romance*, ed. George M. Logan and Gordon Teskey (Ithaca, NY: Cornell University Press, 1989), pp. 257–80.

JOURNALS

The most up-to-date research on Renaissance literature is often published first in academic journals. It is therefore worth becoming accustomed to searching and using them. There are a number of journals which regularly include articles relevant to Renaissance literature, including those listed in the 'Abbreviations' at the start of this book. Most university libraries will have an A to Z list of periodicals which you can use to check whether your university subscribes to these journals. Some journals are freely available via the internet, such as: *Early Modern Literary Studies* (http://www.extra.shu.ac.uk/emls/). This includes articles on various aspects of sixteenth- and seventeenth-century literature, reviews of recent critical books and performances, and links to other useful sites on the web.

Renaissance Forum (http://www.hull.ac.uk/renforum)
This is an electronic journal of early modern literary and historical studies.

ELECTRONIC RESOURCES

Subscription Databases

The following databases are available by subscription only. You will need to check with your university library to see if it has access to them.

OED (Oxford English Dictionary Online) (http://www.oed.com)

This dictionary not only offers definitions of words but shows their historical derivation and gives examples of their use in literature over time.

EEBO (Early English Books Online) (http://eebo.chadwyck.com)

This database contains digital facsimile page images of works printed between 1473 and 1700. You can use it to look at early editions of Renaissance texts.

JSTOR (http://www.jstor.org/)

This is a scholarly journal archive providing full-text access to back-copies of a wide range of journals and journal articles.

LION (Literature Online) (http://lion.chadwyck.co.uk)

You can search LION for full Renaissance texts and for criticism on authors and their works. The database also offers access to full-text journals (such as *Shakespeare Quarterly*).

ODNB (Oxford Dictionary of National Biography) (http://www.oxforddnb.com)

The ODNB includes biographies for more than 50,000 British historical figures, including many Renaissance authors.

Project Muse (http://muse.jhu.edu)

This database provides full-text access to over 380 humanities and social sciences journals.

Internet databases

Early Modern Women Database (http://www.lib.umd.edu/ETC/LOCAL/emw/emw.php3)

This database (compiled by Georgiana Ziegler) provides a free and comprehensive gateway to women's writing, art and society in the early modern period.

ERIC (The English Renaissance in Context) (http://dewey.library.upenn.edu/sceti/furness/eric/index.cfm)

This includes online tutorials on Shakespeare's plays, and free access to a full-text resource of early modern texts from the University of Pennsylvania's Furness Shakespeare Library.

Metasites

Michael Best (University of Toronto), 'Sites on Shakespeare and the Renaissance', *Internet Shakespeare Editions* (http://www.uvic.ca/shakespeare/Annex/ShakSites1.html)

CERES (Cambridge English Renaissance Electronic Service) (http://www.english.cam.ac.uk/ceres/)

This site (maintained by editors Andrew Zurcher, Gavin Alexander and Raphael Lyne) at Cambridge University provides information about electronic resources for research on the Renaissance, and incorporates COPIA (or CERES Online Publications Interactive). The on-line publications include several editions of Renaissance works and an online course about how to read Renaissance hand-writing.

Terry Gray, *Mr William Shakespeare and the Internet* (http://shakespeare.palomar.edu/)
Gray offers an annotated guide to Shakespeare on the internet and background information about Shakespeare and his time.

Alan Liu (University of California), *Voice of the Shuttle* (http://vos.ucsb.edu/)
This offers a guide to web resources for Humanities research, including a section dedicated to the Renaissance and the seventeenth century.

Websites & Online Editions

A Celebration of Women Writers: 1501–1600 (http://digital. library.upenn.edu/women/_generate/1501–1600.html)
This offers access to a collection of electronic texts by Renaissance women writers, edited by Mary Mark Ockerbloom.

Internet Shakespeare Editions (http://internetshakespeare. uvic.ca/index.html)
The Internet Shakespeare project (overseen by co-ordinating editor, Michael Best) provides access to online texts of the plays, background information on Shakespeare, a database of Shakespeare in performance, and a guide to reference works.

Luminarium (http://www.luminarium.org/)
This site, maintained by Annina Jokinen, includes sections on Renaissance and seventeenth-century literature. As well as offering access to online texts, the site includes critical essays, background information on authors and their works, and links to other useful Renaissance websites.

Renascence Editions (http://darkwing.uoregon.edu/~ rbear/ren.htm)
This is an online 'repository of works printed in English between the years 1477 and 1799' (overseen by Richard Bear).

Index